CHURCH, ECUMENISM AND POLITICS

Cardinal Joseph Ratzinger

CHURCH, ECUMENISM AND POLITICS

New Essays in Ecclesiology

Crossroad • New York

1988

The Crossroad Publishing Company
370 Lexington Avenue, New York, N.Y. 10017

Originally published as *Kirche, Ökumene und Politik* © Edizioni Paoline s.r.l., Cinisello Balsamo (Italy), 1987

Translated by Robert Nowell except for Chapter 4, "Anglican-Catholic Dialogue," which first appeared in *Insight* 1, no. 3 (March 1983) and is reproduced by permission of the Rev. Martin Dudley. It was translated by Dame Frideswide Sandemann, O.S.B., of Stanbrook Abbey.

English translation © St Paul Publications, Slough, 1988, and The Crossroad Publishing Co., New York, 1988

Printed in the United States of America

Library of Congress Cataloging-in-Publication Data

Ratzinger, Joseph.
   [Kirche, Ökumene und Politik. English]
   Church, ecumenism, and politics : new essays in ecclesiology /
Joseph Ratzinger.
     p. cm.
   Translation of: Kirche, Ökumene und Politik.
   ISBN 0-8245-0859-9 :
   1. Church. 2. Catholic Church—Doctrines. 3. Christian union.
   4. Catholic Church—Relations. 5. Christianity and politics.
   6. Liberation theology. I. Title.
BX1746.R3513 1988
262—dc19   88-2364
                                    CIP

Contents

Foreword   vii

PART I: THE CHURCH'S NATURE AND
           STRUCTURE   1

1. The ecclesiology of the Second Vatican Council   3
    Appendix: Modern variations of the concept of the
           people of God   21
2. The papal primacy and the unity of the people of God   29
3. The structure and tasks of the synod of bishops   46

PART II: ECUMENICAL PROBLEMS   63

4. Anglican-Catholic dialogue: Its problems and hopes   65
    Postscript   88
5. Luther and the unity of the Churches   99
    Postscript   122
6. The progress of ecumenism   135

PART III: THE CHURCH AND POLITICS   143

    Section I: Fundamental questions   145
7. Biblical aspects of the question of faith and politics   147
8. Theology and the Church's political stance   152
9. Conscience in its age   165

    Section II: Aspects of the concept of freedom:
           Church—State—Eschaton   181
10. Freedom and constraint in the Church   182
11. A Christian orientation in a pluralistic democracy?   204
12. Europe: A heritage with obligations for Christians   221
13. Eschatology and Utopia   237
14. Freedom and Liberation: The anthropological vision
     of the 1986 Instruction *Libertatis conscientia*   255

Sources   277

Foreword

The articles and papers collected here form a kind of second volume to the ecclesiological essays which I published in 1969 under the title *Das neue Volk Gottes* (The New People of God). The basic issues have remained the same: the question of the nature of the Church, its structure, the ecumenical scene, the relationship of Church and world. But in many cases the emphases have shifted and new evaluations have become necessary. The growing number of ecumenical agreed statements has given the dialogue between the Churches an actuality that was not yet foreseeable twenty years ago. The fact that all this agreement has not yet brought about unity necessitates a fundamental consideration of where ecumenism stands and how progress may be made with it. The question raised in general terms at the Council of how Christianity and Christians should serve the world has become dramatically intensified, particularly on the basis of theologies of liberation, and has emerged in the question of the faith and politics and of the relationship between liberation and redemption.

Thus the debate about Christian ecumenism and efforts to achieve the right relationship of faith and politics occupy the foreground of the reflections that make up this volume. Some of the contributions reprinted here aroused vigorous debate when they were first published, and I have tried to do justice to this debate either in additional footnotes or in newly added postscripts. I hope that in this way it will become clear that these essays are meant as a contribution to dialogue with the aim that by listening to each other we shall be able to hear ever more clearly him who in his person is the word and the truth.

Rome, the feast of All Saints, 1986

Joseph Cardinal Ratzinger

PART I

THE CHURCH'S NATURE
AND STRUCTURE

1

The ecclesiology of the Second Vatican Council

Shortly after the first world war Romano Guardini coined the phrase that soon became a byword in German Catholicism: "An event with incalculable consequences has begun: the Church is awakening in people's souls." The fruit of this awakening was Vatican II: it articulated and made available to the whole Church what had matured in the way of insight based on faith during those four decades full of hope and new departures between 1920 and 1960. So in order to be able to understand Vatican II we need to cast a glance over this period and try to discern at least the broad outlines of the trends and tendencies that led into the Council. In doing this my intention will be to start with the ideas that were being thought out at this time so as to develop from them the elements of the Council's teaching on the Church.

1. The Church as the body of Christ

a) The image of the mystical body

"The Church is awakening in people's souls" — this phrase of Guardini's was very carefully formulated, since the important thing about it was precisely that the Church was now recognized and experienced as something within one, not like some machinery that exists over against us but as something that is itself alive within us. If previously the Church had been seen above all as structure and organization, the insight that emerged now was that we ourselves are the Church: it is more than an organization, it is the organism of the Holy Spirit, something alive that embraces us all from within. This new awareness of the

3

Church was articulated in the phrase "the mystical body of Christ". This formula expressed a new and liberating experience of the Church which was formulated yet again by Guardini at the end of his life, in the year when Vatican II adopted its constitution on the Church, in the following way. The Church, said Guardini (*Die Kirche des Herrn,* p. 41), "is not some institution that has been planned and constructed . . . but a living being . . . It goes on living through time, developing as every living thing develops, changing itself . . . and yet in essence always the same, and its core is Christ . . . As long as we see the Church only as an organization . . ., as officialdom . . ., as a corporation . . ., we have not yet got the right relationship with it. But it is a living being, and our relationship to it must itself be life."

It is difficult to communicate the enthusiasm and the joy that was involved in that kind of insight at that time. In the age of liberal thought, up to the first world war, the Catholic Church was regarded as a fossilized machine that persistently opposed the achievements of the modern age. In theology the question of papal primacy was so much in the foreground that the Church appeared essentially as a centrally directed institution which one was dogged in defending but which only encountered one externally. What now became visible once again was that the Church is much more, that in faith we all share in living responsibility for it just as it supports us. It had become clear that it is an organic growth that has developed through the centuries and continues today. It had become clear that through it the mystery of the incarnation remains present and contemporary: Christ marches on through the ages. If we therefore ask what elements remain of lasting worth from this first re-appraisal and have contributed to Vatican II, we could say that the first thing is the Christological definition of the concept of the Church. J. A. Möhler, the great reviver of Catholic theology after the ravages of the Enlightenment, said on one occasion that one could sum a particular false theology up in an admitted caricature by saying: "Christ in the beginning established the hierarchy and by doing so did enough to look after the Church until the end of time." What needs to be set against this is that the Church is the mystical body, in other words that Christ is continually founding it:

that in it he is never only the past but is always and above all the present and future. The Church is the presence of Christ, the fact that we are contemporaneous with him, that he is contemporaneous with us. The source of its life is the fact that Christ is present in people's hearts: it is from there that he shapes the Church, and not the other way round. That is why what it talks about is first of all Christ and not itself: it is healthy to the extent that all its attention is directed towards him. Vatican II put this insight superbly at the head of its considerations when it began its fundamental text on the Church by saying: *Lumen gentium cum sit Christus*, "because Christ is the light of the nations" there exists the mirror of his glory, the Church, that reflects his radiance. To understand Vatican II correctly one must always and repeatedly begin with this first sentence.

The second thing to be grasped from these beginnings is the aspect of the Church's inwardness and its community aspect. The Church grows from the inside outwards, not the other way round. What it means above all is the most inward community with Christ: it takes shape in the life of prayer, in the life of the sacraments; in the fundamental attitudes of faith, hope and love. If therefore someone asks: "What must I do so that the Church may come into being and progress?" the answer must be: "What you must strive for above all is for faith to exist, for people to hope and to love." Prayer builds the Church and the community of the sacraments, in which its prayer reaches us. This summer I met a parish priest who told me that what struck him above all when he took over his parish was that for decades no more vocations to the priesthood had come out of it. What should he do? One cannot manufacture vocations: only the Lord himself can give them. But must we just resign ourselves with folded hands? He decided each year to make the long and ardous pilgrimage on foot to the Marian shrine of Altötting for this intention and to invite everyone who shared his concern to join him in his pilgrimage and prayer. More and more people went each year, and this year to the immense joy of the entire village they were able to celebrate a newly ordained priest's first Mass for the first time in living memory . . . The Church grows from the inside: this is what the phrase about the body of Christ tells us. But it also includes the other point that Christ has built himself a body into which I must fit as a humble member. Otherwise he cannot be found and possessed, but in this way he can be totally, because I am his member, his organ in this world and thus for eternity. The recognition of this fact completely ruled out the liberal idea that Jesus is interesting but the Church is something that went wrong. Christ exists not purely ideally but only in his body. This means with the others, with the community that has persisted through the ages and that is this body of his. The Church is not an idea but a body, and the scandal of the incarnation, over which so many of Jesus's contemporaries came to grief, is continued in the infuriating aspects of the Church. But here too the saying applies: "Blessed is he who takes no offence at me" (Mt 11:6).

This community character of the Church also necessarily implies what may be termed its we-ness. It is not something somewhere: instead, we ourselves are the Church. Of course, nobody can say: "I am the Church." Everyone must and should say: "We are the Church." And once again this "we" is not a group that cuts itself off from others but a group that inserts itself into the entire community of all the members of Christ, living and dead. In this way a group can then really say: "We are the Church." The Church is present in this opened-up "we" that breaks down barriers — social and political barriers, but also the barrier between heaven and earth. We are the Church: from this grew co-responsibility, but also the duty to become genuinely involved; from this came also the right to criticize that must always and primarily be a right of self-criticism. For the Church, we may repeat, is not something somewhere, something other: we ourselves are the Church. These ideas too have matured to contribute directly to the Council: everything that it said about the joint responsibility of the laity and everything that was done to implement this meaningfully in the way of legal provisions grew out of these insights.

Finally, a third idea that belongs here is that of the Church's development and thus of its historical dynamism. A body remains identical precisely by being continually renewed in the process of living. For Cardinal Newman the idea of development was in fact the bridge that made his conversion to Catholicism possible. My own belief is that it belongs in fact to the decisive fundamental concepts of Catholicism which for long have not been given enough consideration, although here too Vatican II has the credit of having formulated it for the first time in a formal statement of the Church's teaching. Anyone who wants to cling merely to the words of scripture or the patterns of the early Church banishes Christ to the past. The result is either a faith that is completely sterile and has nothing to say to today or an arbitrariness that jumps over two thousand years of history and throws it into the dustbin of failure while dreaming up for itself how Christianity was really meant to appear according to scripture or according to Jesus. But what emerges can only be an artificial product of our own making that has no lasting power. Genuine identity with the origin is only to be found where there is also the living continuity that develops in and thus preserves it.

b) Eucharistic ecclesiology

Now we must return once again to the development of the period before the Council. As we have said, the first phase of the rediscovery of the Church centred on the concept of the mystical body of Christ, which was developed from Paul and which brought into the foreground the ideas of the presence of Christ and the dynamism of the living Church. Further research led to new insights. Above all Henri de Lubac made it clear in a splendid work of comprehensive scholarship that the term "mystical body" originally meant the holy eucharist and that for Paul as for the Fathers of the Church the idea of the Church as the body of Christ was indissolubly linked with the idea of the eucharist in which the Lord is bodily present and gives us his body as food. Thus there now arose a eucharistic ecclesiology which people also liked to term an ecclesiology of communion. This ecclesiology of communion became the real core of Vatican II's teaching on the Church, the novel and at the same time the original element in what this Council wanted to give us.

What is meant by this term eucharistic ecclesiology? I shall merely try very briefly to indicate some of its main points. The first is that Jesus's last supper now becomes recognizable as the actual foundation of the Church: Jesus gives those who are his own this liturgy of his death and resurrection and thus gives them the feast of life. In the last supper he recapitulates the covenant of Sinai, or rather what had there been an approximation in symbol now becomes reality: the community of blood and life between God and man. When we say this is clear that the last supper anticipates and at the same time necessarily presupposes the cross and the resurrection, since otherwise everything would remain empty gestures. Hence the Fathers of the Church were able to use a striking image to say that the Church sprang out of the wound in the Lord's side from which blood and water flowed. In reality this is the same, though seen only from another point of view, as when I say that the last supper is the origin of the Church. For what it always means is that the eucharist links men and women not only with each other but with Christ and that in this way it turns people into the Church. At the same time the Church's fundamental constitution is provided: the Church lives in eucharistic communities. Its worship is its constitution, since of its nature it is itself the service of God and thus of men and women, the service of transforming the world.

Worship is its form: that means that in it there is a quite individual relationship of diversity and unity that otherwise would not occur. In every celebration of the eucharist the Lord is completely present. He is indeed risen and dies no more, and so he can no longer be divided. He always gives himself complete and undivided. Hence the Council says: "This Church of Christ is really present in all legitimately organized local groups of the faithful, which, in so far as they are united to their pastors, are also quite appropriately called Churches in the New Testament. For these are in fact, in their own localities, the new people called by God, in the power of the Holy Spirit and as the result of full conviction (cf. 1 Thess 1:5) . . . In these communities, though they may often be small and poor, or existing in the diaspora, Christ is present through whose power and influence the One, Holy, Catholic and Apostolic Church is constituted" (*Lumen Gentium* § 26).

This means that from the starting-point of eucharistic ecclesiology there follows that ecclesiology of the local Church which is characteristic of Vatican II and which provides the inward sacramental foundation for the doctrine of collegiality, to which we will come in a moment.

First we must look more closely at the language the Council uses in order correctly to grasp its teaching. In this passage Vatican II is dealing with ideas from Orthodox and Protestant theology which it integrates into a larger Catholic vision. The idea of eucharistic ecclesiology was expressed first of all in the Orthodox theology developed by Russian theologians in exile and was thus contrasted with supposed Roman centralism. Every eucharistic community, it was being said, is already completely the Church because it possesses Christ completely. Hence external unity with the other communities is not constitutive for the Church, nor, it was concluded, can unity with Rome be constitutive for the Church. This kind of unity is good, because it shows the fullness of Christ to the outside world, but it does not really belong to the essence of the Church, because one cannot add anything to the completeness of Christ. With a different starting-point the Protestant idea of the Church pointed in the same direction. Luther had found himself no longer able to recognize the spirit of Christ in the universal Church and indeed regarded it as the tool of anti-Christ. He could not even regard the Protestant national Churches that arose from the Reformation as the Church in the proper sense of the word. They were merely functional machines that were sociologically and politically necessary under the direction of the political authorities, and nothing more. For him the Church withdrew into the local community. Only the congregation that hears the word of God on the spot is the Church. Hence he substituted the term congregation or community for that of Church, which became a negative concept.

If we now turn back to what the Council had to say we shall be struck by certain nuances. It does not say simply: "The Church exists completely in every community celebrating the eucharist" but uses the formulation: "The Church is really present in all *legitimately organized* local groups of the faithful, which, *in so far as they are united to their pastors,* are . . . called Churches." Two elements are important here: the community must be "legitimately organized" for it to be the Church, and it is legitimately organized "in union with its pastors". What does this mean? First of all it means that nobody can turn himself or herself into the Church. A group cannot simply come together, read the New Testament, and say: "We are now the Church, because the Lord is present wherever two or three are gathered in his name." An essential element of the Church is that of receiving, just as faith comes from hearing and is not the product of one's own decisions or reflections. For faith is the encounter with what I cannot think up myself or bring about by my own efforts but what must come to encounter me. The term we use for this structure of receiving and encounter is "sacrament". And part of the basic structure of a sacrament is that it is received and that no one administers it to himself or herself. Nobody can baptize himself or herself, nobody can ordain himself to the priesthood, nobody can absolve himself or herself from his or her own sins. It is because of this structure of encounter that by its nature perfect repentance cannot remain something internal but needs the sacrament's pattern of encounter. Hence it is not just an offence against external Church discipline if someone administers the eucharist to himself or herself but something that damages the internal structure of the sacrament. The fact that in this sacrament alone the priest should nevertheless give himself communion indicates the *mysterium tremendum* to which he finds himself exposed at the eucharist: acting *in persona Christi* and thus at one and the same time representing Christ while remaining a sinful human being who lives completely from receiving what Christ has to give.

The Church is not something one can make but only something one can receive, and indeed receive from where it already is and where it really is: from the sacramental community of his body that progresses through history. But there is one other thing that helps us to understand this difficult phrase about "legitimately organized communities": Christ is complete everywhere — that is the one very important point which the Council holds in common with our Orthodox brothers and sisters. But he is also only one everywhere, and hence I can only have the one Lord in the unity that he is himself, in the unity with the others who are also his body and are continually to become his body anew in the eucharist. Hence the unity among themselves of the communities that celebrate the eucharist is not an external accessory for eucharistic ecclesiology but its inmost condition: it is only in unity that it is one. In this respect the Council evokes the communities' responsibility for themselves while excluding self-sufficiency. It conveys an ecclesiology for which being Catholic, that is the community of the faithful of all places and all times, is not some external matter of organization but is grace springing from within and at the same time a visible sign of the power of the Lord who alone can give unity across so many barriers.

2. The collegiality of the bishops

Closely tied up with ecclesiology is the idea of episcopal collegiality, which is also one of the main pillars of Vatican II's ecclesiology. This idea too developed from the investigation of the Church's structure of worship. If I am right, the first person to formulate it clearly and thus open the door for the Council on this point was the Belgian liturgiologist Bernard Botte. This is important, because here the connection becomes clear with the liturgical movement of the years between the wars which was in fact the breeding ground for most of the insights mentioned earlier. It is of more than historical importance because it shows the inner connection of these ideas without which one cannot understand them correctly. The dispute over collegiality is not a battle between Pope and bishops over sharing power in the Church, even though it can very easily degenerate into this kind of fight and those involved must continually ask themselves whether they have not let themselves be led down this wrong turning. Nor is it actually a battle over legal forms and institutional structures. Collegiality is of its nature ordered towards that service which is quite simply the proper service of the Church: the worship of God. Bernard Botte drew this concept from the oldest liturgical orders that have come down to us and developed it on these lines. During the Council this was maintained against the opponents of collegiality, who argued that in Roman law and in the law of the early modern period dealing with associations collegiality had a meaning that could not be brought into agreement with the constitution of the Church. In fact what was involved here was a possible version of the idea of collegiality that would have distorted the meaning of the Church's service. Hence it is important to keep on coming back to the core so as to protect it from this kind of distortion.

What then is meant? In his investigations Botte pointed to two levels of the idea of collegiality. The first level consists in the fact that the bishop is surrounded by the college of presbyters. Expressed in this is something we have already touched on before, the fact that the early Church did not know any self-sufficiency on the part of individual communities. The presbyters who serve them belong together: together they form the bishop's "council". The communities are held together among themselves by the presbyters and maintained by the bishop in the larger unity of the universal Church. Being a priest always includes an element of sharing and working with others as well as being related to a bishop in a way that is at the same time being related to the Church as a whole. But this already means that for their part the bishops should not operate shut off from each other for themselves alone but that together they form the *ordo* or order of bishops, to use the language of Roman law which classified society into various different *ordines* or orders. Later the term *ordo* became the formal description of the sacrament of order or ordination, to the essential contents of which belongs entry into a community service, into the "we" of those who serve. The term *ordo* is incidentally interchangeable with *collegium*. In the context of worship both denote the same thing, that the bishop is not a bishop on his own but only in the Catholic community of those who were bishops before him, who are bishops with him and who will be bishops after him. The dimension of time is also included in the meaning of this term: the Church is not something that we make today but something that we receive from the history of those who believe and that we pass on as something as yet incomplete, only to be fulfilled when the Lord shall come again.

The Council blended these ideas with the other fundamental concept of the sacrament of episcopal ordination, the idea of apostolic succession, to form an organic synthesis. It recalled that the apostles too formed a community. Before they were called apostles they appear under the label "the Twelve". The calling of twelve men by the Lord has a symbolic character that every Israelite understood: it recalls the twelve sons of Jacob from whom grew the twelve tribes of Israel. Twelve is thus the symbolic number of the people of God: when Jesus calls twelve men this symbolic gesture says that he himself is the new Jacob/Israel and that now, with these men, a new people of God begins. Mark shows this very clearly in his gospel when he sums up the calling of the apostles by saying: "He appointed twelve" (Mk 3:14). In this context people were aware that twelve was also a cosmic number, the numer of the signs of the zodiac which together made up the year, mankind's time scale. This emphasized the unity of history and the cosmos, the cosmic character of the history of salvation: the twelve were to be the new signs of the zodiac of the final and definitive history of the universe. But to stick with what we are immediately concerned with, the apostles are what they are only by sharing in the community of the twelve, which for this reason is made up to its full complement after Judas's treachery. Consequently one becomes a successor of the apostles by entering into the community of those in whom their office is continued. "Collegiality" belongs to the essence of the bishop's office: it can only be lived and put into effect in the community of those who at the same time represent the unity of God's new people.

If we ask ourselves what this means in practice, the first thing to be said is that the Catholic dimension of the episcopal office (as also of priestly ordination and of every form of congregational life) is very explicitly emphasized. Making it a matter of particularities is a fundamental contradiction of the idea of collegiality. As the Council formulated it, collegiality is itself not immediately a legal thing but rather a theological datum given in advance which is of the first importance both for the Church's law and for pastoral practice. The legal form that provides the most immediate expression of the theological reality "collegiality" is an ecumenical council. Hence in the new code of canon law the latter is fitted into the article dealing with the college of bishops (canons 336–341). All other forms of applying collegiality in practice are not to be deduced directly from this but can only be attempts at a secondary mediation of this great fundamental principle in the context of everyday reality. They must always be measured against the extent to which they correspond to the basic idea that it is all about: transcending the local horizon to enter the community of Catholic unity, to which also the dimension of the history of the faith from its beginnings up to the Lord's second coming has always belonged.

3. *The Church as the people of God*

In dealing with the idea of collegiality we have at last come across the term which I am sure you have long been waiting for: the Church as the people of God. What does it mean? Once again in order to understand it we must go back to the developments that preceded the Council. The first enthusiasm over the discovery of the idea of the body of Christ was followed by a gradual process of deepening and correction in two directions. We have already noticed the first correction: it is to be found above all in the work of Henri de Lubac, who put the idea of the body of Christ in concrete terms as eucharistic ecclesiology and thus opened it up to the actual questions of the Church's legal order and the relationship between the local and the universal Church. The other form of correction began at the end of the 1930s in Germany, where a number of theologians made the criticism that with the idea of the mystical body the relationship of the visible and the invisible, of law and grace, of order and life remained obscure. They therefore put forward as a more comprehensive description of the Church the concept of the "people of God" to which above all the Old Testament bore witness. Among other things this made it easier to deal with sociological and legal categories, while the body of Christ remained an image which was important but which did not satisfy theology's need to form concepts.

What was originally a rather superficial critique of the idea of the body of Christ was then deepened from various points of view from which there developed the positive content with which the concept of the body of Christ entered into the ecclesiology of the Council. A first important point was the dispute over membership of the Church which arose in connection with the encyclical on the mystical body of Christ that Pope Pius XII published on 29 June 1943. He laid down that membership of the Church was linked to three requirements: baptism, orthodoxy, and belonging to the Church's legal unity. This meant that non-Catholics were completely excluded from membership of the Church. In a country where the ecumenical question was so immediately pressing as is the case in Germany this statement naturally led to intense disagreements, especially as the code of canon law opened up a different perspective. According to the Church's legal tradition preserved in that, baptism provided an unlosable form of constitutive membership of the Church. This made it clear that in certain circumstances a legal approach can offer more flexibility and openness than a "mystical" one. It was asked whether the image of the mystical body was not too narrow a starting-point to be able to define the multitude of different forms of Church membership that now existed thanks to the confusion of human history. For membership the image of the body can only offer the idea of member in the sense of limb: one is either a limb or not, and there are no intermediary stages. But in that case, the question was asked, is not this image's starting-point too narrow, since quite clearly there are intermediary stages? In this way people latched on to the term "the people of God", since in this context it was more capacious and flexible. The Council's constitution on the Church adopted precisely this application when it described the relationship of non-Catholic Christians to the Catholic Church by talking about them being "joined in many ways" and that of non-Christians by talking of them "related", in both cases depending on the idea of the people of God (*Lumen Gentium* §§ 15 and 16).

In this way it can be said that the concept of "the people of God" was introduced by the Council above all as an ecumenical bridge. This applies also from another point of view. The rediscovery of the Church after the First World War was to start with a phenomenon common to both Catholics and Protestants, nor did liturgical movement restrict itself in any way to the Catholic Church. But precisely because this development was something shared by the Churches it also provoked mutual criticism. In the Catholic Church the idea of the body of Christ was developed to the point that it became easy to describe the Church as "Christ's continuing life on earth", as the incarnation of the Son continuing until the end of time. This aroused protest and dissent from the Protestants, who saw in it an intolerable self-identification with Christ on the part of the Church in which the Church was as it were worshipping itself and setting itself up as infallible. Without going so far, Catholic theologians gradually found that with this formula a definitive quality was ascribed to all the Church's official statements and actions so that any criticism could appear as an attack on Christ himself and the human and all too human aspects of the Church were simply ignored. The Christological difference, it was said, must once again be clearly brought out: the Church is not identical with Christ but stands over against him. It is the Church of sinners that continually needs purification and renewal, that must continually be becoming the Church. In this way the idea of reform became a decisive element in the concept of the people of God that could not have been developed in this way from the idea of the body of Christ.

Here we touch on a third aspect that played a part in favouring the idea of the people of God. In 1939 the Protestant exegete Ernst Käsemann gave his monograph on the letter to the Hebrews the title "The pilgrim people of God". This became almost a slogan in and around the Council's debates, since it brought out something that became ever clearer in the course of the struggle over the constitution on the Church: the fact that the Church has not yet reached its goal. Its own hope is still ahead of it. The "eschatological" component of the concept of the Church became clear. Above all in this way one could express the unity of the history of salvation that comprehended both Israel and the Church together on their pilgrimage. In this way one could express the historical nature of the Church, which is on the way and will only be completely itself when its paths have traversed the ages and led into the hands of God. One was also able to express the inner unity of the people of God, in which, as in every people, there are various offices and ministries, but cutting across all such distinctions is the fact that all are pilgrims in the one community of the pilgrim people of God. If one wants to sum up in brief phrases the outstanding elements of the concept of the people of God that were important for the Council, one could say that here was made clear the historical character of the Church, the unity of God's history with mankind, the inner unity of the people of God even across sacramental class-distinctions, the eschatological dynamism, the provisional and fragmentary nature of this Church that is always in need of renewal, and finally also the ecumenical dimension, that is the different ways in which being linked and related to the Church are possible and effective outside the boundaries of the Catholic Church.

This has already indicated much that is not to be looked for in the concept of the people of God. Perhaps I may be allowed to indulge in some personal reminiscence here, since in a modest way I found myself involved in the developments that led up to the Council. At the beginning of the 1940s when the idea of the people of God had just been brought into the discussion my teacher of theology had come to the opinion, on the basis of many passages in the Fathers of the Church and other evidence from tradition, that the people of God could actually be the basic concept of the Church to a far greater and better extent than the body of Christ. But because he was a very careful person he was not happy with hunches of this kind but wanted to know more precisely. So he decided to commission a series of doctoral theses on this question in order to investigate the matter layer by layer. Thus I was landed with the task of dealing with the idea of the people of God in Augustine, in whom above all he thought he had located the concept. When I went to work it soon became clear that I needed to bring in too the earlier African theologians who had preceded Augustine, especially Tertullian, Cyprian, Optatus of Milevis, and the Donatist Tyconius. One also needed of course to keep in mind the more important Eastern theologians, at least figures like Origen, Athanasius and Chrysostom, and finally it was imperative to study the biblical foundations too. Here I stumbled on an unexpected finding: while the term "people of God" occurred very frequently in the New Testament, only in very few passages, probably only in two, did it mean the Church, and its normal meaning indicated the people of Israel. Indeed, even where it could denote the Church the fundamental meaning of Israel was retained, though the context made it clear that now the Christians had become Israel. We can therefore say that in the New Testament the term "people of God" is not a description of the Church, but that it can only denote the new Israel in the Christological re-interpretation of the Old Testament and thus by means of its Christological transformation. In the New Testament the normal term for the Church is the word *ecclesia*, which in the Old Testament denotes the assembly of the people through being summoned by the word of God. The term *ecclesia*, Church, is the New Testament's modification and transformation of the Old Testament concept of the people of God. It is used because in it is included the idea that it is only through the new birth in Christ that what was not a people has been able to become a people. Paul then consistently summed up this necessary Christological process of transformation in the concept of the body of Christ. Before I go on to draw the consequences from this I must first note that the Old Testament scholar Norbert Lohfink has meanwhile shown that even in the Old Testament the term "people of God" does not simply mean Israel in the sense in which it is open to empirical observation and discovery. Purely empirically no people is the people of God. To set God up as an indicator of descent or as sociological label could only ever be an intolerable presumption and indeed ultimately blasphemy. Israel is described by the term people of God to the extent that it is turned towards the Lord, not just in itself but in the act of relating and transcending itself which alone turns it into what it is not of itself. To this extent the New Testament development is consistent that makes this act of turning to God concrete in the mystery of Jesus Christ, who devotes himself to us and in faith and sacrament includes us in his relationship to the Father.

What does this mean in actual reality? It means that Christians are not simply the people of God. From an empirical point of view they are not a people, as can quickly be shown by any sociological analysis. And God is nobody's property: nobody can monopolize him for himself or herself. The non-people of Christians can only be the people of God through inclusion in Christ, the son of God and the son of Abraham. Even when people talk of the people of God Christology must remain the core of what is taught about the Church and as a consequence the Church must essentially be thought of on the basis of the sacraments of baptism, the eucharist and holy orders. We are the people of God in no other way than on the basis of the crucified and risen body of Christ. It is only in living relation to him that we become the people of God, and it is only in this context that the term has a meaning. The Council very brilliantly made this connection clear when along with the term "people of God" it brought into prominence another fundamental term for the Church: the Church as sacrament. One only remains faithful to the Council if one always takes and reflects on these two core terms of its ecclesiology together, sacrament and people of God. Here it becomes clear how far the Council is still ahead of us: the idea of the Church as sacrament has hardly entered people's awareness.

It is therefore absurd when from the fact that the chapter on the people of God precedes that on the hierarchy people want to deduce a different conception of the hierarchy and of the laity, as if in fact all the baptized already bore within themselves the powers conferred by ordination and hierarchy were merely a matter of good order. The second chapter of *Lumen Gentium* does deal with the question of the laity to the extent that the essential inner unity of all the baptized in the order of grace is expressed and the Church's character of service is thereby emphasized. But this chapter quite simply does not lay the foundations of the theology of the laity through the fact that everyone belongs to the people of God: what is being dealt with here is the Church as a whole and its nature. Its different classes are presented subsequently, and indeed in the order hierarchy (chapter 3), laity (chapter 4), religious (chapter 6).

If my presentation of the ecclesiology of Vatican II were to be able to make any claim to completeness, I would now have to expound the contents of these remaining chapters and also what is said about the joint vocation to holiness and the relationship of the Church on earth to the Church in heaven. But that would far exceed the limits of a lecture. I have merely been concerned briefly to indicate the foundations on which all applications depend. In conclusion I would like merely briefly to indicate one further point. The Council's constitution on the Church ends with the chapter on the mother of God. The question whether a separate document should be devoted to her was, as is known, the subject of vigorous debate. I think it was nevertheless a good arrangement for the question of Mary to enter directly into the doctrine of the Church. In this way the point that we started out from becomes visible once again: the Church is not some piece of machinery, is not just an institution, is not even one of the usual sociological entities. It is a person. It is a woman. It is a mother. It is living. The Marian understanding of the Church is the most decisive contrast to a purely organizational or bureaucratic concept of the Church. We cannot make the Church: we have to be it. And it is only to the extent that faith moulds our being beyond any question of making that we *are* the Church, that the Church is in us. It is only in being Marian that we become the Church. In its origins the Church was not made but was born. It was born when the intention "Let it be to me according to your word" awoke in the soul of Mary. That the Church should awaken in our souls is the deepest desire of the Council. Mary shows us the way.

APPENDIX

MODERN VARIATIONS OF THE CONCEPT OF THE PEOPLE OF GOD

The emphasis with which the idea of the people of God was seized on during the Council meant that the emotion surrounding this discovery far exceeded what the biblical foundations could bear. Fortunately the Council documents themselves were able to avoid infection with this emotionalism. But it increased all the more in the period after the Council, in which two inter-connected tendencies are to be noted: on the one hand a reductionism which comes close to letting only the term "the people of God" survive from the Council's ecclesiology; on the other a re-casting and expansion of its meaning in the sense of turning the idea of the Church into a sociological entity. In this context "people" appears as a concept to be dealt with in sociological and political terms: if the Church can be defined by the concept "people", then its nature and its legal structure are best determined on the basis of sociological points of view. In this way the "people of God" becomes the vehicle of an anti-hierarchical and anti-sacral idea of the Church, indeed a revolutionary category suitable for dreaming up a new Church.

These post-conciliar developments are certainly classified to some extent by the present spiritual situation in which the question of the biblical heritage and of tradition has continually retreated in the face of pragmatic and sociological categories and those derived from humane studies. All the same, the whole business is not as completely new as all that: it would hardly have been possible with such intensity had it not been prepared for theologically in many different ways over a long period. Extremely important clues to this question are to be found in a book by the great Byzantine scholar Endre von Ivánka which unfortunately has hardly been noticed by theologians up till now: *Rhomäerreich und Gottesvolk* (Freiburg/Munich 1968). It is impossible to

21

indicate with the brevity that is needed here even the broad outlines of this book's relevant findings. What follows can merely serve as an indication of the significance of Ivánka's investigation.

The oldest roots of the transformation of the concept of the people of God into something political are visible in Eusebius of Caesarea: in his idea of Christians as the "third nation" to which the "two others", the pagans and the Jews, lead up. If Clement of Alexandria presented the providential role of the Greeks, what we get with Eusebius is the evaluation of the Roman Empire in terms of salvation history and its classification within God's plan of salvation.[1] On this Ivánka comments: "It is an incredible audacity to regard an actual human community, a genuinely existing state, even if it should be the universal Roman *imperium,* simply as the people of God and to clothe it with the aura of the chosen people of the Old Testament."[2] From this point of view Constantine's empire appears not just as the summit of Roman civilization but as the fulfilment and completion of that line of tradition whose prototype is to be found in Abraham.[3] This nation of people is now at work absorbing the other nations into itself and creating from all of them the "new people of God" promised by the prophets.[4]

Ivánka then shows how this conception persisted and was modified in Byzantine theology and its continuation after the fall of Constantinople in the idea of the third Rome. The decisive turning point when modern national ideologies were directly prepared paradoxically occurred in the Russian *raskol* or schism, when the Old Believers turned away from a hierarchy whose reforms, justified in themselves, were experienced by the simple people as a break of continuity and as the destruction of the faith that had been handed down. This event is so significant for the modern development of the

---

[1] E. von Ivánka, *Rhomäerreich und Gottesvolk,* Freiburg-München 1968, p. 54.
[2] Ibid., p. 57.
[3] Ibid., p. 51.
[4] Ibid., p. 53. For Eusebius's political ecclesiology cf. the fundamental analysis of V. Twomey, *Apostolikos Thronos. The primacy of Rome as reflected in the Church History of Eusebius and the historico-apologetic writings of St Athanasius the Great,* Münster 1982, especially pp. 13 – 229.

concept of the Church that it is justifiable to quote in greater detail how it is characterized by Ivánka: "There is a great element of tragedy in the fact that with the Old Believers the old Byzantine attitude of regarding one's traditional discipline and rite as the criterion of orthodoxy, which for its part had led to the break of 1054, should now be turned against the Greek and the official Russian Church, and that the Old Believers should now themselves break . . . with the official Russian Church and with Greek Orthodoxy on the basis of the same Byzantine tradition of equating national individuality with the orthodox Church as such — in the name of the orthodox *people*, not the orthodox *Church*."[5] In this context Ivánka talks of the "nationalization of the Church": against the Church (against its hierarchy) "the 'orthodox people' upheld as a people, as a nation, the claim to be the sole bearer of orthodoxy . . .".[6]

The attempt to keep things strickly as they were here becomes in reality a revolutionary change in the concept of the Church. In its opposition to the reformist hierarchy the traditionalism that had been forced into dissent leads to a transformation of the faith which fundamentally alters tradition itself.[7] It is no longer the sacrament of apostolic succession that guarantees the identity of the Church and of its message through the ages, but instead the people as such in its unwavering consistency vouches for the Spirit, even against the sacrament. If at first this change, which gives the sociological entity of the people or nation a totally new standing over against the theological category of "sacrament", took place in the restricted circle of the Old Believers with their hostility to education and thus apparently had no effect on history at large, in the nineteenth century a new development brought the idea right into the midst of educated Christianity and finally to western European thought. In opposition to the westernization of Russian intellectual life introduced by Peter the Great a group of

[5] Ivánka, op. cit., p. 132.
[6] Ibid., pp. 133—4.
[7] Similar developments could now occur in the west if "traditionalism" were to lose its links with Rome and the hierarchy of the universal Church or in reverse if the hierarchy were to fail to succeed in making the internal harmony of reform and tradition convincingly understandable even to the simple faithful.

thinkers, among whom the Slavophils stand out as most effective, sought from the middle of the nineteenth century onwards to renew in a way suitable to their times the values of Russia's national tradition. In this context it seemed natural and self-evident to go back to the Old Believers' idea "of the orthodoxy anchored fast in the national consciousness, of the 'national Church' or 'Church of the people' . . . living in the community".[8] "The *raskolniks'* (schismatics') concept of the Church", states Ivánka, "now became translated into the characteristic concept of the Church of Orthodoxy as a whole."[9]

With the Slavophils' "Father of the Church", Alexei Stepanovich Khomyakov (1804 – 1860), these views were given a systematic shape which has appreciably affected western ideas of Orthodoxy, although they are far removed from its historical reality and depend on the radical departure of the Old Believers' schism which turned the Orthodox tradition upside down in the core of its being. For Khomyakov the orthodox people is the guardian of the faith, because it is "the bearer of God": the Holy Spirit "is at work in it and speaks out of its faith; the hierarchy elected and installed by it only has the task of bearing witness to the faith that is alive in it . . .".[10] Setting the people against the hierarchy here also becomes setting the people against the teaching authority, the formation of a pneumatic rather than a hierarchical concept of the Church from which here then arises the idea of a Church of love which is pneumatically, not hierarchically, united. All this is far removed from the classical Orthodox tradition, but, in the process of theological reflection inspired by the Old Believers' movement, it now appears as the true physiognomy of eastern Christianity, which in this form seemed to more and more Catholic and Protestant circles in the west as the ideal image of Johannine Christianity in which the clash between Petrine (Roman Catholic) and Pauline (Protestant) Christianity, a clash that in itself could not be done away with, could be transcended in a higher unity.[11]

[8] Ivánka, op. cit., p. 143.
[9] Ibid.
[10] Ibid., p. 145.
[11] Cf. Ivánka, op. cit., p. 144.

Ivánka draws attention to the fact that Slavophil thinking was not simply nourished by the tap-root of "the faith of the people" but absorbed other traditions which further developed the idea of the people. If one traces the individual lines one is astonished to be able to establish how completely all the post-conciliar developments have been prepared for in advance here. The spiritual idea of the Church may not express the eastern Church's traditional understanding of itself, since it was essentially an episcopal Church and also the Byzantine state church. But it can link up with tendencies in monastic writings in both east and west which among other things were also of significance for Luther's turning against the hierarchy.[12] This spiritual idea of the Church tie in with the ideas of the Old Believers, who had to live without priests and could no longer rely on the apostolic tradition but had to depend on the people's gift of bearing the Spirit.[13] Finally a significant role is also played by the German romantic movement: "Via Schelling, who exercised decisive influence on the Russian intellectual life of the first half of the nineteenth century, the roots of the Slavophil idea of the people being the bearer of God lead to the German romantic movement and its idea of 'the spirit of the people' as the ultimate bearer of spiritual values, and even further back to the ultimate source of European and especially east European romanticism, Herder's concept of nationhood."[14]

The transformation these themes undergo with Khomyakov is far-reaching. For him faith is not the power that makes it possible to accept a revealed doctrine but a power of knowledge and discernment that is higher and more real than merely conceptual thinking. But in his view this power of faith is to be ascribed not to the individual but to the community of the orthodox people. For him there follows from this the claim to the absolute subjection of the individual to the collective — which also applies to the political sphere. The distinction between western democracies and the orthodox people is according to him the fact "that in a democracy a majority imposes its will on the minority, while the orthordox people always decides unanimously

[12] Ibid., pp. 149 and 151.
[13] Ibid., p. 150.
[14] Ibid., p. 152.

because the individual . . . always privately subordinates himself or herself to its decisions . . .". The transformation into the social and political field and the blending together of religious and of social and political ideas in the concept of the people become quite clear when Khomyakov regards the *mir*, the Russian village community, as the only truly Christian form of society; "For you the community is the highest manifestation of being human. In the perfect society the individual must be extinguished." "The absolute value of the human being — yes, if he or she renounces his or her individual personality and subordinates himself or herself completely to the whole. This renunciation . . . is the principle of a truly free human community and concord which is consecrated and hallowed by the presence of the Holy Spirit."[15]

There is no need here to point out how startlingly close such ideas are to the modern ideas that have sprung up after the Council of the grass-roots Church, the "Church from below", the Church of the people, the congregation as the agent of all campaigns that are religious and political and social at one and the same time. But I would like to indicate another strand in intellectual history which has had its effects in the virulence of a concept of the people of God loosed from its biblical basis after Vatican II. Just as the German romantic movement from Herder to Schelling had its effects on Russian thought and in its transformation through other traditions and experiences the whole returned to the west with fresh vigour, so the thought of Latin America has similarly been affected by currents from French intellectual life which found new contexts there and acquired fresh energies to

---

[15] The relevant citations are to be found in Ivánka, op. cit., pp. 153–4. On p. 152 Ivánka draws attention to an important passage in Dostoyevsky's *The Possessed (The Devils)* where the actual theological problem involved in this subordination of the religious to the national becomes visible. The question: "One must believe in God in order to be able to believe in the God-bearing people. Do you believe in God?" and the answer: I believe in the Russian people, I believe in the God-bearing-ness of the Russian people, I want to believe in God" are followed by the riposte: "That does not mean believing in God but turning God into an attribute of the people". In the post-conciliar use of the concept of the people of God this situation has been approached more and more closely and the boundary indicated has in practice not seldom been crossed.

become historically effective. The Brazilian scholar Ricardo Vélez Rodriguez has shown how in South America it was especially Jean-Jacques Rousseau (1712 – 1778) and Claude Henri Saint-Simon (1760 – 1825) who became the "Fathers of the Church" for a new blend of philosophical and theological, political and religious ideas. Saint-Simon stated: "The people of God which already before the advent of Christ received the revelation, the people scattered for the most part over the earth has always known that the Christian doctrine established by the Fathers of the Church is imperfect. It has always looked forward to the coming of a greater age which it has given the name of the kingdom of the Messiah, an age in which religious doctrine will appear in the complete universality of what is available to it and will guide the working of secular as well as of the spiritual power. The whole of mankind will then be united under a single religion and organization."[16] With his "new Christianity" Saint-Simon gave concrete form to Rousseau's concept of a "civil religion" and developed it further. To provide a concept of the Church for this new Christianity, which links the political, the social and the religious and thus promises to bring about complete salvation in this world, what is on offer is "the people of God". What is religious and what is of the people, tradition and modernity can be united in this concept: it allows one to free oneself from tradition while at the same time enlisting it on one's side. Vélez Rodriguez has shown the extent to which the theopolitical heritage of Rousseau and Saint-Simon has remained alive in Latin America so as to be able to become effective as the compost for new conceptions of religion with a political slant.

Anyone who tries to grasp the post-conciliar development of the concept of the Church merely on the basis of the classical theological sources will only with difficulty catch sight of the real problems. The effort to obtain an accurate, biblically based formulation of the concept of the Church must be realized today primarily as an exercise in the self-

---

[16] R. Vélez Rodriguez, "*Politischer Messianismus und Theologie der Befreiung*", in *Internationale katholische Zeitschrift* 13 (1984), pp. 343 – 354; the quotation is on p. 346.

criticism of the intellectual history of the modern age, with its blendings of what is political and what is religious, of biblical tradition and more recent mythologies. To a greater extent than we had thought both the eastern world on the one hand and the American continent on the other belong to this intellectual history. Such an analysis will not only lead to condemnations: it will be able to discover fruitful new knowledge in what is often a displeasing context. It will not only be condemnation but it must always be purification. To make clear how necessary has become a purification of the concept of the people of God on the basis of the biblical foundations and the centre-point of the tradition of the faith: that is the point of the brief suggestions I have been putting forward in this appendix.

2

The papal primacy and
the unity of the people of God

I: THE SPIRITUAL BASIS OF PRIMACY
AND COLLEGIALITY

The papacy is not one of the popular themes of the post-conciliar age. To a certain extent it was something that could be taken for granted as long as it was counterbalanced by monarchy in the political field. But once the idea of monarchy was extinguished in practice and superseded by that of democracy, the doctrine of primacy lost its field of reference in the general presuppositions of our thought. Thus it is certainly no accident that, while the First Vatican Council was dominated by the idea of primacy, the Second was dominated by the dispute over the concept of collegiality.[1] To this, of course, it should at once be added that Vatican II sought to describe the idea of collegiality, with which it took up motives from contemporary ideas, in such a way that the idea of primacy is contained within it. It is probably precisely from this point that we must start today, now that we have had a little experience of collegiality, of its value and also of its limits, so as better to grasp the way in which traditions that appear to diverge in fact belong together and thus to safeguard the wealth of the Christian idea.

---

[1] The context in terms of the history of ideas in which Vatican I is to be seen has been illuminatingly expounded by H. J. Pottmeyer, *Unfehlbarkeit und Souveränität. Die päpstliche Unfehlbarkeit im System der ultramontanen Ekklesiologie des 19. Jahrhunderts,* Tübinger theologische Studien, Band 5, Mainz 1975.

*1. Collegiality as an expression of the "we" structure of the
   faith*

In connection with the Council's debate theology tried for
its part to understand collegiality beyond its purely structural
and functional aspects as the expression of a fundamental law
that reaches back into the most inward essential depths of
Christianity, a law that appears in different ways at the
different levels of the realization of Christianity in practice. It
can be shown that what may be termed the "we" structure is
an essential component of Christianity.[2] The believer is as
such never alone: to become a believer means stepping out of
one's isolation to become part of the "we" of the children of
God; the act of turning towards the God revealed in Christ is
always also a turning towards those who have already been
called. The act of theo-logy is as such always an ecclesial act
for which a social structure is suitable.[3] Initiation into the
Christian life is actually therefore always also socialization in
the community of those who believe, is a process of becoming
"we" that transcends the mere "I" of the ego.[4]
Corresponding to this was the fact that Jesus's calling of the
disciples takes the form of the Twelve, which takes up the
number of the old concept of the people of God, an essential
element of which is once again that God creates a joint

---

[2] I tried to bring out the spiritual background of collegiality in the "we" structure
of Christianity in "The Pastoral Implications of Episcopal Collegiality",
Concilium, vol. 1 no. 1, January 1965, pp. 20 – 34 (reprinted in its original German
in Joseph Ratzinger, *Das neue Volk Gottes*, Düsseldorf 1969, pp. 201 – 224). The
problem is tackled at a fundamental level by the important work by H. Mühlen, *Una
Mystica persona. Die Kirche als Mysterium der Identität des Heiligen Geistes in
Christus und der Kirche Eine Person in vielen Personen*, Paderborn 1964, (^{3}1968).
[3] This was impressively expounded by Henri de Lubac in his work *Catholicisme*,
which first appeared in 1938 (English translation by Lancelot C. Sheppard,
Catholicism: a study of dogma in relation to the corporate destiny of mankind,
London 1950). On this cf. the Regensburg dissertation by H. Schnackers, *Kirche als
Sakrament und Mutter*. In Germany the same starting-point was used particularly
by H. Poschmann in his work on the theology of the sacrament of penance, cf.
especially *Poenitentia secunda*, Bonn 1940; and it was impressively continued by
Karl Rahner in his essay "Forgotten Truths concerning the Sacrament of Penance",
Theological Investigations, vol. II, London and Baltimore 1963, pp. 135 – 174.
[4] Initiation as socialization into the Church is very strongly emphasized in the
section *"Engliederung in die Kirche"* of the *Pastorale Handreichung für den
pastoralen Dienst* compiled by G. Biemer, J. Müller and R. Zerfass, Mainz 1972.

history and deals with his people as a people.[5] Looking at this from the other side, the deepest reason for Christianity having this "we" character is shown to be the fact that God himself is a we: the God confessed by the Christian creed is not thought thinking itself in solitude, is not an absolute and indivisible ego shut in on itself, but unity in the trinitarian relationship of I-you-we, so that being we as the fundamental form of God precedes all earthly forms of this relationship and being made in the image of God is from the start referred to this kind of being we.[6]

In this context a previously largely forgotten essay by E. Peterson on "Monotheism as a political problem" came back into notice. Peterson had tried to show that Arianism was a political theology favoured by the emperors because it guaranteed that the idea of God corresponded to political monarchy while for belief in the trinity to prevail meant exploding this political theology and removing the theological justification of political monarchy.[7] Peterson had broken his explanation off at this point: it was now taken up again and developed to a new idea of correspondence, the basic principle of which was that the Church's action and behaviour must correspond to the "we" of God by following the pattern of this relationship. This general principle that could be interpreted in many different ways was occasionally pushed too far to reach the statement whereby the exercise of the primary by a single human being, the Pope in Rome, was really following an Arian pattern: corresponding to the trinitarian nature of God as three persons the Church too must be led by a college of three who collectively would be the pope. There was no lack of resourceful speculation to work

[5] For the significance of the Twelve cf. Rudolf Schnackenburg, *The Church in the New Testament*, London 1965, pp. 22 – 35; on the way the Council took the subject up see G. Philips, *L'Église et son mystère au II\ème concile du Vatican*, vol. I, Paris 1967, pp. 277 – 290, also pp. 230 – 245.

[6] Cf. Henri de Lubac, *Christian Faith: The Structure of the Apostles' Creed*, London 1986, pp. 19 – 37; Joseph Ratzinger, *Introduction to Christianity*, London 1971, pp. 114 – 137; H. Mühlen, *Una mystica persona* (note 2 above).

[7] First published in 1935, reprinted in E. Paterson, *Theologische Traktate*, Munich 1951, pp. 45 – 147. The historical complex of problems involved in Peterson's thesis becomes discernible in A. Grillmeier, *Mit ihm und in ihm. Christologische Forschungen und Perspektiven*, Freiburg 1975, pp. 386 – 419.

out, no doubt with the support of Solviev's *History of Anti-christ,* that in this way a Roman Catholic, an Orthodox and a Reformed Christian could together form the papal troika. In this way it looked as if theology itself, the concept of God, had provided the key for squaring the ecumenical circle in such a way that the papacy, the chief obstacle for non-Catholic Christians, would have to become the definitive vehicle for the unity of all Christians.[8]

2. *The inner reason for the primacy: faith as witness for which one is personally responsible*

Does this then represent the reconciliation of collegiality and primacy, the answer to the question implicit in our subject—the papal primacy and the unity of the people of God? We should not refuse to recognize anything fruitful and useful in such ideas: it is of course obvious that they represent a distortion of the doctrine of the trinity and an intolerably simplified form of combining confessing one's faith and Church politics. A deeper principle is necessary. What seems to me to be important first of all is once again to link the theology of community which has developed out of the idea of collegiality more clearly once again with a theology of personality, which is something that is no less important for the biblical data. Not only the community nature of the history created by God but also and equally personal responsibility belongs to the structure of the Bible. Its we does not abolish I and you but confirms and corroborates them as something definitive. This is shown already by the position that the name has in the Old Testament—both with God and with men and women. One could almost say that in the Bible the name stands in the place of that which philosophical

---

[8] This kind of thing was occasionally to be heard in conversation, based on a coarsened version of remarks of H. Mühlen, particularly in his work *Entsakralisierung,* Paderborn 1971, pp. 228ff., 240ff., 376–396, 401–440. Although Mühlen's own explanations are impressive and do carry the argument forward, they seem to me not to be free of the danger of a new way of thinking in terms of correspondence that overstretches the ecclesiological applicability of statements about the Trinity.

reflection will finally describe by the terms person.[9] To the God who has a name, in other words who can address people and be addressed in turn, corresponds the human being who is named in the history of revelation and whose responsibility is linked to his or her name.[10] This principle is strengthened even more in the New Testament and brought to its full profundity by the fact that now the people of God comes into being no longer by birth but by being called and responding. Hence it is no longer something that can be addressed collectively as it was before, when the whole people operated with regard to the history of the world as a kind of large-scale individual in collective punishment, in collective responsibility, repentance and pardon. The "new people" is also marked by a new structure of personal responsibility which is seen in the personalization of worship: from now on everyone is called by his or her name in the sacrament of penance, and on the basis of the personal baptism which he or she received as being a particular person is called to personal repentance by name, and for this the general statement "We have sinned" can no longer suffice.[11] Also corresponding to this structure, for example, is the fact that the liturgy does not just talk of the Church in general but presents it by name in the eucharistic prayer, with the names of the saints and of those who bear the responsibility of unity. I would like to point out in passing that on this basis it seemed to me questionable that in the first edition of the lectionary for the German-speaking world the names were deleted (probably for fear of historically false ascriptions) and even Paul's letter to the Romans was not presented with the apostle's responsibility and name but was put forward as if it were an anonymous piece of writing the personal origin of which and the personal responsibility for which remained unclear.[12] Also corresponding to this personal structure is the

---

[9] Cr. Joseph Ratzinger, *Der Gott Jesu Christi,* Munich 1976 , pp. 11 – 21.

[10] Cf. for example the importance of the family trees in the construction of the Bible story.

[11] This has been vividly worked out by Hans-Urs von Balthasar in "Umkehr im Neuen Testament" in *Internationale katholische Zeitschrift* 3 (1974), pp. 481 – 491.

[12] If the aim was to avoid the problem of the authorship of disputed texts, then this involves confusing two different levels and misunderstanding what the liturgy is saying: it must necessarily stand on the firm historical ground of the faith but it should not be seen as the place where historical disputes are decided.

fact that in the Church the leadership of the community or congregation has never been anonymous. Paul writes in his own name as the person who is ultimately responsible for his communities. But he also continually addresses by name those who bear responsibility with him or subordinate to him: one need only think of the lists of greetings in 1 Corinthians and Romans or the notice in 1 Corinthians 4:17: "Therefore I sent to you Timothy . . . to remind you of my ways in Christ, as I teach them everywhere in every Church" — or Philippians, where in 4:2 Paul suddenly switches to the second person singular to address Euodia, Syntyche and his "true yokefellow". On these lines people were already putting together lists of bishops (Hegesippus) in order to put before the scrutiny of history the personal responsibility of the witnesses of Jesus Christ in a verifiable way by naming them.[13] This procedure corresponds at the profoundest level to the central structure of faith of the New Testament: corresponding to *the* witness Jesus Christ are *the* witnesses who, because they are witnesses, vouch for him by name. Martyrdom as response to the cross of Christ is nothing other than the final confirmation of this principle of named personal responsibility that cannot be transferred.[14] Being a witness implies this personal particularity, but as response to the cross and resurrection being a witness is anyway the original basic form of Christian discipleship. With this, however, this principle is now anchored fast in the trinitarian belief in God itself, since the trinity becomes meaningful and in fact recognizable for us through the fact that in his Son as man God himself has become witness to himself and thus his personality has taken actual concrete shape in the radical

---

[13] The structural significance of these lists as embodiments of the concept of tradition for the construction of Eusebius's *Ecclesiastical History* is shown by a dissertation being completed by V. Twomey on ecclesiology in Eusebius and Athanasius.

[14] The essential significance of martyrdom in the structure of the Christian act of faith is well brought out by K. Bommes, *Weizen Gottes. Untersuchungen zur Theologie des Martyriums bei Ignatius von Antiochien,* Cologne/Bonn 1976; cf. also E. Peterson, "Zeuge der Wahrheit", in *Theologische Traktate,* Munich 1951, pp. 165 – 224. The fact that martyrdom can find no place in Hans Küng, *On being a Christian,* London 1977, pp. 573 – 576 (cf. also the summary of his basic thesis on pp. 601 – 602), when seen from this point of view, affects the heart of the matter.

anthropomorphism of "the form of a servant" in "the likeness of men" (Phil 2:7: μορφὴ δούλου, ὁμοίωμα ἀνθρώπου).[15]

It is on this line that the New Testament's Petrine theology is to be found. It is in this that it has its inner necessity. The "we" of the Church begins with the name of the person who in his own name and as a person was the first to confess Jesus as the Christ: "You are the Christ, the Son of the living God" (Mt 16:16). It is remarkable that the primacy text is usually reckoned to start at Matthew 16:17, whereas in the mind of the early Church the decisive verse for understanding the whole is verse 16: Peter becomes the Church's rock as the bearer of its creed, its belief in God, which in concrete terms is belief in Christ as the Son and with that belief in the Father and therein belief in the trinity, something which only the Spirit of God can impart.[16] In the mind of the early Church verses 17–19 were seen as merely the explanation and interpretation of verse 16: to articulate the creed is never something a man or woman does on his or her own, and so someone who in the obedience of confessing says what he or she cannot say from his or her own resources can also do and become what he or she could not do and become from his or her own resources. In this perspective the dichotomy which first appears in Augustine and which has dominated the theological scene since the sixteenth century does not exist: the dichotomy indicated in asking whether the foundation of the Church is Peter as a person or his confession. The answer is that the confession only exists as something for which someone is personally responsible, and hence the confession is linked to the person. To look at it the other way round, it is not a person regarded as what one might call a metaphysically neutral entity that is the foundation but the person as the

---

[15] For the exposition of this fundamental text see J. Gnilka, *Der Philipperbrief*, Freiburg 1968, pp. 111–147.

[16] Failure to notice this is the weakness in the commendable work by J. Ludwig, *Die Primatworte Mt 16,18.19 in der altkirchlichen Exegese* (Neutestamentliche Abhandlungen, edited by M. Meinertz, XIX:4), Münster 1954. This blocks the way to understanding Leo the Great, though all the other Fathers must also be worked through again on the basis of less narrowly formulated questions. The correction to Ludwig's work should be compared: S. Horn, *Petrou Kathedra. Der Bischof von Rom und die Synode von Ephesus und Chalcedon*, Paderborn 1982.

bearer of the confession: one without the other would fail to convey what is meant.

Omitting many intermediate stages, we can therefore say that Christians' unity as "we" which has been established by God in Christ through the Holy Spirit under the name of Jesus Christ and by his witness authenticated in death and resurrection is held together by persons responsible for this unity and is represented once again in a personalized form in Peter—in Peter, who receives a new name and to that extent is raised up beyond what are merely his own abilities and qualities, but at the same time in a name through which his own personal responsibility is laid claim to. In his new name that transcends the historical individual Peter becomes the institution which passes through history (since this ability of this institution to continue and the fact that it has continued is contained in this re-naming), but in such a way that this institution can only exist as a person and in personal responsibility tied to a particular name.

II: THE MARTYROLOGICAL STRUCTURE OF THE PRIMACY

At this point a question arises which has become continually more dramatic since the sixteenth century: does not the claim that is made with the name of Peter completely surpass the dimensions of a human being? Can this final claim and demand of the personality principle still be justified in anthropological terms as well as on the basis of the Bible's fundamental perspective? Or is it not that it applies merely to Christ and that therefore its application to a "vicar of Christ" can only have the effect of damaging the principle of *solus Christus*? This would involve the individual exegetical question, from the perspective of the whole, necessarily being resolved in the sense of a possible Petrine theology of the type sketched out being in contradiction to the New Testament's core statements and thus being labelled degenerate. It is correct that every evaluation of individual exegetical findings depends on a global perspective and that consequently deciding for or against a particular interpretation cannot be done solely within the limits of that interpretation. Beyond this, as F. Mussner has convincingly made clear, it can hardly be disputed today, on the basis of the individual findings, that a Petrine theology intended as a permanent contribution and a Petrine office exist.[17] Moveover the global perspective of the New Testament as a whole seems all the more effectively to oppose the kind of ministry whereby the idea of a purely pastoral primacy without legal rank need not come into consideration on the grounds that in practical terms it is irrelevant.[18]

1. The primacy's structure of witness as a necessary consequence of the opposition of Church and world

I will try to answer the question that has been raised in this way by reference to a historical controversy which in my view has the character of a paradigm and has led to the development of one of the profoundest theologies of the primacy in which the ecumenical claim of the subject is maintained to a degree hardly to be found anywhere else. I am referring to the dispute between Cardinal Reginald Pole on the one hand and on the other King Henry VIII, Cranmer and Bishop Sampson over what happened in the Church of England with regard to the primacy. How real these questions were for Pole can be seen from the fact that on the one hand his life and his homeland were at stake and that on the other he was the most favoured candidate for election as pope in the conclave of 1549—50 and for one moment was regarded as having been elected: in addition, in the last years of his life he was suspected of advocating a Lutheran doctrine of justification and of himself being a heretic.[19] Pole saw himself

[17] Cr. F. Mussner, "Petrusgestalt und Petrusdienst in der Sicht der späten Urkirche. Redaktionsgeschichtliche Überlegungen", in Joseph Ratzinger (ed.), *Dienst an der Einheit*, Düsseldorf 1978, pp. 27—45.

[18] This idea put forward by Luther in the Leipzig Disputation, taken up by Melanchthon and recently revived by Hans Küng, remains unreal. A responsibility that cannot accept responsibility is no responsibility at all.

[19] On this cf. the work by M. Trimpe, *Grundmotive der Theologie des päpstlichen Primats im Denken Reginald Poles* (1500—1558), Regensburg dissertation, 1982. The following remarks about Pole are based on this work. Cf. also W. Schenk, *Reginald Pole, Cardinal of England*, London 1950; D. Fenlon, *Heresy and obedience in Tridentine Italy. Cardinal Pole and the Counter-Reformation*, Cambridge 1971.

opposed to Sampson's thesis that the papal office as such
contradicted Christian humility and could not from the start
be reconciled with this — in other words in fact precisely the
view that we have just now in somewhat different language
described as the central theological objection of Reformed
Christendom.[20] For Pole, on the other hand, it is clear that
denying the primatial principle in fact destroys the New
Testament structure and restores the exclusivity of secular
power. He thus says of Sampson that he "clearly cannot
imagine any other power than that which can kill the body
and rob someone of his outward possessions".[21] In the actual
case of England the denial of the papacy means transferring
to the state the Church's external order, the system of a state
Church and, along with this secular domination over the
Church, the disappearance of martyrdom. In turn this means
that for Pole the martyrs are the unequivocal indication of
where the Church is to be found — and here we touch on the
real reason, both psychological and theological, which turned
Pole into a defender of the papacy. The martyrs, who set
faith in the supranational unity of the universal Church and
its tradition in contrast with the national Christianity of the
realm, provide the indication of where the Christian needs to
stand as a Christian in this dispute. This means two things:

a) The martyrs and the theology of the primacy. In this
way he touches on precisely the early Christian core of the
theology of the primacy as it appeared first in John
21:18 – 19. Dying is something one can only do personally.
The primacy is to be understood first of all as witness to the
confession of Christ on the basis of witness given personal
warranty in martyrdom as verification of testimony for him
who was crucified and victorious on the cross.

b) On the basis of this kind of theology of martyrdom the
primacy represents the guarantee of the opposition of the
Church in its catholic unity to all particular secular power.[22]

[20] Cf. W. Trimpe, chapter 11 § 2 p. 137 and note 51 p. 412.
[21] R. Pole, *Pro ecclesiasticae unitatis defensione libri quatuor,* Rome, no date,
(1553 – 54), 15 r 27.
[22] These two points contain the factual thesis I was concerned to develop in this
lecture: there was thus no question at all of some kind of utopia, as many listeners
thought.

In this context it must now be asked historically what real content can be ascribed to the theology of Peter if one does not see the succession of Peter in the bishop of Rome as its historical fulfilment. The passages in the New Testament are there and demand an explanation. Historically one can establish four answers, and it would hardly be possible to find any more: even if they are capable of individual variation they exhaust the possibilities.

The first answer is that of the Roman tradition of Peter.

The second was given by the early Byzantine theology of the fifth and sixth centuries which referred Matthew 16:16 – 19 and the whole tradition of plenary powers which is tied up with the name of Peter to the emperor. Later this was hardly ever repeated anywhere quite so explicitly, but in fact crops up everywhere that the pattern of a state Church is formed.[23]

A third answer can be found in Theodore of Studios, without it being given by him as an exclusive solution to the question. He sees the saying fulfilled in the monks, in those who are "spiritually spiritual"[24] — a pneumatological solution which has a certain status as expressing the internal dimension of the saying but which cannot stand up on its own.

A fourth answer, prefigured by Augustine and worked out consistently in the Reformation, sees the faith of the community as the rock in which the promises are redeemed. But the specific element of this text is not included in this.[25]

One must therefore say that in reality there are only the

---

[23] On this cf. the material displayed by A. Grillmeier in the section "Auriga mundi" in *Mit ihm und in ihm* (note 7 above), pp. 386 – 419, especially p. 407.

[24] Cf. P. Kawerau, *Das Christentum des Ostens,* Stuttgart 1972, p. 1077: "The honour in which later ages held Basil of Caesarea was so great that he was called a second Peter. Theodore of Studios . . . put it this way: 'You shine in the light of your brilliant life . . .; you yourself took up the key like a new Peter and are the guardian of the entire Church.' It was Theodore's conviction that the monasticism founded by Basil was the foundation of the Church, and history has to a considerable extent confirmed the correctness of this conviction."

[25] On this cf. the remarks of F. Mussner, op. cit. (note 7 above), as well as his book *Petrus und Paulus—Pole der Einheit,* Freiburg 1976. On the exegetical findings see also the contributions of H. Zimmermann, R. Schnackenburg, G. Schneider and J. Ernest in A. Brandenburg and H. J. Urban (ed.), *Petrus und Papst,* Münster 1977, pp. 4 – 62.

alternatives provided by the first and second answers. This means that either (as Pole formulated it) sole and total power on earth is ascribed to the state or that, with the "Roman solution, the papacy is erected as the powerless yet powerful point of opposition to secular power. The latter applies even when, as historically has continually been the case, the attempt is made to clothe the powerlessness of this second "power" in secular might: by this means it has been possible to conceal and jeopardize, but not to destroy, its actual specific nature.

Let us return to Pole. His reference to martyrdom provides the basic answer to Sampson's and to our question. Being the vicar of Christ is a vicariate of obedience and of the cross. It is adapted to and transcends the human just as much as being a Christian.[26]

2. *Sketch of an idea of the primacy seen in martyrological terms*

What is meant by this in practice becomes clearer if as an example we take some features of Pole's image of the pope and thereby look for elements of an answer to the question of how a pope should look today and in general. As a candidate for the papacy Pole was indeed directly confronted by this question, and we are in the historically unique situation of finding the thoughts of a papal candidate during a conclave and his own struggle with the task that might be laid upon him set out in a small book, *De Summo Pontifice,* which he wrote during the conclave for his protégé, the youthful Cardinal Giulio della Rovere.[27] He wanted to help him reach a judgement by providing a kind of mirror of the papacy which now remains as a memorial of his own mental and spiritual struggle and offers a starting-point for reflecting on the dimensions of this office and ministry whose profoundest

---

[26] Hence this kind of presentation of the papal task is just as much and as little utopian as any accurate portrayal of the inner demands of being a Christian.

[27] R. Pole, *De Summo Pontifice Christi in Terris Vicario,* Louvain 1569. For a detailed discussion of the origin and significance of this work see Trimpe, op. cit., (note 19 above).

foundations and reasons are laid bare when its portrait is correctly drawn.

What the pope should be and how he should be it are enquired into in this work in a strictly Christological way. It is from what Christ is that Pole expounds the direction and manner in which the pope should live out the duty of imitating and following Christ. What in relation to Christ is a title of sovereignty — *laudes Christi* — is in relation to the pope a form of requiring him to follow Christ.[28] In this way Pole treats Isaiah 9:6–7 — a text understood as referring to Christ in the Church's tradition of interpretation — as a mirror of the papacy. If Christ appears as *parvulus natus* ("For to us a child is born"), Christologically this means that the Lord has humbled himself for us and that he stands in obedience to the Father and has been sent by him. Christ, "the greatest", has become for us the *parvulus*, "the least". From the point of view of the duty of following and imitating Christ that is laid on the pope, this means: "When you hear that Christ is born for us as a child and sent to us, with regard to his vicar relate this to his election. It is to a certain extent his birth. That means that you must think of him that he is not to such an extent born for himself, that he has not been elected for himself, but for us, that is for the entire flock . . . In the office of shepherd he must regard himself and behave as the least and acknowledge that he knows nothing other than this alone, that he has been taught by God the Father through Christ (cf. 1 Cor 2:2) . . ."[29] Isaiah's next phrase "And the government will be upon his shoulder" refers for Pole to the arduous burden Christ bears for our sake: it is not the word government but the bearing of a more than human burden on human shoulders that for him is the dominant element in this image. The honorific "strong hero" is interpreted by the English cardinal on the basis of what "strength" ultimately means in the Bible. This he finds in the Song of Songs: "For love is strong as death" (8:6). The strength in which the vicar of Christ must become like his Lord is the strength of the love that is ready for martyrdom.[30]

---

[28] *De Summo Pontifice*, p. 27 r – v.
[29] Ibid., pp. 28 v and 32 r – v.
[30] Ibid., p. 52 r – v.

Within the titles to be analysed here Pole discovers a structure which links the whole once more with the starting-point that has just been sketched out and brings out its actual core. There are titles that are to be labelled titles of humility and abasement (*parvulus natus, filius datus, principatus super humerum*) and titles of sovereignty (*magni consilii angelus, princeps pacis,* etc.). Both are related to each other irreversibly, first in the case of Christ himself and then rightly in the case of him who in his faith is to serve Christ as his vicar. The titles of sovereignty belong to Christ essentially as God; but in keeping with his humanity it is only after he has lowered himself that he receives them. This applies analogously to Christ's vicar: the titles of sovereignty are only effective and possible in and beyond his abasement. Sharing in Christ's sovereignty occurs in no other actual way than by sharing in his lowness and humility, which is the only form in which his sovereignty can be made present and represented in this time. In this respect the cross is the real *locus* of the vicar of Christ: standing in the place of Christ is standing in the obedience of the cross and thus the representation of Christ in the secular age, keeping his power present as a counter-balance to the power of the world . . .[31]

In keeping with this Pole, with reference to Peter and on this basis, has made *sedes* (chair, or see as in apostolic see) and cross identical for the pope. To Rovere's question: "What similarity is there now between the see of Peter on which the vicar of Christ sits and the cross on which Christ was nailed?" he makes the following answer: "This we shall recognize easily once we have grasped that the see of the vicar of Christ is that which Peter established in Rome when he implanted the cross of Christ there . . . During the entire exercise of his pontificate he never descended from it, but, 'raised up with Christ' according to the Spirit, his hands and feet were pinioned by the nails in such a way that he did not want to remain where his own will drove him but where

---

[31] Ibid., p. 55 r: . . . *nemo possit sequi Christum in iis quae ad gloriam spectant: nisi prius illum sequutus sit in eo, quod in hominum oculis nullam gloriae speciem obtinet.* Cf. also p. 43 r: . . . *hanc praeclaram Christi personam . . . a nemine referri posse: qui non Christum ante in prioribus illis infirmitatis titulis . . . fuerit imitatus.*

God's will led him (cf. Jn 21:8), and he knew that his mind and his thinking were fixed there . . .''[32] In another passage the English cardinal expresses similar ideas: "The papal office means the cross, and indeed the greatest possible cross. For what could have more to do with the cross . . . than care and responsibility for all the Churches of the globe?" In this context he recalled Moses, who groaned under the burden of all Israel, a burden he could no longer bear and yet had to bear.[33] Being bound to the will of God and to the Word whose messenger he is is that being bound and led against one's own will spoken of in John 21. This being nailed to God's Word and will is however what turns the see or chair into the cross and thus reveals the vicar as the representative, standing in obedience and thus in personal responsibility for him the confession of whose death and resurrection is his entire task, his personal responsibility, in which the common element of the Church is represented in a personally binding way through the person who is bound . . .

This personal responsibility which forms the core of the doctrine of primacy does not therefore stand in opposition to the theology of the cross, nor to Christian humility,[34] but follows from these and is the point where they become ultimately actual. At the same time it is the public contradiction of the power of the world as the only power and the elevation of the power of obedience against secular power. Vicar of Christ is a title that is profoundly concerned with the theology of the cross and thereby provides an interpretation that illuminates the inner unity of Matthew 16:16−19 and John 21:15−19. On the basis of John 21 being bound is to be described as a characteristic that defines the papal office, and without a doubt part of this is that being bound to the will of God that is expressed in God's word

---

[32] Ibid., pp. 132 v − 133 r.

[33] Ibid 133 v: . . . *munus ipsum Pontificatus Crucem esse et eam quidem omnium maximam. Quod enim magis ad Crucem et sollicitudinem animi (pertinere) dici potest, quam universarum orbis terrae Ecclesiarum cura atque procuratio?* Cf. ibid., p. 50 v 1.

[34] By humility in such contexts is meant not simply humility as a moral virtue but as the objective recognition of the fact that justice is not the product of one's own achievement but the fruit of justifying grace.

means being bound to the "we" of the entire Church: collegiality and primacy refer to one another. But they are not dissolved in each other in such a way that personal responsibility ultimately disappears in anonymous committees. It is precisely in the fact that this cannot be separated off that it serves unity, which surely it will achieve all the more the more it remains loyal to its pattern based on the theology of the cross. In this way Pole also defended the thesis that the person most suited to become pope was the person who was least likely to come into consideration from the point of view of a human choice of candidates, on the basis of the ideals of political cunning and clout. The more someone is like the Lord and thus (objectively) comments himself as a candidate, the less will he be regarded by human reason as capable of government, since reason cannot recognize the abasement, the cross.[35]

Conclusion: A look at the situation of Christendom

It would certainly be foolish to expect a general re-union of Christendom based on the papacy in the foreseeable future in the sense of a recognition of the succession of Peter in Rome. Perhaps it is also part of the necessary connections and limitations of this task that it cannot be completely fulfilled and that hence it must also experience the opposition of Christian believers, who emphasize in him what is not his power as vicar but his own power. Nevertheless this kind of papal function of unity transcending the community of the Roman Catholic Church can come into effect. Even when the claims of his office are disputed the pope remains a point of personal reference in the world's sight for the responsibility he bears and expresses for the word of faith, and thus a challenge perceived by everyone and affecting everyone to seek greater loyalty to this word, as well as a challenge to struggle for unity and to be responsible for the lack of unity. In this sense even in division the papacy has a function of establishing unity, and ultimately no-one can imagine the

[35] *De Summo Pontifice*, pp. 79 r – v; 82 r; 90 r.

historical drama of Christendom without this function. For the papacy and for the Catholic Church the criticism of the papacy offered by non-Catholic Christendom is a spur to seek an ever more Christ-like realization of the Petrine ministry; for non-Catholic Christendom the papacy is the permanent visible challenge to the actual unity to which the Church is committed and which should be its characteristic sign in the eyes of the world. On both sides may we succeed in accepting more and more unreservedly the question we are faced with and the task we are given and thus, in obedience to the Lord, become that area of peace which prepares the new world, the kingdom of God.

3

The structure and tasks
of the synod of bishops

Already during the Council the question was touched on whether in the Catholic Church too there should not be something like a "permanent synod" which would aid the pope in leading the universal Church and provide a permanent link between the principles of primacy and collegiality. The synod of bishops created by Paul VI and included in the new code of canon law does indeed take up the idea of regularly involving the bishops of the universal Church collectively in the formation of policy on major questions affecting the Church as a whole, but canonically and theologically it follows a different model. It advises the pope; it is not a small-scale Council, and it is not a collegial organ of leadership for the universal Church. But it is in the nature of things that the question should continually come up in the synod itself and in the synod council whether more should not be attempted. Thus in 1983 Pope John Paul II invited the synod council to give this question a thorough discussion and in due course to put forward proposals. The papers given on this occasion have been published.[1] This chapter is an abbreviated version of the paper I originally drew up in Latin. The aim of simply providing material for discussion explains the very schematic and technical construction of this essay: I have left out what was merely included to suggest how the discussion should be structured and what was concerned with the purely technical aspect of the synod's procedure. I have long hesitated over including

---

[1] J. Tomko (ed.), *Il Sinodo dei Vescovi..Natura—Metodo—Prospettive,* Libreria Editrice Vaticana 1985.

here a text that from the literary point of view has undergone so little revision, but in view of the fact that the question of the synod has remained a matter for discussion I did not finally wish to abandon it. I hope that even in the skeletal form in which it is offered something will become clear of the nature of the synod, of its pastoral significance and of its essential canonical limitations.

I: THE SYNOD OF BISHOPS ACCORDING TO THE NEW CODE OF CANON LAW

1. The synod's nature and aims

The present legal status of the synod of bishops is described in canons 342—348 of the new code. In interpreting these it is important first of all to notice the place the code allots to the synod in its systematic presentation of the Church's law. It is found in the second part of the second book; the second book is entitled "The People of God" and its second part "The Hierarchical Constitution of the Church" (the hierarchical ministry is seen as fitting in this way into the totality of the "people of God"). This second part in its turn is divided into two sections, of which the first deals with "the supreme authority of the Church" and the second with "particular Churches and their groupings". In keeping with this the synod, according to the code's systematization, belongs to the area of the "supreme authority of the Church". As the agent (or agents) of this authority the first chapter presents "the Roman Pontiff and the college of bishops"; subsequent chapters deal with the synod, the cardinals, the Roman curia, and papal legates. Here the question arises of the relationship the synod is seen in with regard to the pope on the one hand and on the other the college of bishops; prior to this is the other question of how the pope and the college of bishops are related to each other — in other words, the question of the sense in which this undeniable duality is represented as the one authority in the one Church.

We approach the answer to this question by considering

the theological structure presented in canon 342 and subsequently the juridical structure presented in the following canons, and by relating these to each other. Canon 342 does not of course provide a proper definition; it describes the purpose of the synod and thus explains its nature on the basis of its goals. Three aims are listed:

1) It is stated that in the synod bishops selected from different parts of the world meet together to promote a closer relationship between the bishops and the pope.

2) By its advice and counsel the synod assists the pope both in the defence and development of faith and morals and in the preservation and strengthening of ecclesiastical discipline. If we look a little more closely at this nuanced statement it becomes clear that both the legal character of the synod's work and the framework and aims of its content are quite clearly described:

a) as its legal character there emerges the task of advising the pope or assisting him with counsel;

b) the framework of its content is formed by (i) the field of faith and morals on the one hand and (ii) on the other the question of the Church's discipline, or how it orders its life;

c) and as the aims of its work there emerges (i) the task of preserving the deposit of faith and protecting the Church's discipline while (ii) there is also the positive goal aimed at expressing the internal dynamism of the gospel, of not just protecting but also developing the faith, of not just protecting but also strengthening discipline, and therefore animating the Church's organization in keeping with the demands of history as it unfolds.

3) The synod should consider questions that concern the Christian involvement in the world.

If one tries to understand as a unity this canon with its varied statements, it becomes clear that the synod is seen in a threefold orientation which corresponds to the three fundamental aspects or relationships which characterize the concept of the Church after the Council. The first is the internal relationship of the pope and the college of bishops. To put it another way, the synod serves the right relationship of the Church's unity and catholicity and therefore of that living unity which corresponds to the vitality of the living organism that is living and growing in the many cells of the local Church. The second consists of assisting and co-operating in the task of the pope; the third in the Church's activity with regard to the world. One could talk of the Church's collegial, primatial and external aspects: the relationship of the college of bishops to the pope, of the pope to the universal Church, and of the Church to the world. According to the canon this triple framework of relationships forms the one object that bears the name "synod of bishops".

If in this way canon 342 describes the synod's theological and pastoral purpose, the question remains how it categorizes this juridically. The analysis of this canon has already let it be clearly seen that the second aim — advising the pope in leading the universal Church — is given by far the most detailed and precise presentation. This suggests from the start that it is here that the nub of the problem is to be found. In fact the synod's threefold aim is comprised in the one juridical category of the assistance which the bishops from all over the world give the pope in his duties towards the universal Church. By doing this they tighten the links between the pope and the bishops and between the bishops themselves; by doing this they make the Church's activity in the world more effective. In this it is important that according to the code it is not the synod itself which initiates this kind of activity in the world: it merely discusses the questions connected with it.

2. Supplementary definitions

The legal status that is quite clearly presupposed in canon 342 is explicitly presented in canons 343 and 344. Canon 344 thus states that the synod is directly subordinated to the authority of the pope, and it spells out what this means. In the same way canon 343 says that the synod discusses the questions put before it and draws up recommendations but does not make decisions or issue decrees. This legal status is not altered by the additional provision that in certain cases the pope can confer on the synod a power of decision. The reason is that this deliberative power remains dependent on the pope: it is assigned to the synod by the pope and is not the expression of powers inherent in the college of bishops.

The detailed provisions concerning general and particular synods — the latter concerned only with particular regions — need not be considered here. But on the other hand what canon 348 has to say about the synod's general secretariat, which is assisted by a council composed of bishops, is important. The secretariat's job is to prepare meetings of the synod and to implement things undertaken by it and connected with it. The co-operation in this of bishops who for the most part are elected by the synod itself guarantees coherence with the needs and desires of the local Churches. But it is obvious that this "council' does not offer any kind of pre-figuration of a "permanent synod" in the way that many would like to understand it; it serves the secretariat and is in no way an organ for sharing with the pope in governing the Church, however important it may be for him to meet these representatives of the universal Church regularly.

3. Conclusions

To conclude this first section, which has dealt simply with interpreting the current law, we must take up once again the question of the relationship between the theological and the legal definition of the synod in these canons and probe it more deeply. A survey of what has been said so far shows that the theological and the legal patterns do not overlap completely and that often the theological framework is drawn more broadly than the legal. In the theological definition we see not only the primatial aspect of the constitution of the Church but also the aim of linking the college of bishops with the pope and also a concern for the Church's responsibility towards the world. But on the other hand looked at legally the synod belongs totally and exclusively to the legal sphere of the pope as primate; it advises the pope, and any possible decrees and decisions it may make are by delegation of papal powers and do not derive from the college of bishops.

Of course the critical observer will at once ask if this must be so, or should not the legal pattern have the same breadth as the theological aims? Is there not here perhaps a starting-point for extending and reforming the synod? One can only answer this if one explains why the legal framework is drawn more tightly than the theological and pastoral one and in what form the college of bishops can become effective as a legal source. The answers given by the code of canon law are simply those of the Second Vatican Council, which for its part brings together the Catholic Church's conciliar and legal traditions. According to the Council there are only two ways in which the college of bishops can act with legal force, that is, as plenipotentiary for the universal Church: an ecumenical council, and by all the bishops dispersed around the world acting together.[2] The Council discussed in detail and stated conclusively how the limitations to these two ways of acting was not something positively determined and therefore capable of being changed but was founded in the nature of the college of bishops itself and could not therefore be extended.

If things are so, then the college of bishops cannot delegate its powers; it can only exercise them itself, as a whole, either in a council or in practice. Included in this once again is the corollary that the college may be able to be involved generally in some process as a spiritual reality but that it cannot ever be a legal source for any kind of representation of itself. This however means that in actual fact it is only the pope who can be the legal source for the synod and that the dichotomy between the theological and pastoral framework and the legal framework is inevitable.

The decisive element that underlines this is therefore the fact that there cannot be any delegation of the responsibility with regard to the universal Church which belongs to the college only as a united whole. We shall have to consider this further in the second part. In the meantime the basic principles of ecclesiology allow us to say the following. The essential meaning and sense of the college of bishops from an ecclesiological point of view does not consist in forming a central government for the Church but precisely the reverse, in the fact that it helps to build up the Church as a living organism which grows in living cells and is a unity. Individual

[2] *Lumen Gentium* § 22.

bishops share in the government of the universal Church not by being represented in some central organ but by leading as shepherds their particular Churches which together form and carry in themselves the whole Church and in doing so lead the Church as a whole, whose health and right government does not simply depend on some central authority but on the right living of the individual cells both in themselves and with relation to the whole. It is in governing the particular Church that the bishops share in governing the universal Church, and not otherwise. The idea that it is only by being represented at the centre that they will have significance for the whole represents a fundamental misjudgement of the nature of the Church; it is the expression of a centralism which the Second Vatican Council in fact wanted to overcome. If one wanted to pursue this idea in order to overcome papal centralism, then all that would be introduced would be a new and much coarser centralism which would bring the Church's real nature to disappearing-point and subordinate it to the logic of contemporary political theories of the state.[3] Overcoming a one-sided centralism must happen the other way round: not by everything being drawn into the centre but by means of the internal bipolarity of the nature of the Church. This nature consists of the working together of the plenary powers of the primacy, which express the Church's unity in diversity, with the living diversity of the local Churches, whose bishop is indeed *episcopus ecclesiae catholicae* by virtue of the fact that he heads the Catholic Church in his Church and heads it as something specifically Catholic.

II: QUESTIONS CONCERNING THE REFORM OF THE SYNOD

After having in the first part attempted to interpret the current law we must now discuss some problems concerned

---

[3] This is why Karl Rahner's attempt to define the bishop on the basis of the college of bishops thought of as a central authority is wrong. A bishop is someone who represents so important a part of the Church that he deserves to belong to the college that is responsible for the Church as a whole.

with the possible future development of this law. It will chiefly be a question of elucidating the ecclesiological principles of canon law by clarifying the concepts involved. But first it must be shown why some widely canvassed models lead us astray and are therefore unusable.

1. Unusable models

a) The simplest model for raising the status of the synod and giving it more weight seems to be the proposal to ascribe a right of decision to it not just in individual cases but generally. But if one looks more closely it is clear that nothing would be gained by this either from the theological or from the practical point of view.

i) The theological reason for this has already become evident. Such a right of decision would — unavoidably, as has been shown — be by delegation from the pope and not the right of the synod itself. In reality such a synod would represent simply a second Roman curia, and it is difficult to see what would be gained by this.

ii) The practical reason consists of the fact that within the short period of time during which a synod can meet the thorough preparation of documents or decrees is not possible. Only one synod, that of 1971, has so far succeeded in issuing some documents which are of real importance but which nevertheless have gained little influence on the life of the Church as a whole. To this one could answer: "Fair enough, that's true — four weeks isn't long enough. But why don't we just extend the length of the session?" Here it is important to mark the difference between a council and a synod. A council is something rare and exceptional in the life of the Church and can thus justify for this special case a bishop's lengthy absence from his see — though of course not so long as to turn him into the delegate of a central body from being the bishop of a local Church. That in fact is the limit we have already come up against. But the synod as a regular component of the life of the Church would by lengthening its sessions affect the nature of the episcopal ministry itself. Here we should recall that an essential element of the

Tridentine reform of the Church was the restoration of the
bishop's duty to reside in his diocese. This duty should not in
any way be seen as purely a matter of discipline but is at its
core a requirement of divine law, that is, derives from the
sacrament itself: to be a bishop means to be the shepherd of
one's Church, not its delegate at some centre. The details are
of course subject to variation, but the fundamental principle
of a bishop's duty to reside in his diocese is not something for
the Church to make its mind up about as it pleases. The
language of the decree of 13 January 1547 has lost nothing of
its force: "The apostle lays down that they (bishops) must
labour and perform their service in everything. But they
should know that in no way can they fulfil this if they
abandon . . . the flocks entrusted to them . . . The synod
therefore decided to re-affirm . . . the old canons . . . against
non-residents."[4]

In this way the practical reason against this proposal in fact
coincides with the theological reason. This can be
represented, if a little schematically, in the following argument.

Within the limited duration of a synod the right of decision
cannot, apart from exceptional cases, be exercised
responsibly. But to extend the duration so as to make this
possible cannot be reconciled with the inner nature of the
episcopal ministry (*iuris divini*). Consequently the exercise of
the right of decision cannot be the normal legal form of the
synod of bishops.

To put it another way: bishops remain bishops, responsible
to their particular Churches. The variable elements of the
Church's constitution do not include the possibility of
building up a second central power within it that would do far
less damage to the importance of the papal ministry than to
that of the episcopal ministry and would in fact eliminate the
latter.

b) The same applies to the proposal to develop the council of the synod secretariat into a permanent synod.

[4] Council of Trent, Session VI, 13 January 1547, *Decretum de residentia
episcoporum et aliorum inferiorum,* cap. 1, in *Conciliorum oecumenicorum decreta,*
Bologna ³1973, p. 682.

Once again, either its members would stay in Rome or they would not. If they stay in Rome then they cease to be resident bishops and become a second curia with an international composition. Or they do not stay in Rome, in which case they cannot do the work that is needed and do not form any kind of permanent synod. To this extent the proposal is unreal. But the positive element in it is that what is desirable is for the existing curia to have as international a membership as possible, with the opportunity for its members to change places. This would in fact bring about what is called for under the wrong label of a permanent synod. Similarly another positive element is the call for an exchange of views between the curia and the world episcopate, an exchange that needs to be as lively and forceful as possible. However open to criticism the curia may be, it can be said that it is developing along these lines.

2. *The clarification of fundamental elements in the Church's constitution*

The unsatisfactory nature of the models discussed above shows that every discussion of reform has to be preceded by a clarification of what is permanent and what is changeable in the constitution of the Church. It will readily be understood that only hints are possible within the limited framework of this essay.

a) The college of bishops and the communion of particular Churches

Let us go back again to that particular reform introduced by the Council of Trent, the substance of which, as we saw, consisted in restoring the bishop's duty of residing in his diocese. At a deeper level what is involved here is the renewal of the individual life and significance of particular Churches presided over by a bishop. They need a shepherd who is not looking to be a bigger fish somewhere else but is simply their shepherd and pastor who knows his own and stays with them. In this sense one can call the Tridentine reform truly pastoral;

princes had to become shepherds, *pastores,* once again. Today one can occasionally hear it said that Vatican II went in the opposite direction. Its central concept was not the shepherd but the college of bishops, and that does not demand shepherds who remain stuck in their dioceses but wandering shepherds who visit each other and together find ways for the whole to follow. The wrongness of playing the two councils off against each other in this way is plain from a serious reading of the documents. The concept of the college of bishops, which describes the hierarchical aspect of the Church, presupposes the reality of communion as the Church's vital and constitutional fundamental form. A collegial structure exists in the Church because the Church lives in the communion of Churches and because this structure of communion implies bishops belonging to one another and thus forming a college. If this is how things are, if the Church as an organism builds itself up from the inside in particular Churches which are one through being in communion in the word and the body of the Lord, then one can deduce two practical fundamental rules from this:

i) The necessity of the particular Churches as vital fundamental expressions of ecclesiastical life must be seen as a fundamental pre-condition and as a goal of the Church's constitution.

ii) This individual life of the particular Churches must of course be of such a nature that they do not live shut in on themselves but are in themselves "Catholic" and so are open to the whole in the living out of their life.

Because the Church is constructed in this way, it is not governed by a central parliament or by an aristocratic senate or indeed by a monarchical head but is entrusted to bishops who (i) lead the Catholic Church in its particular Churches and thus lead the universal Church, and (ii) hence the particular Churches are not in competition with one another but are directed at each other and at the single Catholicity of the whole. The organ for this relationship of the Churches with each other and for the fact that all the particular Churches are in communion in the one Church is once again the bishop of a particular Church, that of Rome, who as such makes the Church's unity visible and upholds its realization.

The Second Vatican Council formulated this doctrine as follows: "It is an established fact of experience that, by ruling well their own Churches as portions of the universal Church, they (the bishops) contribute efficaciously to the welfare of the whole Mystical Body, which, from another point of view, is a corporate body of Churches."[5] To put it another way, the first and fundamental collegial action consists of a bishop governing his Church well according to the responsibility assigned to him in the sacrament and as a good shepherd maintaining the vitality of his portion of the universal Church by leading it towards the Lord and thus into the co-operative community of the whole. If this foundation of particular Churches living separately and in co-operation is weakened or destroyed then the foundation of collegiality is done away with: all meetings and conferences are built on nothing and are working in a vacuum. Let us repeat that governing the local Churches is to share in governing the Church as a whole. Other actions of this sharing in governing have their urgent importance for the realization of this co-operative enterprise, but by their nature they merely supplement this fundamental action.

b) Representation-Discussion-Decision

The synod of bishops serves this relationship of the Churches among themselves and to this extent it belongs theologically to the sphere of collegiality, although, as we have seen, it derives its legal basis from the primacy. Once again we are faced by the question whether it would not be possible to turn it into a genuine organ of the college of bishops. We saw that the real reason why this is not possible is that the college's right of governing cannot be delegated because by its nature it cannot be centralized. There are however ideas about how one could get round this, and we must now consider these. The proposal has been made that individual bishops' conferences should discuss the synod's agenda, decide on it as conferences, and mandate their

---

[5] *Lumen Gentium* § 23.

delegates only to put forward and support these decisions of the bishops' conference. The logic of this proposal is that the delegates would then be complete representatives of their conferences, and all together would then have to represent the entire college of bishops. In this way the assembly of delegates could regard itself as a genuine council and act on the legal basis of an ecumenical council.

At first sight this is a tempting proposal. But when we look at it more closely it becomes clear that it could neither be implemented in practice nor be sustained in theory; once again the practical and the theoretical arguments are two sides of the same coin.

i) The proposal presupposes that individual delegates are mandated by their conferences to speak and vote according to each conference's decision and in no other way. But if individual bishops' conference do not come to identical decisions—something we must take for granted — then the assembly is condemned to a complete impasse. Nobody can let himself be convinced by other people's arguments, because he is bound by his mandate. All genuine debate and all moves towards reconciliation are excluded. The practice of democracy thus rejects this kind of absolute mandate in the political field, although it is urged by certain ideologues, because it would be the end of democracy. Although a synod and a council are something different from a parliament, they too need genuine debate; they too could not survive under the domination of an absolute mandate.

ii) On matters of faith and morals no-one can be bound by majority decisions. This is also the reason why bishops' conferences do not have any teaching authority and cannot as conferences make teaching binding. Because this is so, even ecumenical councils can only decide on matters of faith and morals in moral unanimity, since one cannot establish the truth by resolution but can only recognize and accept it. The pattern whereby truths are defined as such is not the majority decision but the recognition becoming generally clear that the guardians of the faith united in sacramental communion jointly recognize a statement as the consequence of this faith they hold. Where this kind of unity arises it should be judged as a sign that this really is an expression of the faith of the

Church which as the Church and as a whole cannot err in matters of faith. This is the inner foundation of theological definitions. The idea of consciences being bound by a teaching through a majority decision is an impossibility in human as well as theological terms.

iii) Because the conscience is where faith dwells, both the local and the universal Church are most fully represented by someone who follows his or her conscience—naturally not an ego raised to an absolute but an open, alert and listening conscience of faith. Hence hearkening to one's conscience contributes more to genuine "representation" than majority decisions that are often prepared by few and accepted by many more for the sake of peace than out of any deep inner conviction. This does not in any way mean to label as meaningless or superfluous the work done jointly by bishops' conferences. But their meaning cannot consist of devising absolute mandates but rather of jointly informing the conscience, making it keen and alert, and thus discovering unity from the inside. My view is that the work of bishops' conferences should by its nature be directed not towards a lot of resolutions and documents but rather towards consciences becoming more enlightened and thus on the basis of the truth more free. It is only in this way that the true liberation of mankind to which the Church is summoned can be accomplished.

iv) Debate at the synod can therefore by its nature not be an exercise in persuasiveness along party lines, as is often the case in parliaments. It must rather be an effort jointly to hearken to the conscience of faith and thus help jointly to understand the faith better so as to be able better to bear witness to it on the basis of this kind of joint understanding. In councils and synods it is not a question, as in the work of scholarly research, of bringing out something new, but of becoming free of what is purely individual and divides us from each other and so discovering the common answer of faith that already occurs more or less openly in our baptismal faith and thus becoming capable of expressing this in the language of our times. The decisions of synods thus obtain their weight not so much from the great number of people voting (which can and often will be a clue but which as a total is not in itself decisive) but from illuminating and articulating the truth present in the conscience.

c) What does "being the head of the Church" mean?

Our considerations so far bring us up against the quite general question of what "being the head of the Church" really means. How does this happen and what happens? It is a theological commonplace that the only true head of the Church is Christ and we are all merely his tools. But how can this principle, so correct in theory, be put into practice? This question is the real core of the whole question of ministry and authority, which we cannot go into here. But the context of what we have been discussing so far enables us to make two observations which may be helpful.

i) Christ governs by means of the conscience. Christ is therefore able to exercise his governance over the Church more effectively the more open and pure are above all the consciences of those to whom is entrusted the care of their flocks.

ii) A second consideration occurs to me ever more urgently. By doing far too much ourselves and running things far too much ourselves we could perhaps get in the way of the leadership of the Holy Spirit and set our work up against him. This disturbs the period of maturation, of quiet development. The field of education suggests a comparison. Education should not try to relieve the other person of everything; it must have the humility to go along with what is the other person's and to help it mature. By doing too much ourselves we quickly find ourselves on the path of justification by our own works and we forget the profound truth that the Lord has put before those in authority throughout all ages: "The kingdom of God is as if a man should scatter seed upon the ground, and should sleep and rise night and day, and the seed should sprout and grow, he knows not how. The earth produces of itself ($\alpha\dot{\upsilon}\tau o\mu\acute{\alpha}\tau\eta$)" (Mk 4:26 – 28). I also recall the wonderful passage with which Hilary of Poitiers concludes the first book of his work on the Trinity. He beseeches the divine mercy "that you will want to fill the outstretched sail of our faith and acknowledgement with the breath of your Spirit".[6] This is precisely the real core of

---

[6] Hilary of Poitiers, *De Trinitate* I:37, *Corpus Christianorum* LXII p. 35.

what "being the head of the Church" means: to stretch out the sail of our faith and acknowledgement of this faith so that the Holy Spirit may fill it with his breath.

I am aware that these observations are far too fragmentary for so important a subject. But perhaps it is not completely inappropriate today to indicate the limits and the dangers of our activism that from time to time could shut the doors on the Spirit.

3. Final considerations: What are synods for?

Finally there remains the question: what purpose can synods serve in practice? Now of course the real goal is an increase of faith, hope and love: an increase in the real presence of the gospel in the Church and in the world. The actual intermediate aim which precedes this real main aim I would sum up under three heads: to inform, to correct, to encourage.

a) A fundamental task of the synod is without a doubt an exchange of information. Bishops' conferences inform the pope and the curia, the pope informs the bishops, the bishops inform each other. What is involved here is of course more than just an exchange of items of news that one could learn from reading the newspapers. It is a mutual process of forming oneself in learning to understand the ideas, the actions, the urgent questions and the difficulties of the other person. Informing oneself in this way in learning to share in the ideas of others so as to become capable of acting together thus becomes a process of communication in the truth, the maturing of that awareness which the shepherd needs in order to know his own and to be known by them.

b) This kind of informing oneself also includes a process of mutual self-correction: lack of knowledge on both sides, which becomes lack of understanding, must be overcome. If discussion at the synod is to be "a process" then it should know no other incontrovertible datum than the truth of faith. To enter into this more deeply one must be ready to learn: to accept something different, to re-examine what is one's own and if necessary to change it. Anyone who has taken part in a

synod knows that this happens there and that this is the finest
experience of the syn-od, the "common way". *Correptio*
("correction") is part of the bishop's duties according to the
apostolic tradition,[7] whether this is mutual fraternal
correction, particular Churches putting each other to rights,
or the Church rebuking the world. The prophetic ministry of
rebuking and reprimanding, both within the Church and
outside it, is of increased importance in this age of ours. It
seems very urgent to me that the voice of the universal
Church on the major questions of our time should through
the synod be heard powerfully and in unison.

c) The third task of the synod could be described as
"encouragement" (*promovere*). However necessary the
critical element may be it is not enough on its own. The synod
must above all encourage and strengthen the positive forces
inside and outside the Church and foster all activities that let
hope and love grow and thus contain hope.

If one considers a little more deeply the synod's tasks that
have been briefly outlined here it becomes automatically clear
that its primary problem cannot lie in the question how it can
develop its own rights over against a Roman centre that
appears all too strong. The common effort in favour of the
gospel in this age demands all our powers, and the men and
women living in this world of today await from us not
discussions of the relationship among themselves of our
various rights but the contribution we are enabled by the
gospel to make for the salvation of the world. That is what
God has called us to do.

---

[7] Cf. 2 Tim 4:2; Augustine, *Epist.* 53:7.

PART II

ECUMENICAL PROBLEMS

4

Anglican-Catholic dialogue: Its problems and hopes

INTRODUCTION: AGREED STATEMENTS AND THE POSITION OF THE ROMAN CONGREGATION FOR THE FAITH

In a series of sessions between January 1970 and September 1981 the Anglican-Roman Catholic International Commission drew up statements on the Eucharist, Ministry and Ordination, and Authority in the Church. The aim of the Commission was to prepare a way for the restoration of intercommunion between the two Churches. There was no intention of solving *all* controversial issues, but it was hoped under these headings to get to grips with the major causes of division. Even here no claim was made to have achieved complete agreement in every detail[1] but conviction was expressed that the statements provided a fundamental common approach to these questions which might be termed "substantial agreement", since fundamental principles were developed in them, whereby any remaining particular disagreements in these areas might be resolved.[2] The document accordingly concludes with the confident assertion that now — in 1981 — it is more than evident that "under the

---

[1] *Anglican-Roman Catholic International Commission, The Final Report:* Windsor, September 1981. The admitted limitation of the document with regard to achieved consensus is clearly expressed especially in *Authority in the Church II* (1981), section *Jurisdiction,* 16 – 33. Also in other places, e.g. Elucidation to *Eucharistic Doctrine* (1979) 8, 9, certain limitations are mentioned.

[2] Cf: *Eucharistic Doctrine* (1971) 12: "We believe we have reached substantial agreement on the doctrine of the eucharist . . . if there are any remaining points of disagreement they can be resolved on the principles here established . . ."

Holy Spirit, our Churches have grown closer together in faith and charity. There are high expectations that significant initiatives will be boldly undertaken to deepen our reconciliation and lead us forward in the quest for full communion".[3]

At the same time the Commission was fully aware that the ultimate decision as to the ecclesiastical relevance of its findings did not rest with itself. All along it had intended, according to the ecclesiastical mandate which had called it into being, to submit its statements to the "respective authorities". Since its purpose was not merely academic but focused on ecclesiastical reality, the statements had to go through an official ecclesiastical process of examination and judgement.[4] This took place when the sessions came to an end in September 1981. It was also clear that, since ecclesiastical authority is structured differently in each case, examination and decision making would also have to be conducted on quite different lines by the respective authorities. Perhaps one should remark at this point that any presentation of the theme "Authority in the Church" which was really intended to lead to unity, would have to take into account in a much more concrete way the actual form of authority in order to do justice to the question. For if there was surprise afterwards at the fact that the Roman Catholic Church can give an authoritative answer more immediately than Anglican structures allow for, this is surely an indication that too little attention had been paid to the actual functioning of authority. It was probably not made clear enough that the pope — especially since Vatican II — has a special authentic teaching function for the whole Church: it is not indeed infallible but does make authoritative decisions.[5] On the other hand the text left one completely in the dark as to the concrete structure of authority in the Anglican community. Those well acquainted with Anglicanism know that the Lambeth Conference, originally instituted in 1867, was not due to meet for several years, according to its regular timing,

---

[3] Conclusion, 1981.
[4] E.g. *Authority in the Church I*, 26 (conclusion).
[5] Cf. *Lumen Gentium* II, 12; III, 22; especially in this context III, 25.

and that no authoritative pronouncement could be made before that date. But ought not the text to have mentioned this structure in order to give a true explanation of the problem of authority without stopping short of the concrete reality? Would not the right and indeed necessary thing have been to explain what sort of teaching authority and jurisdiction belongs or does not belong to this assembly of bishops? Should one not also have gone into the question of the relation between political and ecclesiastical authority in the Church which first touches the nerve-point of the question of the Catholicity of the Church or the relation between local and universal Church? In 1640 Parliament decided as follows: "Convocation has no power to enact canons or constitutions concerning matters of doctrine or discipline, or in any other way to bind clergy or religious without the consent of Parliament." That may be obsolete, but it came to mind again in 1927 when on two occasions a version of the Book of Common Prayer was rejected by Parliament.[5a] However that may be, these concrete questions should have been clarified and answered, if a viable agreement about "Authority in the Church" was the aim in view. For it is of the essence of authority to be concrete, consequently one can only do justice to the theme by naming the actual authorities and clarifying their relative position on both sides instead of just theorizing about authority.

But to go back to our starting point: this parenthesis was only inserted because, after there had been theoretical substantial agreement about authority in the Church, the actual intervention of authority resulted in misunderstanding and bad feeling. What had happened? According to the express intention of ARCIC, the Congregation for the Faith, commissioned by the pope as central organ of ecclesiastical authority, had set to work examining the texts as soon as they were completed, and then on 29 March 1982 promulgated a

---

[5a] Th. Schnitker, *The American Book of Common Prayer* (Th Rev 78, 1982, 265 – 272) points out that as a result of "Church of England (Worship and Doctrine) Measure 1974", the Church of England itself, without ratification from Parliament, can make decisions about its liturgical books. With Schedule 2 of this document the Act of Uniformity 1662, like almost all liturgical enactments of state controlled churches, has become invalid (a.a.O., Note 3, col. 266f).

detailed statement of their opinion. This was first despatched to the Bishops' Conference as a "Contribution to the current dialogue", and then on 6 May 1982 published in the *Osservatore Romano*.[6] Pursuing the matter further, one can say that this was an example of the functioning of precisely that structure of authority sketched out by Vatican II. One can clearly recognise three characteristic elements of that structure—the office of Peter's successor, the worldwide college of bishops, and relation in dialogue to other Christian Churches and denominations. In this case we see ecumenical dialogue raised from the sphere of particular groups — which are not yet authoritative, however important and well authorised they may be — and transferred to the level of matters concerning the whole Church in a universal and obligatory way. Then the See of Peter speaks through one of its central organs, not indeed in a definitive manner, yet with an authority which carries more weight in the Church than a merely academic publication about the question would. Based on the teaching of the Church, the document provides guidelines for further development of the dialogue. And finally the whole college of bishops, as successors of the apostles, are drawn into the dialogue in their capacity of responsibility for the whole Church.

THE FUNDAMENTAL PROBLEM OF THE DIALOGUE: THE AUTHORITY OF TRADITION, AND THE CENTRAL ORGANS OF UNITY

1. Preliminary note on the situation of the discussion

The above statements have already brought us right to the heart of the problem with which Anglican-Catholic dialogue is concerned. A first reading of the ARCIC documents might

---

[6] The essential content of the text was pre-announced in a letter, published on 31.3.1982 in the *Osservatore Romano,* from the Prefect of the Congregation for the Faith, to the Catholic Chairman of ARCIC, Bishop Clark.

well convey the impression that nothing but Vatican I's teaching about papal primacy, and the more recent Marian dogmas stood in the way of complete agreement. The reaction of the media, which are always bound to be on the look-out for something striking and quickly grasped, intensified this impression which only too easily turned into the opinion that reconciliation was held up only by particular nineteenth century dogmas on the part of Rome. Were this the case, it would certainly be hard to understand why Rome laid so much stress on such recent, particular doctrinal developments, apparently even wishing to raise them to a touchstone of ecumenism. In point of fact, both the aforesaid dogmas are only the most tangible symptoms of the overall problem of authority in the Church. The way one views the structure of Christianity will necessarily affect in some measure, great or small, one's attitude to various particular matters contained within the whole. For this reason I do not wish here to go into the particular points which surfaced in the dialogue between Catholics and Anglicans, and which have already been dealt with in the ARCIC Report as well as in the comments of the Congregation for the Faith. I would prefer to approach one single point from various aspects — the point which has already emerged from a simple account of the course of events as the core of the problem, namely the question of authority. This is identical with the question of tradition and cannot be separated from that of the relation between the universal Church and a particular Church. Even this problem cannot receive comprehensive, systematic treatment here. Within the limits of this short essay it would seem more to the point to dispense with systematic procedure and simply juxtapose a series of observations which will nevertheless, each in its own way, reflect something of the whole.

But first it would seem fitting to comment briefly on the general nature of the statement of the Congregation for the Faith and of the Agreed Statements of ARCIC which underlie it. Almost everywhere newspapers and reports tell how the communication from the Roman Congregation begins with a few short, meaningless and florid compliments, and that everything is merely negative and critical, so that by the end of it one is left with a discouraging impression. Such an assertion could only be the result of a very superficial reading of the text. In the relatively short first section, dealing with the subject as a whole, the positive side is stated first and then followed up by criticism. This pattern is retained throughout the sections dealing with particular subjects. Attention is first drawn to the important steps forward that have been made in dealing with the particular questions, and then guidelines are laid down to show the way ahead if a really viable basic "substantial agreement" is to be reached. Actually it is impossible to read through the ARCIC statements without feeling a great sense of gratitude, for they show how far theological thought has matured in the last decade as regards shared insight. Recourse to scripture and the Fathers has brought to light the common foundations of diverging confessional developments, and so opened up that perspective in which apparently irreconcilable elements can be fused together into the wholeness of the one truth. The desire for unity is plain: one might say that the hermeneutics of unity have made a new understanding of the sources possible, and conversely, recourse to the sources has evoked hermeneutics of unity. All this is indisputable and makes the ARCIC documents so outstanding that they could be, and had to be, transferred from the sphere of private preparatory work into the forum of the Church's public dialogue. But all this must serve too to justify the courage needed to face the questions squarely and fully both in statement and deliberation. Approbation and criticism are not mutually exclusive: each demands the other. It is only when both are joined together that we get an authentic vehicle for true dialogue. This will be taken for granted as I proceed now to deal with the most urgent questions.

2. The authority of Tradition

The complex of questions we are concerned with here cannot possibly be contained with the single concept "primacy". It includes, over and above, determining the co-ordination of scripture — tradition — councils — episcopate —

reception. The two last ideas refer to the respective roles of bishops and laity in the formation of Christian doctrine. It is a universal tenet amongst Christians that scripture is the basic standard of Christian faith, the central authority through which Christ himself exercises his authority over the Church and within it. For this reason all teaching in the Church is ultimately exposition of scripture, just as scripture in its turn is exposition of the living word of Jesus Christ: but the ultimate value of all is not what is written but the life which our Lord transmitted to his Church, within which scripture itself lives and is life. Vatican II formulated these mutual relations very beautifully: "Through tradition the complete canon of sacred books is made known to the Church. Within her the Holy Scriptures are themselves understood at greater depth and ceaselessly put into action. So it is that God who spoke of old, never ceases to converse with the Bride of his beloved Son, and the Holy Spirit — through whom the living voice of the Gospel resounds in the Church and through her in the world beyond — leads the faithful into all truth and causes the word of Christ to dwell amongst them in full measure" (cf. Col 3:16).[7] There is a priority of scriptures as witness and a priority of the Church as the vital environment for such witness, but both are linked together in constantly alternating relationships, so that neither can be imagined without the other. This relative priority of the Church to scripture obviously presupposes also the existence of the Universal Church as a concrete and active reality, for only the whole Church can be the locus of scripture in this sense. So the question of defining the relation between a particular Church and the universal Church has obviously already claimed a place amongst the fundamental problems.

The mutual dependence of a community living the Bible, and of the Bible in which the community finds the inward standard of its being, is first represented as a subtle spiritual reality, but it becomes a very practical issue with the question: How is scripture recognised in the Church? Who decides whether what you say is in accord with scripture or not? It is rather ambiguous when ARCIC says: "Neither

[7] *Dei Verbum* II, 8.

general councils nor universal primates are invariably preserved from error even in official declarations.[8] It is still more emphatic in another place: "The Commission is very far from implying that general councils cannot err and is well aware that they sometimes have erred".[9] The Synods of Ariminum and of Seleucia are quoted as examples of this. Then it goes on to say: "Article 21 (i.e. of the Anglican Articles of Religion) affirms that general councils have authority only when their judgements 'may be declared that they be taken out of Holy Scripture'. " The ARCIC text adds that according to the argument of the Statement also, "only those judgements of general councils are guaranteed to exclude what is erroneous or are protected from error which have as their content fundamental matters of faith, which formulate central truths of salvation and which are faithful to Scripture and consistent with Tradition".[10] Moreover there is need for reception; about this it says in what seems a rather dialectical way that "reception does not create truth nor legitimize the decision", the authority of a council is not derived entirely from reception on the part of the faithful; on the other hand it also teaches that a council is "not so evidently self-sufficient that its definitions owe nothing to reception".[11] Another passage is even more explicit: "If the definition proposed for assent were not manifestly a legitimate interpretation of biblical faith and in line with orthodox tradition, Anglicans would think it a duty to reserve the reception of the definition for study and discussion".[12]

The phrase "manifestly a legitimate interpretation of biblical faith" catches one's attention. The dogmas of the pre-Reformation Church are quite certainly not "manifestly legitimate" in the sense in which "manifest" is used in modern exegesis. If there were such a thing as the "manifestly legitimate", obvious enough to stand in its own right out of range of reasonable discussion, there would be no need at all for councils and ecclesiastical teaching authority. On this

---

[8] *Authority in the Church* II, 27 (1981).
[9] *Authority in the Church* I, Elucidation 3 (1981).
[10] Ibid., "which have as their content, fundamental matters of faith."
[11] Ibid.
[12] *Authority in the Church*, II, 29.

point questions raised by the continental European Reformation are fully present amongst the Anglicans. It is true they are modified by the fact that the survival of the episcopate retains the fundamental structure of the pre-Reformation Church as the form of life within the ecclesiastical community to this day. This assures a fundamentally positive attitude to the doctrinal tenets of the pre-Reformation Church. Originally this was the intention also of the continental denominations but the pull away from tradition was much stronger in their communities, so that there was far less ability to hold fast. This modification of the principle of "scripture only" has, however, long been more on the level of fact than of principle; it is true that fact could facilitate the step down to the fundamental level. This should not be too difficult, considering the actual authority of tradition. In any case further dialogue must get to grips in real earnest with this fundamental issue.

3. The Universal Church and its central organs as the condition of tradition

But to return once again to our starting point in the analysis of the text. Nothing "manifest" can be derived from intellectual discussion or from the mere fact of general opinion in the Church. Ultimately we come up against an anthropological question here; beyond what is purely objective, nothing is "manifest" to anyone save what he lives. For that reason interpretation is always a question of the whole complex of life.[13] To transfer authority in this way to what is "manifest", as is done in the passage already quoted, means linking up faith with the authority of historians, i.e. exposing it to conflicting hypotheses. Quite the contrary — keeping in view the faith testified to in the New Testament itself and the life of the early Church, we

---

[13] Cf. especially the important essays from J. Pieper, *Buchstabierübungen,* München 1980, 11–30; E. Coreth, *Grundfragen der Hermeneutik,* Freiburg 1969; H. Anton, *Interpretation,* in J. Ritter-K. Gründer, *Historiches Wörterbuch der Philosophie* IV (1976), 514–517.

must hold fast to the conviction that there can be no second sifting through of what the universal Church teaches as universal Church. Who would presume to undertake such a task? One can read greater depth into a pronouncement of the universal Church; one can improve on it linguistically; one can develop it further by focusing on the centre of the faith and on new perspectives opening up a way forward, but one cannot "discuss" it in the ordinary sense of the word.

At this point it becomes clear what the episcopal office means and what exactly "tradition" is in the Church. According to the Catholic way of thinking, a bishop is someone who can express the voice of the universal Church in his teaching, or to put it another way: the episcopate is the supreme court in the Church as regards both teaching and decision, because it is the living voice of the universal Church. An individual bishop has full authority as pastor of a particular Church because, and in so far as, he represents the universal Church.

"Apostolic succession" is the sacramental form of the unifying presence of tradition.[14] For this reason the universal Church is not a mere external amplification, contributing nothing to the essential nature of Church in the local Churches, but it extends into that very nature itself. Here it is necessary to contradict the ARCIC Report where it says "The Second Vatican Council allows it to be said that a Church out of communion with the Roman See may lack nothing from the viewpoint of the Roman Catholic Church except that it does not belong to the visible manifestation of full Christian communion".[15] With such an assertion wrongly claiming the

[14] J. Ratzinger *Theologische Prinzipienlehre*, München 1982, 251–263; 300–314.

[15] *Authority in the Church* II, 12. The text of *LG* I, 8, quoted here in support, is far from expressing such a conviction. The text runs: "Haec est unica Christi Ecclesia, quam in Symbolo unam, sanctam, catholicam et apostolicam confitemur . . . Haec Ecclesia, in hoc mundo ut societas constituta et ordinata, subsistit in Ecclesia catholica, a successore Petri et episcopis in eius communione gubernata, licet extra eius compaginem elementa plura sanctificationis et veritatis inveniuntur, quae ut dona Ecclesiae Christi propria, ad unitatem catholicam impellunt." (This is the unique Church of Christ which in the Creed we avow as one, holy, catholic and apostolic . . . this Church, constituted and organised in the world as a society, subsists in the Catholic Church, which is governed by the successor of Peter and by the bishops in union with that successor, although many elements of sanctification or truth can be found outside of her visible structure. These elements, however, as

support of Vatican II, Church Unity is debased to an unnecessary, if desirable, externality, and the character of the universal Church is reduced to mere outward representation, of little significance in constituting what is ecclesial. This romantic idea of provincial Churches, which is supposed to restore the structure of the early Church, is really contradicting the historical reality of the early Church as well as the concrete experiences of history, to which one must certainly not turn a blind eye in considerations of this sort. The early Church did indeed know nothing of Roman primacy in practice, in the sense of Roman Catholic theology of the second millennium, but it was well acquainted with living forms of unity in the universal Church which were constitutive of the essence of provincial Churches. Understood in this sense, the priority of the universal Church always preceded that of particular Churches.

I will just instance here three well known phenomena: letters of communion, which bound Churches together; the symbolism of collegiality at the consecration of a bishop. This ceremony was always linked up with living tradition by cross-questioning and acceptance of the Creed, while the imprint of the universal Church was manifest in the fact that bishops of prominent sees were represented: mere neighbourly recognition would not suffice; it had to be made clear that the prominent sees were in communion with each other, as it fell to them to guarantee the character of the universal Church in the case of this particular one. Finally one should include here what people today like to call the conciliarity of the Church, though they often have romantically simplified ideas about it. For it is a known fact that conciliarity has never functioned simply of its own accord by the pure and spontaneous harmony of plurality, as

gifts properly belong to the Church of Christ, possess an inner dynamism towards Catholic unity). Neither does *Unitatis Redintegratio* III, 13, quoted in the same context, say anything of the kind. It gives a typology of *divisions,* and ends the description of communities resulting from 16th century divisions with the sentence: "Inter eas, in quibus traditiones et structurae catholicae ex parte subsistere pergunt, locum specialem tenet Communio anglicana." (Among those in which some Catholic traditions and institutions continue to exist, the Anglican Communion occupies a special place).

many present day statements would seem to suggest. Actually the authority of the emperor was necessary to summon a council. Take away the person of the emperor, and you can no longer discuss the conciliar reality of the medieval Church but only a theological fiction. Closer consideration shows that the participation of Rome, the See centred on the place where SS. Peter and Paul died, was of great significance for the full validity of a council, even if this factor is less in evidence than the position of the emperor. All the same, Vincent Twomey has already shown in a very well documented piece of research, that already in the contest at Nicaea two opposed options stand out clearly: the Eusebian and the Athanasian, i.e. the idea of an imperial universal Church as against a really theological conception in which it is not the emperor but Rome which plays the decisive role.[16] However that may be, the imperial Church has vanished, and with it the emperor too: Thank God, we may say. Meanwhile, if one wants to discuss the conciliarity of the Church in a way that is realistic and meaningful, the question inevitably arises: what office is important enough from a theological point of view to replace and sustain the function fulfilled by the emperor?[17]

At this point the question about the later development of history must inevitably be faced as a theological issue; a mere return to the medieval Church is no solution even from a theological point of view. Jean Meyendorff has recently

---

[16] V. Twomey, *Apostolikos Thronos. The Primacy of Rome as reflected in the Church History of Eusebius and the historico-apologetic writings of St Athanasius the great*, Münster 1982. This extremely thorough work (to my mind) marks a turning point in the approach to this subject in dogmatic history. Here perhaps for the first time it is again brought to light how profoundly imbued the pre-Reformation Church was with the Petrine idea and its connection with the See of Rome, and also how soon the conception of a state church began to break away from it. A recently published book by St Horn, *Petrou Kathedra*, Paderborn 1982, throws similar light on the 5th century. Now that both these books have appeared, the commonplace judgements of the present day on the subject will have to be thoroughly re-examined and possibly revised. Cf. also by St Horn *La "Sedes Apostolica": Theological outlook of the East at the beginning of the sixth century*, in *Istina* 1975, pp. 435–456.

[17] The same objection applies especially to the Catholic-Orthodox joint statement, *Le mystère de l'Eglise et de l'Eucharistie à la lumière du mystère de la Sainte Trinité*.

tackled the whole subject with an uninhibited realism which might well serve as a model for research with an eye to the future. He shows how, once the central organs of unity, founded on a theological basis, were given up after the break up of the old imperial Church, this led in fact with compulsive inward logic to state churches springing up everywhere. These did not correspond at all to the medieval idea of local Church or parish, though an attempt was made to justify them theologically in that way. Instead they brought in their train a tendency to particularize Christianity, contrary to the essential idea of "Church" in the New Testament and pre-Reformation Church.[18] Once the universal Church had disappeared from view as a concrete reality actually leaving its mark on the local Church, and a link had been forged with some political or ethnic reality as a framework for the latter, the whole pattern of ecclesiastical government changed — including the evaluation of episcopal office, and so involving alteration in the structure of the Church. It was not only an outward "manifestation" which fell away but a power which had influenced from within. It is in this context that Meyendorff wonders whether it would not actually be better to devote more attention to the idea of development in the Church, and use that as an approach to the theological content of primacy. The latter is offset by the negative legalism which resulted from the tendency to particularise and was in evidence after the break up of the old empire wherever the link with the unifying function of the papacy had been severed.[19]

Reflections like these must on no account lead to one sided assertion of the "Roman" point of view. They do point towards the principle of a unifying office, but they also call for self criticism on the part of Roman Catholic theology. Without a doubt there have been misguided developments in

---

[18] J. Meyendorff, *Kirchlicher Regionalismus: Strukturen der Gemeinschaft oder Vorwand des Separatismus?* in G. Alberigo-Y. Congar-H. J. Pottmeyer, *Kirche im Wandel. Eine kritische Zwischenbilanz nach dem Zweiten Vatikanum*, Dusseldorf 1982 pp. 303 – 318; cf e.g. p. 311: "one can see how modern nationalism has deformed legitimate ecclesiastical provincialism and turned it into a cloak for ethnic separatism."

[19] Ibid., pp. 316ff.

both theology and practice where the primacy is concerned, and these must be brought to light with the same perspicacity and frankness that Meyendorff has shown with regard to misguided developments in a theology and practice geared simply to the local Church. By this means the theological core could really be brought to view and be seen as acceptable. The principle of the primatial office in the universal Church, in my opinion, must not be weakened to the extent of being reduced to mere manifestation, while the reality of the universal Church is theologically dissolved. On the other hand the outward ways of putting the office into practice are subject to alteration and must always be tested afresh by the principle. The consequences of this for the Catholic-Anglican dialogue became evident to us rather as a side-result of the introductory report on its last phases. In order to reach a viable unity, the form of authority in the Anglican Church must be spelt out with complete realism, and there must be no shirking the question of the relationship between episcopal and political authority, for that was after all the start of the separation. The fact that since then the Anglican community has spread all over the world, has anyway led automatically to modifications of the original pattern, so that history itself has helped to rectify history. Parallel to these considerations, most careful thought must be given to variations in practice, potentially contained in the principle of primacy.

4. Tradition and belief

With all that has been said, it should have become clear that the question of the universal Church and of the primacy as its real central organ is not simply a matter of an isolated Roman problem, of varying significance to different people. It is at heart a question of the most powerful and communal presence of the Word of God in the Church, and as we have said, this question includes that of the universal Church and its authority as well as the official instruments of this authority. To put it in a different way: it is a question of what one actually means by "tradition". In this connection I think a comment on terminology might bring us further. In quite a number of places in the ARCIC papers the two dialoguing parties—Anglican and Catholic—are referred to as "our two traditions".[20] "Tradition" has become a key-word in recent ecumenism and is used in theological classification of the difference between various churches and denominations: they are referred to as "our traditions". This terminology expresses a quite definite idea about the degree of separation and the way to restore Church Unity. The different forms of the reality "Church" are according to this "traditions" in which the heritage of the New Testament has found manifold realisation. This means that divisions are regarded theologically as of secondary importance, even when historically seen as venerable and noteworthy realisations of common Christianity. One might say that in the most recent publications about dialogue "tradition" is the new name for "confession", which certainly means that a fundamental change of model has taken place in the vision of Church and faith. Wherever "tradition" is substituted for "confession" the question of truth is resolved into reconciling concern for what history has brought about.

One more thought comes to mind which will take us back to the theological question from which we started. If two such different subjects as the Catholic Church and the Anglican Church are grouped together under the common term "our two traditions", the profound difference in estimation of the phenomenon "tradition"—such a hallmark of the identity of each—is obliterated. But unfortunately one searches in vain through the ARCIC texts for an analysis of what "tradition" means to each. Roughly speaking one might summarise it like this: in the Catholic Church the principle of "tradition" refers, not only and not even in the first place, to the permanency of ancient doctrines or texts which have been handed down, but to a certain way of co-ordinating the living word of the Church and the decisive written word of scripture. Here "tradition" means above all, that the Church, living in the form of the apostolic succession with the Petrine office at its centre, is the place

[20] Cf. Elucidation (1979) to *Ministry and Ordination*, para. 3: "both traditions"; *Authority in the Church* I, 18: "both our traditions" so also ibid. 19; ibid. 25: "our two traditions", and *Authority in the Church* II, 8; ibid. 15: "both our traditions".

in which the Bible is lived and interpreted in a way that binds. This interpretation forms a historical continuity, setting fixed standards but never itself reaching a final point at which it belongs only to the past. "Revelation" is closed but interpretation which binds is not.[21] There can be no appeal against the ultimate binding force of interpretation. So tradition is essentially marked by the "living voice"—i.e. by the obligatory nature of the teaching of the universal Church.

If, on the other hand, one consults the Articles of Religion or the "Lambeth Quadrilateral" of 1886, the difference strikes one immediately. The similarity of Art. 19 on the Church with Art. 8 of the Augsburg Confession hits one in the eye in the same way as the similarity of Art. 20 on Authority in the Church with the corresponding Art. 15 of the Confessio Augustana. Now both the Confessio Augustana and the Articles of Religion assume that Creed and dogmas are taken over from the pre-Reformation Church. One cannot strictly speaking apply *sola scriptura* here in the face of a fundamental recognition of tradition. But for all that, the tendency is to regard tradition as a recognised heritage of texts from the past. At the same time the right of the living voice of the Church is minimised in theology by the demand for testing against scripture, while in practice it is reduced to the sphere of mere discipline, which is thereby cut off from its true foundations. This restriction is to a certain extent projected into the past in the Articles of Religion, in so far as it is expressly stated that just as the Church of Jerusalem, Alexandria and Antioch erred, so also the Church of Rome has erred in matters of faith, and general councils too (Art. 19 and 21).

5. *Tradition can never be closed*

At this point another omission in the ARCIC documents should be noted: it has to do with the concrete realities of

---

[21] Cf. My own contributions in K. Rahner — J. Ratzinger, *Offenbarung und Uberlieferung*, Freiburg 1965.

each Church. It is true that ARCIC defends itself against accusation that it has contradicted Art. 21 of the Articles of Religion.[22] But it does not explain anywhere what force these Articles and the Book of Common Prayer actually have. In this case too, as in the question of authority, one can only grasp the concrete situation by investigating these matters, for obviously we are touching here on what an Anglican would regard as "tradition". In the discussion about the texts it was evident that both the Articles of Religion and the Book of Common Prayer have great influence as standards. It seems to me all the more strange that from the reverse point of view the Catholic ecumenical paper *Irénikon* felt obliged to criticise the Congregation for the Faith severely in an editorial because in its analysis of the Agreed Statements it had brought in definitions promulgated in the Catholic Church since the separation. *Irénikon* speaks (in a quite unirenic way) of the "painful" impression that the Congregation has made. With finger raised in reproach it continues: "If this attitude has already had consequences in dialogue with the Anglicans, one can imagine how it would block the way towards restoring canonical and sacramental communion with the Orthodox Church".[23]

A kind of ecumenical dogma seems to be developing here which needs some attention. Quite likely it began with this train of thought: for intercommunion with the Orthodox, the Catholic Church need not necessarily insist on acceptance of the dogmas of the second millennium. It was presumed that the Eastern Churches have retained in the traditional form of the first millennium, which in itself is legitimate and, if rightly understood, contains no contradiction to further developments. The latter after all only unfolded what was already there in principle in the time of the undivided Church. I myself have already taken part in attempts to work things out like this,[24] but meanwhile they have grown out of hand to the point at which councils and the dogmatic decisions of the second millennium are supposed not to be regarded as ecumenical but as particular developments in

---

[22] Elucidation (1981) to *Authority in the Church.*
[23] *Irénikon* 55 (1982) 161f. quotation 162.
[24] Cf. *Theologische Prinzipienlehre*, München 1982, pp. 109–211 (text from 1976).

the Latin Church, constituting its private property in the sense of "our two traditions". But this distorts the first attempt to think things out into a completely new thesis with far-reaching consequences. For this way of looking at it actually implies denial of the existence of the Universal Church in the second millennium, while tradition as a living, truth-giving power is frozen at the end of the first. This strikes at the very heart of the idea of Church and tradition, because ultimately such an age test dissolves the full authority of the Church, which is then left without a voice at the present day. Moreover one might well ask in reply to such an assertion, with what right consciences, in such a particular Church as the Latin Church would then be, could be bound by such pronouncements. What once appeared as truth would have to be reduced to mere custom. The great age-long claim to truth would be disqualified as an abuse.

All this means that a far-reaching thesis, the principles and consequences of which have not been thought out, has been raised to the level of a self-evident axiom. To belittle it is to incur ungracious censure. But this very self-evidence which convinced *Irénikon* that it was its duty to pass censure from its lofty look-out on the Congregation for the Faith, demands decisive response. To my mind the central truth of what they are trying to get at is this: unity is a fundamental, hermeneutic principle of all theology, and we must learn to read the documents which have been handed down to us, according to the hermeneutics of unity, which show up much that is new and open doors where only bolts were visible before. Such hermeneutics of unity will entail reading the statements of both parties in the context of the whole tradition and with a deeper understanding of scripture. This will include investigating how far decisions since the separation have been stamped with a certain particularisation both as to language and thought—something that might well be transcended without doing violence to the content of the statements. For hermeneutics are not a skillful device for escaping from burdensome authorities by a change of verbal function, (though this abuse has often occurred), but rather apprehending the word with an understanding which at the same time discovers in it new possibilities.

Ecumenical dialogue does not mean opting out of living, Christian reality, but advancing by means of the hermeneutics of unity. To opt out and cut oneself off means artificial withdrawal into a past beyond recall; it means restricting tradition to the past. But that is to transfer ecumenism into an artificial world while one goes on practising particularisation by fencing off one's own thing. Since this preserve is regarded as immune from dialogue but is still clung to, it is lowered from the realm of truth into the sphere of mere custom. Finally the question arises as to whether it is a matter of truth at all, or just of comparing different customs and finding a way of reconciling them. In any case, the remark that the introduction of dogmatic decisions passed since the separation should not be regarded as the high point of the dialogue denotes a flight into the artificial which should be firmly resisted.

6. Tradition and eucharist

Now to get back to the ARCIC document after this detour. Everything said so far has revolved round the question of authority and tradition. I have tried to show that here and nowhere else really lies the fundamental problem. To solve it would be decisive for the question of unity. It would not be hard to show that this question affects also the particular areas in which full agreement has not yet been reached, and which were noted in the communication from the Congregation for the Faith: eucharist with emphasis on sacrifice, transubstantiation and, according to circumstances, adoration of the consecrated species; sacramental nature and content of the priesthood (with the question in the background of the institution of the sacraments and of their actual number); theological substantiation and concrete ecclesiastical content of the Petrine office. It is not possible to deal with all these things here. But let me just add one remark about the question of the eucharist. The great reformed denominations and the Anglican community accepted the ancient creeds as part of their own belief, and so the Trinitarian and Christological faith defined in the councils of the early Church has been kept out of the debate. Side by side with scripture and combined with it, this is the actual nucleus of the unity which binds us together and gives us hope of complete reconciliation.

For this reason we must for the sake of unity strenuously resist any attempt to break up this central ecclesial deposit or to discard as outmoded the practice based on it of reading scripture together. A mere fundamentalist approach to the Bible, adopted these days by quite a number of people, would not bring us together but would soon break up the Bible itself. Without this centre the Bible would cease to be one book and would lose its authority.

So, although unity remained in the Creeds, the break in the form of eucharistic liturgy had its full effect. But in point of fact, in spite of all textual and ritual differences, the consistent unity of structure and understanding of the eucharistic liturgy in the pre-Reformation Church (together with the baptismal liturgy) was the vital habitat in which the Christian dogma of that Church was rooted. The authority of tradition in the case of eucharistic model carries no less weight than in the case of councils and their creeds, even though it is differently expressed —through constant living enactment instead of by conciliar decree. It is really only possible to make an artificial separation between the two: in both cases it is the one basic form of the pre-Reformation Church expressing itself. Unfortunately this connection was no longer easily recognisable in the late medieval Church and its celebration of Mass. But all the same one can imagine what it would mean for ecumenism if the inseparability of this union were again both manifest and recognised. If we had today to "prove" the Trinitarian dogma and Christological faith from scripture in the same controversial way as the sacrificial character of the eucharist, our endeavour to reach common conclusions would certainly be no less arduous. On the other hand, if the basic form of the liturgy of the early Church were accepted as a lasting heritage, ranking with conciliar creeds, this would provide unifying hermeneutics which would render many points of contention superfluous. The Church's liturgy being the original interpretation of the biblical heritage has no need to justify itself before historical reconstructions: it is rather itself the standard, sprung from what is living, which directs research back to the initial stages.[25]

I do not think that this sort of consideration is merely an intellectual game. Fundamentally it again points to the question of mere history and the significance of its content (*Geschichte*), of growth and life, i.e. the problem of authority and tradition which has occupied our minds throughout these ruminations. It is essential to have the most accurate knowledge possible of what the Bible says from an historical point of view. Progressive deepening of such knowledge can always serve to purify and enrich tradition. But what is merely historical remains ambiguous. It belongs to the realm of hypothesis, whose certainty is intellectual, not certainty by which to live.[26] To live by faith and die for faith is possible, only because the power of the living community, which it created and still creates, opens up the significance of history and renders it unequivocal, in a way that no amount of mere reasoning could do. The two levels we are referring to can be well illustrated by a formula in the ARCIC documents. As the authors unfold their theological vision, they repeatedly use the phrase "we believe."[27] If I understand them aright, what it actually means is "it is our opinion": it is expressing the opinions of theologians. But it is only when "we believe"

---

[25] Cf. J. Ratzinger, *Das Fest des Glaubens,* Einsieden 1981.

[26] Cf. R. Spaemann, *Die christliche Religion und das Ende des modernen Bewusstseins,* in the international Catholic periodical *Communio* 8 (1979) pp. 251 – 270, especially pp. 264 – 268.

[27] To give just some examples, though the meaning of the word is perhaps not exactly the same in each case: *Ministry and Ordination* (1973) 6: "we believe"; *Elucidation* to it (1979) 6, para. 2: "The Commission believes"; Co-Chairman's Preface to *Authority in the Church* (1976), para. 4: "we believe"; *Authority in the Church* I, 25: "we believe". I find it difficult to answer the question as to the exact force of the claim made for the contexts, especially because for the actual teaching of the Church a terminology is used that is very similar to those expressions of the Commission in the aforementioned texts, cf. e.g. *Authority in the Church* II, 27: "The welfare of the koinonia does not require that all the statements of those who speak authoritatively on behalf of the Church should be considered permanent expressions of the truth. But situations may occur where serious divisions of opinion on crucial issues of pastoral urgency call for more definitive judgement. Any such statement would be intended as an expression of the mind of the Church . . .". This inevitably gives rise to the question as to how the mind of the Church and faith of the Church relate to each other, which means that the respective levels of faith and theology must be further clarified.

is transformed from "this is our opinion" to "this is our faith" by what has been thought out theologically that it is caught up into the full life stream of the Church; only in this way can unity be achieved. The task that lies before us is to find a way to effect this transition. The document from the Congregation for the Faith was intended as a contribution towards this.

Conclusion—Prospect for the future

This brings me to my conclusion. Perhaps what I have said sound in places rather depressing. It may have given the impression that there are far more problems than signs of hope. But here too it is true that the problems belong to the realm of thought, the hopeful signs to the realm of life. The pope's visit was a clear indication of this: because it was a lived event, it was also a gesture of hope. Of course thought and life belong together; to separate them would destroy both. The hopes of all in our days have come from those who have lived the faith and suffered for it. Hope has directed thought along new ways and made unifying hermeneutics possible. In this sense Catholic theology can and must agree to the idea of reception. Unity can grow only if particular communities live out their faith with unity as their goal. There must always be interplay between thought and life, ministry and community. Although at times things have been held up, there is much that is hopeful, precisely with regard to the fundamental problem of the authority of living tradition and its central organs in the universal Church, and also in what concerns the intimate mutual relationship between the universal Church and each particular Church. The fact that most of the communities which were once national or state churches have transcended the frontiers of countries and continents means that there is a new openness to the meaning of "catholicity" in the original sense of the word. In the same way actual experience of lived ecclesial community has moderated exaggerated fundamentalist notions with regard to scripture and facilitated new understanding of the meaning of tradition and of doctrinal authority on a sacramental basis.

In both cases contact with the Orthodox Church has proved stimulating. The Eastern Church has enabled reformed communities to experience a form of Catholicity free from the burden of Western history; and on the other hand, thanks to their common structure, it has enabled the Catholic Church of the West to detect a number of its own exaggerations and prejudices and helped it to differentiate better between what is essential to its character and what is merely accidental. Much is on the move, and the ARCIC papers are part of an endeavour to seize the opportunity of the moment, follow the way opened up for us and carry possibility through to actuality. No one can predict when convergence will end in unity, just as no one could have forseen the ways which have brought us so far. History shows us that a superficial unity which jumps the gun without inward preparation through actual living could only prove harmful. Greater unity is really to be found in the fact that the separated communities are passionately seeking the truth together with the firm intention of imposing nothing which does not come from the Lord on the other party, and of losing nothing entrusted to us by him. In this way our lives advance towards each other because they are directed towards Christ. Perhaps institutional separation has some share in the significance of salvation history which St Paul attributes to the division between Israel and the Gentiles—namely that they should make "each other envious", vying with each other in coming closer to the Lord (Rom 11:11).

As regards practical measures for the future progress of affairs between Anglicans and the Catholic Church, the Pope and Archbishop Runcie in their joint declaration at Canterbury on 29 May 1982 announced the next step to be taken: "We are agreed that it is now time to set up a new international Commission. Its task will be to continue the work already begun: to examine, *especially in the light of our respective judgements on the final report,* the outstanding doctrinal differences which still separate us, with a view towards their final resolution; to study all that hinders the mutual recognition of the ministries of our Communions; and to recommend what practical steps will be necessary when, on the basis of our unity in faith, we are able to proceed to the restoration of full communion".[28]

That is a modest statement as well as a hopeful one. The task it sets before us cannot be accomplished by a commission alone; it needs the prayerful support of the whole Church, which in the last resort is always the inspiration of any hope of unity.

POSTCRIPT

I: REFLECTIONS ON THE DEBATE AROUSED BY MY ARTICLE

There was an extraordinary lively reaction to these reflections on the Anglican-Catholic dialogue that were first published in 1983. They appeared in the recently founded journal *Insight*, and this devoted a whole issue to the debate. Among those taking part were such important representatives of the Church of England as Christopher Hill and the Bishop of London, Graham Leonard, while among Catholic contributors were Cecily Boulding O.P., Alberic Stacpoole O.S.B., and Edward Yarnold S.J. Finally there was an impressive contribution from a representative of the Catholic wing of the Church of England, William Ledwich.[1] Jean Tillard O.P., one of the outstanding Catholic theologians on ARCIC, took the dialogue up in *The Tablet*, and a wealth of material was provided by the founder and editor of *Insight*, Martin Dudley.[2]

The debate focused on three key areas: the question of

---

[28] *Acta Apostolicae Sedis* 74 (1982), 8, p. 925. The above mentioned Editorial of *Irénikon* (see note 23) when naming the first task significantly omits the phrase "especially in the light of our respective judgements on the Final Report"; it contradicted too obviously the polarity suggested by the said article between the text of the Congregation of the Faith and the utterances of the pope — not a very fair way of conveying information to the reader.

[1] All these contributions are to be found in *Insight: A Journal for Church and Community*, vol. I no. 4, December 1983, "Authority — Tradition — Unity; The Response to Cardinal Ratzinger".

[2] J. Tillard, "Dialogue with Cardinal Ratzinger: Tradition and Authority" and "Christian Communion", in *The Tablet*, 7 and 14 January 1984, pp. 15–17 and 39–40; Martin Dudley, "Waiting on the Common Mind: Authority in Anglicanism", in *One in Christ*, vol. 20 (1984), no. 1, pp. 62–77.

authority in the Church; tradition and traditions; and the relationship between the local and the universal Church. My impression was that the debate on the first of these subjects, the question of authority, was the most productive. Christopher Hill emphasized that it would in fact be nonsense to suppose that the Church in the second millennium has lost its voice. He also established that "tradition" could not simply consist of bits and pieces that had been handed down. He saw the answer to this problem in the Lambeth Quadrilateral of 1888, which points to an internal inter-action of scripture, the creeds, the sacraments and the historic episcopate. In his view these in their mutual internal relationship guarantee both the link between the Church and its origin and the contemporary relevance of its voice. To see the present nature of the Word in its totality one would need to go further and understand this "quadrilateral" against the background of the consensus of the faithful, which for him expresses the participation of the whole Church in the life and continuity of the faith.[3] Martin Dudley went into even greater detail on this question. He carefully worked out the individual elements of the concept of authority from recent statements of the Anglican Communion in order then to evaluate their position theologically within the Christian ecumenical scene on the basis of the classical concept of the *via media*. In this Dudley went back to Newman's ideas before his conversion. According to these the Anglican *via media* would be represented as follows: Protestantism limited the external means (of making the word of God present) to the text of the bible, the interpretation of which was left to private judgement or simple reason. The Roman Church pushed· reason, scripture and antiquity to one side and thus staked everything on the authority of the Church as it exists now. The Anglican Communion by contrast held reason, scripture, antiquity and catholicity in balance with an emphasis on the authority of antiquity, but where this was silent on the voice of the present Church.[4] Dudley then for his part tries to fill out these somewhat schematic ideas and at the same time to deepen them. For

[3] Christopher Hill, "Reflections on Cardinal Ratzinger's article", in *Insight*, loc. cit., pp. 5 – 13; the reference is to p. 12.
[4] Dudley, art. cit., p. 71.

him, as for Christopher Hill, the interaction of a variety of factors is important. Authority is distributed among scripture, tradition, the creeds, the ministry of the word and the sacraments, the witness of the saints and the *consensus fidelium,* "which is the continuing experience of the Holy Spirit through his faithful people in the Church". In Anglicanism we have what is a dispersed rather than a centralized authority, "having many elements which combine, interact with and check each other". They are organized in a process of mutually supporting and checking each other[5] and thus form a "system of checks and balances (in which) the truth of God makes itself known and accepted in a consensus or common mind".[6] The system may seem complicated but is in fact very simple in its fundamental idea, the expression of God's multiform loving provision against the temptations to tyranny and the dangers of unchecked power.[7]

These important and pregnant statements are however powerfully confronted by the passionate questions raised by William Ledwich in his article "With Authority, not as the Scribes". Ledwich too traces a line from Newman to the present, but in contrast to Dudley he does not confine himself to Newman's attempt to defend the Anglican principle of the *via media* but puts the whole Tractarian dispute in relation to the struggles of the present day. It is impossible in a few lines to give an idea of the dramatic picture that emerges. I would therefore like briefly merely to indicate what I feel is the decisive point. In Newman's day every kind of interpretation of the Thirty-nine Articles was permitted except for an explicitly Catholic one.[8] Conversion became imperative for Newman once the Anglican hierarchy had explicitly rejected as unacceptable his attempt at a Catholic interpretation.[9] No doubt it is progress that in contrast today a Catholic interpretation has become possible. But in Ledwich's eyes this progress is very relative if one considers the

---

[5] Dudley, art. cit., p. 77.

[6] Dudley, art. cit., p. 76.

[7] Dudley, art. cit., pp. 76 and 77.

[8] William Ledwich, "With Authority, not as the Scribes", *Insight,* loc. cit., pp. 14–23; the reference is to p. 16. (Translator's note: Rev. William Ledwich left the Church of England in the summer of 1984 over the Bishop of Durham affair to join the Orthodox Church.)

[9] Cf. C. S. Dessain, *John Henry Newman,* London, 1966, p. 75.

manner in which Catholicism can now occupy a place within Anglicanism: "That Catholicism is a party within Anglicanism no one can realistically deny . . . But it remains true that Jesus did not found a Catholic party in a cosmopolitan debating society, but a Catholic Church to which he promised the fulness of truth . . . A body which reduces its catholics to a party within a religious parliament can hardly deserve to be called a branch of the Catholic Church, but a national religion, dominated by and structured on the principles of liberal tolerance, in which the authority of revelation is subordinate to democracy and private opinion."[10] I do not presume to give any judgement on this depiction. Certainly it would not be right to want to see in Ledwich the sole and final word on the Anglican Communion of today. But it would be equally wrong simply to leave on one side as disruptive this voice marked by personal experience, by passion and by passionate love both for the Anglican Church and for Catholic truth. It remains that the debate has produced important exemplifications of detail and has illuminated the question of authority a good bit more. But it also remains that the problem has not been solved but continues to form the chief question of the Catholic-Anglican dialogue. However one may judge in detail Ledwich's findings, it will be difficult to contradict his central contention. The question that is really at issue in the Church today has remained precisely the same as in the days of the Tractarians: the place of authority and the value of dogma as opposed to private judgement.[11]

II: TWO FUNDAMENTAL ELEMENTS OF MODERN ECUMENICAL THEOLOGY AND THE PROBLEMS CONNECTED WITH THEM

While the debate on authority in the Church was abundantly fruitful precisely in its differences, the outcome on the two other points—tradition (traditions) and the relationship between the local and the universal Church—strikes me rather as meagre. Much of what was said rests on misunderstandings, while much

[10] Ledwich, art. cit., p. 21.
[11] Ledwich, art. cit., p. 17.

also overlooked the heart of the matter. What disappointed me above all was what was said in response to my remarks about tradition. It was not a question here of terminological quarrels, as could be deduced from the reactions. Rather I had maintained that lurking behind the new concept of tradition was the elimination of the question of truth. The difference between the Churches is reduced to a difference of "traditions" (customs). This puts the ecumenical dispute on a completely new track: it is no longer man's great struggle for the truth but the search for compromise in the matter of tradition, for a balancing out of different customs. I had expected so large a claim to be bound to evoke a passionate debate: instead I was reminded that talk of "our traditions" had been customary in ecumenical circles for some decades. Since for the past forty years I have been trying to share in theological activity I was of course aware of this. This does not mean that I want to dispute that on these points some interesting and important things were said on matters of detail, but it would not seem to me appropriate to bother the reader with learned details of a controversy that is now already several years old. Instead I would like to choose a simpler and, I think, more fruitful way by trying, independently of the preceding debate, briefly to state my position on two fundamental elements of ecumenical theology which are often presupposed without being questioned but which in reality contain a host of unsolved problems.

1. The "conciliarity" of the Church

Today the model of the Church's "conciliarity" increasingly surfaces in order to clarify the relationship between the universal Church and the particular Church. From two points of view this strikes me as a mistake. In my book *Das neue Volk Gottes* I was able, on the basis of detailed philological analysis, to demonstrate the profound semantic and factual difference which in the language and thought of the early Church separated the concepts of *communio* and *concilium* from each other.[12] While *communio* can virtually act as an equivalent for

---

[12] Joseph Ratzinger, *Das neue Volk Gottes,* Düsseldorf 1969, pp. 151–163.

Church and indicates its essential nature, its mode of life and also its constitutional form, the same does not in any way apply to the concept *concilium*. In contrast to communion, to union in and with the body of Christ, council is not the act of living of the Church itself but a particular and important act within it which has its own great but circumscribed significance but which can never express the life of the Church as a whole. To put it another way, the Church is not a council. A council happens in the Church but it is not the Church. A council serves the Church but not *vice versa*. From the point of view of the Fathers of the Church it is completely nonsensical and unthinkable to describe the whole Church as some kind of permanent council. A council discusses and decides but then comes to an end. The Church, however, is not there to discuss the gospel but to live it. Hence a council presupposes the constitution of the Church but is not itself that constitution. The idea of a perpetual conciliarity of the Church as the basic form of its unity, of its existence as a unity, springs rather from the idea, to use Ledwich's polemical description, of a "cosmopolitan debating society"[13] than from the thought of scripture and the Fathers.

But even the inner idea of the council presupposed in the slogan of "conciliarity" is wrong. What is assumed here is that the council, the harmony of all the local Churches, is at the same time the only form of expression of the universal Church *qua* universal Church, its only constitutional organ. I have already pointed out in the preceding contribution on the Anglican-Catholic dialogue that one cannot see how under such conditions a universal council could come into being at all. The difficulties which the Eastern Church is facing on the road to a pan-Orthodox synod provide a quite concrete verification of this problem. In fact the Church of the Fathers never saw itself as a pure combination of particular Churches with equal rights. One can roughly distinguish in it three basic ideas of the constitution of the universal Church, though admittedly these were slow to take on their specific forms and become separated from each other. The East knew two fundamental models: one was the pentarchy, a fourth-

[13] Ledwich, art. cit., p. 21.

century expansion of the three primatial sees of the Council of Nicaea in which a foundation of Petrine theology was united with practical political aims. Rome and Antioch are Petrine sees: Alexandria in the shape of St Mark is also able to claim a Petrine origin for itself. If originally Jerusalem was excluded from the authoritative sees on the basis of the idea of its mission being translated to Rome, it now returns among their circle as the place of origin of the faith: at the same time the recent *translatio imperii* from Rome to Constantinople, the imperial city on the Bosphorus, made it possible for the latter to be included among the primatial sees. The reference to Andrew then became a kind of theological variant of the idea of translation and the idea included in it of the brotherly equality of the two cities. Be that as it may, the early episcopal Church was aware of itself against the background of the Petrine idea and its historical variations as a pentarchy, but not as a general conciliarity or as a "federation of love" (as *sobornost*).[14] The mixed theological and political model of the pentarchy, which was not in any way seen as the fruit of mere historical accidents or political expediency, was then admittedly increasingly overlaid by the imperial model of the state Church in which the functions of the Petrine ministry devolve upon the emperor: the emperor becomes the actual executive organ of the universal Church.[15] In keeping with this the pentarchy in the Byzantine state Church markedly regressed to become the monarchy of the Ecumenical Patriarch. If we should regard this connection between the monarchy of the emperor and that of the Ecumenical Patriarch as a second model, then finally the idea of the succession of Peter at Rome—in no way restricted to the city itself and its immediate sphere of influence—must be classed as the third model. For this model the single successor of Peter, the bishop of Rome, is the properly biblically based executive organ of the universal Church, without at first the pentarchy and the position of the emperor being seen as totally incompatible with it.

[14] Cf. E. von Ivánka, *Rhomäerreich und Gottesvolk,* Freiburg/Munich 1968, p. 146.
[15] Cf. the examples in A. Grillmeier, *Mit ihm und in ihm. Christologische Forschungen und Perspektiven,* Freiburg 1975, pp. 386–419, especially p. 407.

My conclusion from the whole of this is that the model of conciliarity is unsuitable for the oneness of the universal Church in and from the particular Churches and should be given up. The dialogue should be conducted much more explicitly against the background of the actual history of the Church and the experiences it has undergone, as Meyendorff has expressly indicated.[16] Then my conviction is that the indispensability of the Petrine principle would come to light and at the same time we would also see the breadth of its possible forms of realization.

2. Traditionibus *or* sola scriptura? *A new ecumenical formal principle*

Anyone who reads attentively the ever growing number of ecumenical agreed statements gets ever more clearly the impression that the classic criterion of *sola scriptura* is hardly ever still applied but that in place of this a new formal principle seems to be developing that I would tentatively like to describe by the label *traditionibus*. This seems to me to be most clearly the case in what is called the Lima text on Baptism, Eucharist, Ministry, which appeared in 1982. What is meant by this? The impression arises that scripture—torn to pieces by the disputes of different confessions and different exegetes—is regarded as too insecure for one really to be able to base oneself on it. But what is available are the "traditions", i.e. the actual forms of Christian life in which individual confessions live. These are "traditions". This factual datum thus becomes the starting-point and also the inner standard of the ecumenical dialogue. The "traditions" are there, and because they are there one must come to terms with them. Ecumenical irenism excludes simply rejecting actual historical interpretations of Christianity. The effort must rather be directed at bringing them into a relationship of amicable tolerance. In this it is completely unimportant to ask when and how a tradition arose. The fact that it could and can sustain Church life gives it its right in the ecumenical

---

[16] See note 18 (p. 77) to the preceding essay on "Anglican-Catholic Dialogue".

quest. Thus what is factual—the existence and persistence of a practice—obtains a hitherto unknown weight.

A few examples may make this clear. In Africa, we are told by BEM (the Lima document), there are communities which baptize only by the laying on of hands, without water.[17] The consequence? One must study the relationship of this practice to baptism with water. In some "traditions" it is the custom to give children merely a blessing in order to link them to the Church: only when they can make a confession of faith themselves are they baptized. Other communities baptize their children, who then later, when they are mature enough, make their own confession of faith. What should one do? See both "traditions" as fundamentally of the same kind. Some Churches have started ordaining women while others refuse to do so. What follows from this? The blessing that clearly lies on the ordination of women also justifies it, but not everyone has to adopt it. The sacramental understanding of the ministry in the threefold form of diaconate, presbyterate and episcopate is ancient and proper to the entire Catholic form of the Church. In general it is not recognized by the Churches of the Reformation. What should one do? The Churches of the Reformation should seriously consider entering the form of ministry of the apostolic succession, but at the same time both forms of ministry should be recognized as completely valid, and entry into the sacramental ministry should take place in a non-sacramental form, for example by means of a certificate. These examples may suffice to make clear the nature of the new formal principle: "traditions" are simply to be accepted as such at first; they are the reality with which the ecumenical scene has to deal. The task of ecumenical dialogue is then to seek fairly the necessary compromises between the different traditions, compromises that do not destroy anyone's identity but make it possible for everyone to recognize each other.

This is no longer Luther's or Calvin's principle of scripture; we do not have to waste any words over that. But it

---

[17] BEM, Baptism, Commentary 21b. In view of the ease with which they can be tracked down there is no need to list individually the references to the various instances quoted.

is also something quite other than the Catholic (or Orthodox) principle of tradition. In the latter it was a case of "apostolic traditions" which were "of divine right"; in other words, traditions which rested on revelation without their being explicitly recorded as such in scripture. Purely "human traditions", the existence of which nobody disputed, could demand respect but could not be brought up to the level of revelation. Today, however, the crisis of exegesis seems to mean that the idea of a real origin from Jesus (institution) and thus of a real quality of relevation has become so uncertain that recourse is hardly still had to it. What is certain are the "traditions", and now it no longer counts for very much whether they arose in the first, in the tenth, in the sixteenth or in the twentieth century, nor in what way they arose. Once again we must be cautious about making a judgement. Even classic doctrine had established that even in scripture there were traditions that could be purely of human right (for example the obligation on women to cover their heads) and that on the other hand what had belonged to the essential nature of the whole from the start without having been stated explicitly could become visible in the living tradition of the Church as the agent of tradition. But in this there always remained the requirement that this kind of context of development must exist and thus an inner connection with the origin and that to this extent a certain justification in the light of the original sources was needed. But where the common agent of tradition disappears, the idea of development thereby becomes untenable and actual traditions become the sole bearers of Christian reality, one finds oneself on a different plane which is neither that of the Reformers nor that of the Catholic Church.

This kind of openness to factual data certainly has its positive side. Old prejudices lose their power; a new impartiality arises that is able to see and to understand others' ideas. So in the event realizations became possible that could only with difficulty have been imagined under the domination of the old principles. In this climate precious rapprochements have succeeded precisely in the concept of ministry and in the understanding of sacrifice, two apparently insuperable focuses of controversy. To this extent one can grant this principle a heuristic intermediate function that is helpful. But in no way can it or should it mean anything more. For if one were to agree completely on regarding all the different confessions simply as traditions, then one would have cut oneself completely loose from the question of truth, and theology would now be merely a form of diplomacy, of politics. Our quarrelling ancestors were in reality much closer to each other when in all their disputes they still knew that they could only be servants of one truth which must be acknowledged as being as great and as pure as it has been intended for us by God.[18]

Anyone who wants to see in these remarks an attack on recent ecumenical work has understood nothing of what I am concerned about. What has been achieved in the way of agreements is precious and must not be lost but must be deepened and extended. But we must see to it that in this we do not silently make ourselves the absolute rulers of our faith and thus by pressing on thoughtlessly destroy the living thing that we cannot create but can only cherish. It is good that the traditions have entered into the ecumenical scene. But if we cannot link them with scripture in a single principle we have lost the ground from under our feet. Every hope bears its own danger within it. It only remains hope if we do not refuse to face up to the danger.

---

[18] I refrain from adding here another separate section on the local Church and the universal Church: the most important aspect of this is at least hinted at in the first part of this book. I should also refer to the section "Kommunion — Kommunität — Sendung" in my book *Schauen auf den Durchbohrten*, Einsiedeln 1984, pp. 60 – 84. It would also be important to take more notice once again of the important exegetical work of recent decades. To cite just one example, I refer to O. Michel's book that appeared in expanded form in 1983, *Das Zeugnis des Neuen Testamentes von der Gemeinde,* and recall H. Schlier's major commentary on Ephesians (Düsseldorf [2]1958).

5

Luther and the unity of
the Churches*

*What is the present position of Catholic research on Luther?
Beyond the historical approach has there been an exploration
of his theology?*

This question cannot be answered in a few sentences, and
beyond that it would need a great deal of specialized
knowledge which is not at my disposal. But perhaps it could
be useful briefly to indicate some names that represent
various stages and trends in Catholic research on Luther. At
the beginning of this century we have the markedly polemical
work of the Dominican Heinrich Denifle, who however
deserves the credit for having placed Luther in the context of
the scholastic tradition which Denifle knew like no-one else,
among other things on the basis of material only available in
manuscript. He was followed in a much more conciliatory
fashion by the Jesuit Hartmann Grisar, who admittedly drew
a variety of criticism on account of the psychological
characterizations with which he sought to elucidate the
problem of Luther. The founding father of recent Catholic
research on Luther was Joseph Lortz, who continues to be
regarded as the turning-point in the struggle for a historically
accurate and theologically appropriate picture of Luther.
Against the background of the movement of theology in the
period between the two world wars Lortz was able to develop
new ways of asking questions which led to a new overall
picture. The liturgical, biblical and ecumenical movements
had in the mean time changed much on both sides. On the
Protestant side there was a new searching for sacrament and
Church, for the "Catholic Luther" in K. A. Meissinger's

* An interview with the *Internationale Katholische Zeitschrift Communio.*

phrase; Catholics were concerned about a new direct
approach to scripture and in connection with this with a piety
that was shaped by the standard of the classical liturgy. Thus
there was much criticism of many religious forms that had
developed during the second thousand years of Christianity
and particularly during the nineteenth century. This kind of
criticism found a great deal of affinity with Luther; it tried to
bring out the "Protestant" side of Catholicism. In this
atmosphere Lortz was able to describe the great impulses
which fuelled the Reformer and demonstrated theological
understanding for Luther's criticism against the background
of the crisis in the Church and theology that arose in the late
middle ages. On this basis Lortz coined the famous phrase to
describe the period of the great transformation in the
Reformer's thinking: "Within himself Luther wrestled and
overthrew a Catholicism that was not Catholic."[1]
Paradoxically he was able to base himself on Denifle for this:
Denifle had adduced the proof that Luther's revolutionary
interpretation of Romans 1:17, in which Luther himself
subsequently wanted to see the real turning-point of the
Reformation, corresponded in reality to the main line of the
mediaeval tradition of interpretation. Even for the period
around 1525, when after Luther's excommunication and
after his attacks on the core of Catholic doctrine the outlines
of the new Evangelical Church order were becoming
apparent, Lortz thought he was able to say that Luther was
not yet aware "that he was outside the Church".[2] Although
Lortz himself did not underestimate the profound gulf that in
reality opened up in the Reformation dispute, following on
from his work and by coarsening what he had said it became
tempting to develop the thesis that the schisms had really
been a misunderstanding which could have been avoided if
pastors had been more watchful.[3]

---

[1] Joseph Lortz, *The Reformation in Germany,* London 1968, vol. 1 p. 200.
[2] Lortz, op. cit., p. 287.
[3] To my surprise P. Manns (*Martin Luther. Reformator und Vater im Glauben*
[Beiheft 18 of the publications of the Institut für europäische Geschichte, Mainz]),
Stuttgart 1985, p. 5) has expressed the opinion that he is being attacked here,
whereas I had merely been thinking of a widespread stereotyped idea that lies at the
root of not a few ecumenical utterances. The work cited above does however

The generation which followed Lortz developed a variety of emphases. Names like E. Iserloh, P. Manns, and R. Bäumer show how Lortz's starting-point could be further developed in quite different directions. Younger theologians like O. H. Pesch or J. Brosseder from the school of H. Fries have essentially remained on the lines laid down by Lortz.[4] I would like to mention two outsiders who, standing apart from professional theology, have tackled the phenomenon of Luther on the basis of their personal questions.[5] First there is

show that in fact Manns supports the misunderstanding theory in a somewhat more nuanced form: "It simply cannot be disputed that to contemporary theology and to the magisterium on the historically fixed view of what was 'Catholic' Luther appeared as a heretic. On the other hand it was also true of Luther that in the historical situation of a profound lack of theological clarity he did not always succeed in formulating important principles of his teaching without distortion and exaggeration" (pp. 45 – 46). Manns' position becomes even clearer later on: "Luther is therefore just as much in advance of the old Church, which would gladly have had him burnt, as he is of the 'reforming' Church, which appeals to his concern and yet thereby distorts it. Luther is in advance of both Churches without for that reason leaving them" (pp. 57 – 58).

[4] This attempt to draw up a brief genealogy of Lortz's successors has run into particularly sharp criticism from Manns (op. cit., p. 5). He takes especial exception to the fact that I include R. Bäumer, a pupil of Jedin, in the "Familia Lortziana". Because of the fact that I do not mention the controversy that raged between him and O. H. Pesch in 1967 he feels he is justified in remarking that "not even by way of a hint" do I know anything of it, while at the same time one is stuck by the zealousness of the conclusions and attributions in what is probably a little too emotional a contribution from the Mainz scholar. So I can let matters rest when he talks of "the cardinal's lack of interest for the really important questions, a lack of interest stemming from ignorance". That is the self-assurance of the guild member for whom the non-specialist can only be a poor ignoramus. As far as my idea of the "Familia Lortziana" is concerned, I admit that an attempt of this kind to indicate how different tendencies are related to each other is always problematical because it necessarily omits much (perhaps too much) and presupposes much. The fact that Bäumer is a pupil of Jedin I am of course aware of as a former colleague of Jedin's at Bonn. But at the same time it is known to Manns that, at least for the period in question, Jedin completely adopted Lortz's portrait of Luther, as has recently been confirmed meanwhile by Jedin's memoirs. Beyond this I did not talk of Lortz's *pupils* but of the generation that followed Lortz and how they developed in their different ways from the starting-point the doyen had provided. There is nothing for me to correct here. Nor does my presentation exclude the fact that all the rest are not to be lumped together and that "violent disagreements" are possible between them. All I am asserting is merely a common basic orientation, and I maintain this assertion.

[5] The relatively detailed presentation of these two "outsiders" most aroused the undisguised wrath of the "insider" Manns: he is only able to explain it on the basis of my "ignorance" and my "lack of interest for the really important questions". Of

the expert on Indian questions. Paul Hacker, a convert, who in this book on Luther *Das Ich im Glauben*[6] has also documented his own spiritual journey. He was concerned to investigate the structure of the act of faith in Luther; he found the real turning-point of the Reformation to consist in the transformation of the basic shape of the act of faith, and on this basis passionately opposed the theory of misunderstanding along with all ideas of convergence and complementarity. The former Leipzig parish priest Theobald Beer with dogged persistence devoted his life to reading Luther and the immediately preceding theology of the late middle ages. He has studied the change in theological thinking in the difference between Luther and scholasticism but also between Luther and Augustine, and thereby he established important shifts in the conception of Christology which, on the basis of the fundamental idea of the "holy exchange", is completely linked with how one understands man and with the doctrine of grace. This new structure or altered basic pattern of the holy exchange (which Beer finds maintained with great consistency from early to late Luther) expresses as far as he is concerned what is completely different and new in the Reformer's attitude to faith, something which in his view does not ultimately admit of any harmonizations.[7]

course, for guild members questions posed by outsiders are always unimportant questions. But the attempt based on all too great an awareness of belonging to a specialists' guild simply to condemn such voices to non-existence forces one to oppose the official commandment of silence. Meanwhile in the person of B. Hallensleben a suitably qualified scholar has brought back into discussion what she describes as "the very remarkable work of Paul Hacker, even if hardly noticed by Luther scholars", while noting that as a philologist of standing he knew how to handle texts (" 'Das heisst eine neue Kirche bauen': Kardinal Cajetans Antwort auf die reformatorische Lehre von der Rechtfertigungs-gewissheit", in *Catholica* 39 [1985], pp. 217–239; the quotation is from p. 230). Moreover Manns seems to overlook the fact that I was asked about *Catholic* research on Luther, in which context it had to be mentioned that voices were being raised from outside which called into question the basic consensus of the "Familia Lortziana". By doing so I did not want to canonize the two books — in fact I would not be competent to do so; but I wished to underline the seriousness of their questions as "really important" as against the "lack of interest" of members of the specialists' guild. Despite all my "ignorance" my general theological education is sufficient for that.

[6] Graz 1966.

[7] T. Beer, *Der fröhliche Wechsel und Streit. Grundzüge der Theologie Martin Luthers,* Leipzig 1974; second edition, heavily revised, Einsiedeln 1980.

With this it should be clear that there can be no investigation of Luther without an investigation of his theology and that it is quite manifestly not possible to encounter him only in the distance of historical perspective. His theology may indeed need to be analysed and interpreted historically, but for the historian who is a Christian it inevitably steps out of the past and affects him or her in the present. As far as their directions are concerned, my opinion is that today one can observe two fundamental decisions in which Harnack had already seen the fundamental alternative. On the one hand, with his catechisms, his hymns, and his directions for worship Luther founded a tradition of Church life on the basis of which one can see him as the "father" of this kind of Church life and interpret him in the sense of an Evangelical ecclesiastical tradition. But Luther also created a theological and polemical work of revolutionary radicality which he in no way retracted with his political link with the princes and his turning against the left wing of the Reformation. So one can conversely understand him on the basis of this revolutionary breach of his with tradition and one will then come to a very different overall view. What one should strive for would be a reading which would keep in mind the revolutionary background in the case of his writings dealing with the Church and his piety in the case of the polemical works.

Is the idea realistic of the Catholic Church lifting its excommunication of Luther on the basis of the results of recent research?

To do justice to this question one must distinguish between excommunication as a measure taken for the sake of order by the Church as a legal community against a particular person and the factual content that forms the occasion for such a procedure. Since the Church's legal power obviously affects only living people the excommunication ceases with the death of the person concerned. To that extent the question of lifting the excommunication directed against the person of Martin Luther is otiose: it came to an end with his death, since after

death judgement belongs to God alone. The excommunication directed against the person of Luther does not
need to be lifted; it has long since ceased to exist.

But the question whether the doctrines put forward by
Luther still have the effect of dividing the Church today and
thus exclude from the community of communion is
something completely different. It is this question that the
ecumenical dialogue revolves around; the mixed commission
established following the Pope's visit to Germany in 1980
intends to study precisely the problem of the sixteenth-
century exclusions from communion and whether they
continue in fact to be valid or can be overcome. For one must
observe that there are not only Catholic anathemas against
Luther's teaching but also quite emphatic rejections of the
Catholic approach on the part of Luther and his followers
which reached their culmination in his saying that "we are
divided for ever". One does not have to take what Luther
wrote when seething with anger about the Council of Trent in
order to show how categorically he rejected the Catholic
thing: "We should take them—the pope, the cardinals, and
whatever riffraff belongs to His Idolatrous and Papal
Holiness—and (as blasphemers) tear out their tongues from
the back, and nail them on the gallows . . . Then one could
allow them to hold a council, or as many as they wanted, on
the gallows, or in hell among all the devils."[8] After the final
breath Luther did not just categorically reject the papacy but
saw idolatry in the Catholic doctrine of the sacrifice of the
Mass because in the Mass he saw a relapse into the law and
thus the denial of the gospel. Simply to trace all these
differences back to misunderstandings is in my eyes a
presumptuousness that has its roots in the Enlightenment and
that cannot do justice either to that person's passionate
struggle or to the weight of the realities at issue. The real
question can therefore only be how far it is possible for us
today to transcend the positions adopted then and to attain a
perception that overcomes that of the past. To put it another

---

[8] *Wider das Papsttum in Rom, vom Teufel gestiftet,* quoted from A. Läpple,
Martin Luther. Leben. Bilder. Dokumente, Munich/Zürich 1982, pp. 252–253. The
English translation comes from Luther's *Works,* vol. 41, Philadelphia 1966, p. 308.

way, unity demands new steps; it cannot be contrived by tricks of interpretation. If at that time separation and schism came into being through contrary religious experiences that could find no place in the environment of Church teaching as it had been handed down, so too today unity is not to be created through doctrine and discussion alone but only through religious power. Indifference is only an illusory means of binding the two sides together.[9]

Can one say that the pluralism of theologies that exists today in the Catholic Church as it does in the Churches of the Reformation makes it easier for the Churches to approach each other or merely for Catholic and Protestant theologians to approach each other?

What is needed here first of all is to clarify the concept of pluralism, while the question of the relationship between theology and the Church also needs to be raised. It is an

---

[9] I regard myself as confirmed in this view by the letter which Pope John Paul II sent to Cardinal Jan Willebrands to mark the Luther quingentenary, published in *Osservatore Romano* of 11 November 1983. P. Manns (op. cit., pp. 39 – 42) subjects the papal letter to some remarkable treatment. Since part of what is said clearly does not fit in correctly with his ideas he tackles the text with the tried and tested means used by literary criticism in such cases of authoritative texts that do not fit in with one's own system. He distinguishes between "the document's original purport", which he approves, and a revision, which apparently he would like to ascribe at least in part to me. This revision comes in for criticism while the original meaning that he has been able to distil allows him cheerfully to assert a difference between the pope and me (as he does also on p. 8) and to bring the authority of the pope into play against me. I hope that other ventures by Manns into the field of literary criticism have greater success: all I can say on the basis of my own knowledge of prehistory of the text in question is that Manns is wrong. But quite apart from that kind of division and allocation of authority is a frivolous manoeuvre which a scholar of the standing of someone like P. Manns really should not stoop to. Quite a different tone from Manns is taken by E. Herms (*Einheit der Christen in der Gemeinschaft der Kirchen,* Göttingen 1984, p. 184 note 7): without distinguishing between sources and attributing the text to different authors he talks of the "outstanding remarks of the present pope in his letter . . . to mark the five hundredth birthday of Luther" and expresses the hope that "in the long term" these "will lead to new emphases and goals being set". Interestingly enough he picks out as especially helpful precisely the passage in the letter that Manns is most concerned to blame me for and thereby strip of its ecumenical relevance: the statement that the schism that began with the Reformation is not simply to be traced back to mutual misunderstandings but goes much deeper in its decisive factors.

indisputable phenomenon that on the basis of the data provided by the historical critical method or by newer methods based on literary criticism Catholic and Protestant exegetes have drawn so close together that the ecclesiastical allegiance of the individual interpreter for the most part hardly still plays any part in determining his or her findings. Indeed they even exchange positions; in certain circumstances a Protestant exegete takes a more "Catholic" line and one more conscious of tradition than does a Catholic. Thus Protestant and Catholic exegetes contribute to new biblical works of reference according to their particular expertise; what distinguishes them seems really only to be their respective fields of study. The same development is shown by the *Evangelisch-Katholischer Kommentar* that has been appearing for some years now. In this it is interesting that Protestant exegetes refer back more strongly to their "Fathers" (Luther, Calvin) and draw them in as contemporary partners in dialogue into the struggle to understand scripture than do Catholic exegetes, who seem to a considerable extent to be of the view that Augustine, Chrysostom, Bonaventure and Thomas cannot contribute anything to exegesis today.

One must of course ask what community can be created by this kind of agreement among the exegetes. While Harnack was of the opinion that there could not be a more solid basis than the common ground of the historical method, Karl Barth lampooned this attempt to provide a basis for unity as completely illusory. In fact the unity of method makes common ground possible but at the same time it can always create fresh differences. Above all agreement in the findings of scholarship denotes a different level than the unity of ultimate convictions and decisions which is what Church unity is all about. The unity of the findings of scholarship is of its essence open to revision at any time; faith is something durable. The history of Reformed Christendom shows the limits of exegetical unity very clearly; Luther to a considerable extent abolished the boundary between the teaching of the Church and the findings of theology. Church teaching that is in opposition to exegetical evidence is for him no Church teaching. Hence throughout his life his doctorate of theology was for him a decisive means of legitimation in his opposition to the teaching of Rome. The evidence of the exegete superseded the plenary powers of the Church's teaching authority; teaching authority was to be found with the scholar and with nobody else. The fact that in this way Church teaching was linked to the evidence of exegesis became from the start of the Reformation a continual questioning of Church unity in itself. This evidence that was fundamentally capable of revision necessarily became a device for exploding unity conceived of as depending on content; but unity without content remains void and collapses. In this way the effect on unity of theological pluralism is only temporary and limited; it belongs to the essential nature of pluralism that it cannot be the ultimate foundation of unity.

Regardless of this it is true that agreement between exegetes can overcome differences encrusted with age and disclose their secondary nature. It can create new opportunities for dialogue on all the major subjects of dispute between Christians: scripture and tradition, ministry in the Church, the Petrine ministry, the eucharist, etc. In this sense hope certainly exists for the Church too in this movement. The only thing is that the real solutions that are aiming at a more profound certainty and agreement than that of scholarly hypotheses cannot come from there alone. On the contrary, when a complete dissociation of Church and exegesis develops both find themselves in danger; exegesis becomes purely a matter of literary criticism and the Church loses its intellectual foundations. Hence the cohesion of the Church and theology is the real heart of the matter; when this fundamental unity ceases to exist every other unity has no roots.

Are there still between the Catholic Church and the Churches of the Reformation differences that divide, and if so what are they?

The fact that differences that divide continue to exist is shown precisely by the agreed statements that have been produced in great numbers of recent years. This becomes clearest in the dialogues that have made most progress: the Anglican-Catholic dialogue and the Orthodox-Catholic dialogue. The agreed statements of the Anglican-Roman Catholic International Commission (ARCIC I), published together in 1982 as its final report, may claim to have found a basic pattern on the basis of which the controversies become capable of being solved, but they do not in any way claim to be able to present these solutions without exception. Not only the official response of the Congregation for the Doctrine of the Faith but also other publications have pointed beyond this to serious problems within this report. Similarly, for example, the Catholic-Lutheran document on the Lord's Supper, while noting many important cases of convergence on old controversies, does not hide the fact that unsolved differences remain.[10] A forced march towards unity, such as Heinrich Fries and Karl Rahner have recently offered with their proposals, cannot lead to the goal.[11] Church unity lives from the unity of fundamental decisions and fundamental convictions; the unity in action shown by Christians in the world is something other. It already, thank God, exists in part, and even without solution of the real questions of unity it could be very much stronger and more comprehensive.

In answer to your main question, what the differences that divide really are, whole libraries have been written; to answer it concisely and yet accurately is very difficult. One can of course without more ado adduce a sheaf of questions in which differences persist: scripture and tradition or scripture and the Church's teaching authority; linked with that the question of the Church's ministry in general, apostolic succession as a sacramental form of tradition, and their combination in the Petrine ministry; the sacrificial character of the eucharist and the question of transsubstantiation as

---

[10] Joint Roman Catholic/Evangelical Lutheran Commission, *Das Herrenmahl*, Paderborn/Frankfurt ³1979.
[11] Heinrich Fries and Karl Rahner, *Einigung der Kirchen — reale Möglichkeit*, Freiburg 1983. Some first critical remarks on this can be found for example in the review which H.-J. Lauter published in the *Pastoralblatt* 9 (1983), pp. 286 – 287. More detailed discussion of this book's proposals and of subsequent discussion will be found in the postscript to this interview, pp. 122 – 134 below.

well as the persistence of the presence of the Lord in the elements and thus eucharistic worship outside the Mass (while fundamental agreement exists on the real presence of Christ in the actual celebration of the eucharist); the sacrament of penance; differences of perception in the field of Christian morality, in which of course the problem of the teaching authority once again plays a major role, etc. This kind of enumeration of controversial points of doctrine does not however solve the question of the basic decision: does all this depend on a fundamental difference, and if so can it be labelled? When during the celebrations to mark the four hundred and fiftieth anniversary of the Augsburg Confession Cardinal Willebrands stated that in the divisions of the sixteenth century the root had remained one, Cardinal Volk was being both humorous and serious when he remarked: "What I would like to know is whether what we are talking about was a potato or, for example, an apple-tree." To put it another way, is everything apart from the root really only foliage or is the tree that has grown from the root important? How deep does the difference really go?[12]

Luther himself was of the conviction that the separation from the teaching and customs of the papal Church to which he felt himself obliged affected the basic form of the act of faith itself. For him the act of faith as presented by the Catholic tradition had been moved back and shut up in the law, when it was meant to be the expression of accepting the gospel. In his opinion it had therefore been turned into the reverse of itself, since for him faith was liberation from the law, whereas in its Catholic form it looked to him like subjugation under the law. Thus he thought he was now

[12] P. Manns, op. cit., p. 6 describes this passage as "shocking" and regards it as showing me in clear opposition to Cardinal Willebrands and to the pope himself. He has overlooked the fact that I was not putting forward any thesis of my own here but merely repeating a question of Cardinal Volk's that had struck me rather forcefully. What was intended by the formula which Cardinal Willebrands was not the first to use was never at any time disputed by us: the fact that by clinging to the Trinitarian and Christological faith of the old Church the core of the content of the faith remained common to both sides. The question asked here merely draws attention to the fact that the image of the root does not explain everything but that instead the argument about the relationship between the root and the whole remains open.

obliged to wage against Rome and against the Catholic tradition in general the war which Paul in his letter to the Galatians had fought against the Judaizers. The identification of the positions of his age with those of St Paul (and thereby a certain identification of himself and of his mission with Paul) belongs to the fundamental elements of his way. Today it has become common to say that no difference yet remains any longer in the doctrine of justification. In fact the form in which Luther posed his question can hardly still be understood today; Luther's consciousness of sin and fear of hell persist just as little as do his being shattered by the majesty of God and his cry for grace. His idea of the unfree will, too, which already provoked the decided opposition of Erasmus of Rotterdam, appears today understandable only with difficulty. On the other side the Council of Trent's decree on justification emphasized the primacy of grace so emphatically that Harnack was of the opinion that, if this document had been in existence at the start of the Reformation, it would have had to take a different course. But since Luther throughout his life fixed the central difference with such emphasis in the doctrine of justification the supposition seems to me to remain justified that it is on the basis of this issue that the real fundamental difference will soonest be found. I cannot present all this in the context of an interview. So I will try to give an indication which will necessarily be one-sided and fragmentary but which can perhaps at least point to the right perspective.

It seems to me that the decisive origin of the break cannot be found only in the changed intellectual climate and the shifts in theological theory connected with this, however important these elements are. For it remains true that religion can always only be brought forth by religion and that a new religious movement only comes into being through a new religious experience which is perhaps favoured by the total situation of a particular epoch and makes use of its means without being absorbed by it. The fundamental element, so it seems to me, is the fear of God which affected Luther in the tension between the demands of God and his consciousness of sin; it affected him right to the core of his being — so much so that God appeared to him *sub contrario,* as the opposite of himself, as the devil that wanted to annihilate man.[13] Liberation from this fear of God became the real problem of salvation. This liberation is found in the moment in which faith appears as being saved from the claim of one's own righteousness, as a personal certainty of salvation. This new axis of the concept of faith becomes quite clear in Luther's *Small Catechism:* "I believe that God has created *me* . . . I believe that Jesus Christ . . . is *my* Lord who has redeemed *me* . . . so that *I* may be his own . . . and serve him in eternal righteousness, innocence, and blessedness." What faith provides now is above all certainty of one's own salvation. Personal assurance of salvation becomes its decisive means—without it there would not be redemption. This brings about an essential change in the mutual relationship of what are termed the three divine virtues of faith, hope and love, in the interaction of which something like the formula of Christian existence may be seen; certainty of hope and certainty of faith, until now distinct of their nature, become identical. For Catholics the certainty of faith is related to what *God* has done and what the Church attests to us; certainty of hope relates to the salvation of the individual person and thereby of one's own self. For Luther, on the contrary, it is precisely this latter that is the real trigger without which all the rest does not count. Hence love, which for Catholics forms the inward aspect of faith, is completely excluded from the concept of faith to the point of the polemical formulation of the great commentary on Galatians, *Maledicta sit caritas.*

The formula *sola fide,* "by faith alone", on which Luther so insisted, means precisely and exactly this exclusion of love from the question of salvation. Love belongs to the sphere of "works" and to this extent becomes "profane".[14]

[13] P. Manns, op. cit., p. 6, is of the opinion that T. Beer "clearly inspired" me to make this statement, which is his way of condemning it. I can put Manns' mind at rest by pointing out that I gradually came to this conclusion on the basis of all my reading of the sources and subsequent literature and have finally been confirmed yet again by H. Obermann, *Luther: Mensch zwischen Gott und Teufel,* Berlin 1982. Perhaps it has not become quite clear to Manns that in my view this is a very positive statement: Luther's theology and the path he took with regard to the Church rest on a personal encounter with the living God, not on ideas worked out at his desk.

[14] P. Manns, op. cit., p. 6, is quite succinct on this: "Seldom has a theologian of the cardinal's standing so massively misrepresented an opponent's theology as

If one wants to, one can call this a radical personalization of the act of faith, which consists of an exciting and, in a certain sense, exclusive face-to-face encounter between God and man. In this man must continually hold out against the God or Christ appearing *sub contrario,* as the devil, the God who demands and judges, and cling to the forgiving God. This dialectic of the image of God corresponds to a dialectic of existence which Luther himself once summed up in this way: "Christianity is nothing other than perseverance in this point of doctrine, namely to feel that you have no sin although you have sinned, that your sins are borne by Christ."[15] This "personalism" and this "dialectic", together

happens here in these brief statements." In this sentence at least the assumption that I saw an "opponent" in Luther is false. Or has Manns secretly identified Luther with his own picture of Luther and meant himself as the misrepresented "oponent"? However this may be, the force of this statement made me all the more curious to see the "refutation" of my "mistaken principle" in the second part of this treatise. A first disappointment here was Manns' admission that he "still owes his colleagues as well as the public . . . proof for this outline" (p. 57). While matters are like this he would do better to speak more softly: the tone he adopts against Frieling is even rougher than that used against me (cf. p. 68 note 127 and p. 69 note 135). However I was re-assured by reading Manns' study because when he quotes texts he does in fact confirm my interpretation. On p. 50 he describes as Luther's "highly original principle" the view that "faith represents . . . love that is not yet complete until death". On p. 51 he writes: "If we ask about the actual growth of love, Luther clearly is a little afraid of the fulfilment that is tantamount to the perfect fulfilment of the law. Hence Luther pushes the goal of development as far as possible into the future: only in death or beyond death does our love experience its ultimate fulfilment." On p. 56 he writes: "Behind this principle lies Luther's concern lest 'faith working through love' (Gal 5:6) could rob faith of its power as *fides iustificans* and call it into question. It is on this basis that with reference to justification he emphasises the absolute primacy of faith over love: only the 'divine' *fides absoluta* compared with the Godhead brings about our justification; *fides incarnata* belongs to life . . . without affecting justification as such . . . It is on this basis that we are to understand Luther's anathema: *Maledicta sit caritas,* or his demand for action: *Loco caritatis ponimus fidem."* It was precisely this that I was putting forward in my interview. The noteworthy essay by B. Hallensleben mentioned in note 5 above offers an impressive confirmation and deepening of what I was only able to hint at. On p. 235 she points out that "man's action . . . appears as an event without God" and that in this way "the secular sphere freed from its relationship to God suddenly" falls victim to "the whim of him who seizes power over himself". Especially interesting too are her remarks about the concept of sacrifice and about the separation of spirituality and ethics (p 236). Her indications of how on the basis of Cajetan's theology an acceptance of Luther's intentions is possible are ecumenically valuable (pp. 237ff.).

[15] Weimarer Ausgabe, vol. 25, p. 331:7.

with his understanding of man, have in greater or lesser measure transformed the remaining structure of doctrine. This fundamental principle means that in Luther's view faith is no longer, as it is for Catholics, of its essence a sharing in faith with the entire Church; for him at least the Church can neither assume the guarantee of certainty for one's personal salvation nor decide in a definitively binding manner about the content of faith. For Catholics on the contrary the Church itself is contained in the inmost principle of the act of faith; it is only by sharing in faith with the Church that I have a part in that certainty on which I can base my life. Corresponding to this, scripture and Church are inseparable in the Catholic view, whereas with Luther scripture becomes an independent standard by which the Church and tradition can be measured. This in turn brings with it the question of the canon of scripture and of the unity of scripture. From a certain point of view this is indeed the starting point of the whole movement, since it was precisely the unity of scripture—the Old and New Testaments, the gospels, the Pauline and the catholic epistles—through which Luther felt himself to be confronted by a devil-God which he had to oppose and succeeded in opposing with the help of the divine God he found in Paul. The unity of scripture, which had hitherto been seen as a unity of stages in the history of salvation, as a unity of analogy, was now dissolved by the dialectic of law and gospel. This dialectic obtained its intensity from the fact that of the two complementary concepts of gospel in the New Testament, that of the gospels themselves and that of the letters of Paul, it was only the latter that was taken up, and then radicalized in the sense of the formula "by faith alone" that we have already described. I would say that this dialectic of law and gospel expresses Luther's new experience in the most rigorous possible way and also explains in the most concise way possible the opposition to the Catholic conception of faith, the history of salvation, scripture and Church.

To sum up: Luther already knew what he meant when he described the doctrine of justification, which for him was identical with the "gospel" as against the "law", as the real point of division. The only thing is that one has to take justification in as radical and as profound a way as he did, as tracing one's whole understanding of man and with that all other items of doctrine back to the dialectic of law and gospel. Since then much has opened up in all individual statements, so that it is possible to hope that we may be at the point where the fundamental decision can be considered afresh and integrated into a larger vision. But so far, unfortunately, this has not yet happened. To skip the question of truth, which is posed here in a clear either/or, by means of a few manoeuvres of ecclesiastical politics, as fundamentally Fries and Rahner seem to propose, would be completely and totally irresponsible. One may hope all the more that the commission which was set up following the pope's visit and which is concerned precisely with this central point and the mutual excommunications that accompany it will come closer to the goal, even if it probably cannot yet reach it itself.

With regard to the relationship of the Catholic Church to the Churches of the Reformation today, could one use the Pauline formula of "the Church of Corinth", "the Church of Rome" and "the Church of Wittenberg"?

The answer is quite plainly no. This is already the case purely on the basis of the sociology of the Church. "The Church of Wittenberg" as such does not exist at all. Luther did not have in mind founding a Lutheran Church. For him the focus of the concept of the Church was to be found in the congregation. For relationships that transcended the congregation, in view of the logic of developments at that time, one depended as far as organization was concerned on the political structure, in other words on the princes. Thus there arose the *Land* or provincial Churches in which the political structure took the place of the structure of its own which the Church lacked. Much has changed in this field since 1918, but the Church continues to exist in provincial Churches which are then united in Church federations. It is obvious that when the concept Church is applied to this kind of accidental historical formation the word takes on a different meaning from that which is envisaged in the case of the expression "Catholic Church". Provincial Churches are not "Church" in the theological sense but organizational forms of Christian congregations which are empirically useful or even necessary but which can be swapped for other structures. Luther was only able to transfer Church structures to the princedoms because he did not regard the concept of the Church as established in these structures. But for Catholics, on the contrary, the Catholic Church, that is the community of the bishops among themselves and with the pope, is as such something established by the Lord which is irreplaceable and cannot be swapped for anything else. Here the concept of the Church forms part of this sacramental structure which is visible because it is sacramental and at the same time makes what is visible a sign of something greater. Belonging to this symbolic function are the unity across the ages and the transcending of the various different political and cultural spheres in the communion of the body of Christ, which proves itself to be the communion of his body in the physical reality of the community of the bishops of all places and times. In keeping with this it is clear that the plural of local Churches, which together are the Catholic Church, means something different from the plural of confessional Churches, which is not based on any actual singular and behind which are to be found different institutional expressions of the Christian thing and different theological ideas of the spiritual reality of the Church.

Is grassroots ecumenism a way of ecumenism?

In my opinion the term "grassroots" cannot be applied to the Church in this way. Talking of the grassroots is based on a sociological and philosophical idea according to which in the construction of society a top and a bottom arise in opposition to each other, with the top denoting the established and exploiting power and the bottom, the grassroots, meaning the forces that really carry society and that by their achievement can alone bring progress about. When one talks about grassroots ecumenism the emotions generated by such ideologies continue to have their effect. In fact what is involved is in general for the most part rather an adaptation of the idea of the congregation which regards only the congregation as the Church in the real sense; large-scale Churches are seen as an organizational roof that can be shaped this way or differently. Now of course local congregations are the actual cells of the life of faith in the Church and thereby also sources of inspiration for its way. The Second Vatican Council has this to say about the Church's development of faith: "There is a growth in insight into the realities and words that are being passed on. This comes about in various ways. It comes through the contemplation and study of believers who ponder these things in their hearts (cf. Lk 2:19,51). It comes from the intimate sense of spiritual realities which they experience. And it comes from the preaching of those who have received, along with their right of succession in the episcopate, the sure charism of truth."[16] Three chief factors of progress in the Church are thus adduced: contemplation and study of the sacred texts; insight from spiritual experience; and the proclamation of teaching by bishops. To this extent there is not in any way to be found in the tradition of th Church that monopolizing of doctrine and life by the episcopal ministry that is so often claimed. When mention is made of insight drawn from spiritual experience this includes the entire contribution of the Christian life and thus also the special contributions of the grassroots is recognised, that is of congregations of the faithful as a *locus theologicus*. On the other hand it is clear that these three factors belong together: experience without reflection remains blind; study without experience becomes empty; proclamation by bishops without being rooted in the soil of these two has no effect. All three together build the life of the Church, and in this process in different times sometimes one element, sometimes another can stand out more strongly, but none may be entirely lacking. For the rest, looking at it purely sociologically, it would be an incredible idea that making the congregations autonomous could bring about the united Church. The opposite is the case. That kind of creation of autonomy leads to

---

[16] *Dei Verbum* § 8.

atomization. Already in relevant cases experience has shown that the bringing together of hitherto separated groups has at the same time the effect of creating new separations: a united "great Church" is precisely what does not grow spontaneously out of this kind of thing.

Does the Johannine unity of Christians also mean in every case the unity of the Churches?

One must first of all guard against simply projecting our situation and our set of questions into the text of St John. The first thing to do is to understand the relevant verses of St John's gospel on the basis of their own perspective; then one can try with all due caution to extend the lines to our own time. But in this case the correct interpretation of the Johannine prayer for unity is very much disputed. I do not claim to know the only correct interpretation. All the same some basic elements held in common can be established in the clash of interpretations. A first one is that the unity of those who believe is not, according to John, anything that could be brought about by human agency; it remains a plea, it forms part of a prayer that indeed as such also implies a commandment for Christians. It forms part of a prayer because the unity of Christians comes from above, from the unity of the Father with the Son. It is a sharing in the divine unity. I think Käsemann is fundamentally right when he states: "For John, unity is a mark and a quality of the heavenly realm in the same way in which truth, light and life are the quality and mark of the heavenly reality . . . Unity in our Gospel exists only as heavenly reality and therefore in antithesis to the earthly, which bears the mark of isolations, differences and antagonisms. If unity exists on earth, then it can only exist as a projection from heaven, that is, as the mark and object of revelation."[17] The completely theological setting of unity does not of course mean that the question of unity is put off into the future or the next world; the particular individuality of the Church is precisely that in it what is heavenly reaches into

---

[17] Ernst Käsemann, *The Testament of Jesus: A Study of the Gospel of John in the Light of Chapter 17*, Philadelphia 1968, p. 68.

what is earthly. The Church is the occurrence of human
history being drawn into the sphere of the divine. Hence there
becomes possible in the world what cannot come from the
world — unity. And for this reason too unity, as that which
characterizes only what is heavenly, is also a sign of the
Church's divine origin. If one corrects the too narrow
concentration of the "Word", then one can agree completely
with another statement of Käsemann's: "The accepted Word
of God produces an extension of heavenly reality on earth,
for the Word participates in the communion of Father and
Son. This unity between Father and Son is the quality and
mark of the heavenly world. It projects itself to the earth in
the World in order to create the community there which,
through rebirth from above, becomes integrated into the
unity of Father and Son."[18]

This however already makes it clear that all this is not
meant in a purely spiritual sense but has in mind actual
Church unity, otherwise the symbolic character it is
concerned with (Jn 17:20) would be completely without
content. Schnackenburg has gathered together a whole series
of elements which show clearly the "Catholic" orientation of
the fourth gospel in the direction of the great Church: the
passages about the acceptance of Samaritans and Greeks into
the community based on Christ; the saying about the
gathering together of the scattered children of God (Jn
11:52); the discourse about the one shepherd and the one
flock (Jn 10:16); the acceptance of the tradition of Peter; the
story of the miraculous draught of the hundred and fifty-
three fish (Jn 21:11).[19] Beyond this Käsemann has drawn
attention to certain analogies between St John's gospel and
the vision of unity of the letter to the Ephesians. The latter he
characterizes as follows: "In Ephesians 4:5 a formative
orthodoxy asserts itself which considers itself to be
constitutively bound to heaven and in this respect to be the
institution of salvation . . . The unity of this orthodoxy now
becomes identical with the truth of the right doctrine which it

---

[18] Ernst Käsemann, op. cit., pp. 69–70.
[19] Rudolf Schnackenburg, *Das Johannesevangelium*, vol. III, Freiburg 1975, pp.
241–245.

must administer as the mystery of divine revelation. Earthly reality may show its nature as dispersion and division. The heavenly reality is of necessity one and indivisible."[20] Even if one does not overlook the element of exaggeration, almost of caricature, in this, it remains an important statement. Käsemann describes the position of St John's gospel with regard to early Catholicism in a rather mixed and confused manner: on the one hand he talks of the "closeness to the rising early Catholicism",[21] on the other he says that John "is at least spatially remote from the beginnings of early Catholicism and theologically he does not share its trends" while at once going on to add that "he shares a number of its premises".[22] What is in any case clear is that John wrote his gospel for and in the context of the great Church as a whole and that the idea of a unity of Christians in separated Churches is completely alien to him.

Is the unity of Christians in the sense of the farewell discourses possible in time, and is that of the Churches possible only at the end of time?

I think the answer to this question is clear in the light of what I have just explained. The unity of the Church is the unity of Christians. To separate these two kinds of unity from one another or even to set them against one another is a modern fiction the content of which is extremely indistinct. Even if in John interest in the individual institutional aspects of the Church seems to be small, nevertheless his gospel quite obviously presupposes the actual context in terms of salvation history of the people of God, the context in which God performs his action of salvation. To take only one example, the discourse about the vine (Jn 15:1–10) takes up the image of Israel as the vine to be found in Hosea,

[20] Ernst Käsemann, op. cit., p. 57.
[21] Ibid., p. 73.
[22] Ibid., pp. 66–767.

Jeremiah, Ezekiel, and in the psalms. "Vine" is thus an image taken from tradition for "the people of God", which is here given a new core, the figure of Jesus Christ; the echo of the eucharist in the image of the vine gives a very realistic Church framework to what may seem a quite "mystical" train of thought.[23]

Something quite different, of course, is the question of what actual goals the ecumenical movement can strive to reach. Twenty years after the Council one should in fact re-think this problem. It is perhaps not completely pointless to begin by noticing that the Catholic tradition, as it has been re-stated by the Second Vatican Council, is not characterized by the idea that all existing "Churchdoms" are merely fragments of a true Church which does not exist anywhere but which one must now try to form by putting all these fragments together; this kind of idea would turn the Church into purely the work of man. Even the Second Vatican Council, and precisely this Council, says explicitly that the one Church of Christ "subsists in the Catholic Church, which is governed by the successor of Peter and by the bishops in communion with him".[24] As is well known this word "subsists" replaces the earlier "is" (the one Church "is" the Catholic Church) because even outside the Catholic Church there are many true Christians and much is truly Christian. But this latter perception and recognition, which form the basis of Catholic ecumenism, do not mean that from now on as a Catholic one has to regard the "true Church" as merely a utopia which may emerge at the end of time; the true Church is a reality that exists, even now, without one on that account having to deny that other Christians are Christians or to dispute an ecclesial character on the part of their com-munities.

After this digression let us return to the question of actual ecumenical goals. The real goal of all ecumenical efforts must of course remain the transformation of the plural of confessional Churches separated from one another into the plural of local Churches that are in their diversity really one Church. But it

[23] Cf. Schnackenburg, op. cit., pp. 118–123.
[24] *Lumen Gentium* § 8.

seems to me that in the situation which exists in fact it is important to set realistic intermediate goals, since otherwise ecumenical enthusiasm could suddenly turn into resignation or even into a new embitterment which would seek to pin on the others the blame for the failure of the great aim. Then the last state of things could be worse than the first. These intermediate goals will vary according to the progress that has been made by individual dialogues. The witness of love (charitable and social work) is something that fundamentally should always be able to be borne jointly or at least be co-ordinated if for technical reasons separate organisations seem more effective. In addition one should make the effort to give joint witness on the great moral questions of the day. And finally a joint fundamental witness of faith should be given in a world shaken by doubt and fear, and the more comprehensive the better; but even when this can only happen in a relatively narrow compass one should in any case say jointly what is possible. All this must then lead to people recognizing and loving their common Christianity in and despite their divisions, and to division and separation no longer being a reason for opposition but rather a challenge to an inward understanding and acceptance of the other that means more than mere tolerance—a belonging to each other in loyalty to Jesus Christ. Perhaps in this kind of attitude, which does not lose sight of the ultimate goal but meanwhile does what is immediately at hand, the process of ripening towards complete unity can take place at a profounder level than in a hectic chase after reunion that remains superficial and often has the effect merely of make-believe.

The question when the union of all Christians will at last come about is in the event in my conviction unanswerable. And one should not forget that to this also belongs the question of the unity of Israel and the Church. At any rate as far as I am concerned the idea that one could establish this unity by means of a "really general (ecumenical) council" is a hybrid; it would be like building the tower of Babel and could only end with all the greater confusion. The complete unity of all Christians is something that in this age will only exist with difficulty. But that unity of the one Church that already indestructibly exists guarantees for us that this greater unity is coming one day. One is all the more a Christian the more one approaches this unity with all one's power.

POSTSCRIPT

This interview drew criticism from three directions. *Herder-Korrespondenz*—as is so often unfortunately the case more concerned about party polemics than about factual theological debate—thought it was obliged to give the fundamental position of my contribution the label "ecumenism in reverse".[1] Even a superficial reading would have been enough to see how nonsensical this insinuation is. I concluded by speaking out emphatically against too hasty and unprepared a stampede towards reunion and said that division must no longer be opposition to each other but rather a challenge to a mutual understanding that is more than tolerance: belonging to each other in loyalty to Jesus Christ. In this context I also spoke of an indestructible unity that is already given. Meanwhile on the basis of my entire corpus of theological writings H. Schütte has generously refuted *Herder-Korrespondenz*'s thesis, first in a series of shorter essays and then in a book which has rightly received a great deal of attention, *Ziel: Kirchengemeinchaft,* and has drawn on an astonishing knowledge of my work to put things in a correct perspective. P. Manns, too, in spite of his attacks on my interpretation of Luther, has come out against the charge of "ecumenism in reverse".[2] No more words need therefore be wasted on this topic.

Manns' spirited attacks on my remarks about Luther mark the second field in which what I said ran into opposition. Manns even suggested I should go in for a "recantation" or palinode, but then said that "for other reasons" this request was unrealistic. Nevertheless I should tacitly surrender my position, especially as it could possibly "be interpreted as a confirmation of the other side in its appeal to the 'Protestant Luther'."[3] To this I am bound to say that when it is a matter of what is

[1] U. Ruh in *Herder-Korrespondenz* 38 (1984) p. 4. Cf. H. Schütte, *Ziel: Kirchengemeinschaft. Zur ökumenischen Orientierung,* Paderborn 1985, pp. 22–25.
[2] Manns, op. cit., p. 65 note 25.
[3] Ibid, p. 8.

primarily a historical problem, as is now the case with regard to the interpretation of Martin Luther, I do not recognize any "other side" but only the common search for accurate knowledge, even in the case of controversial results, when everyone must remain open to correction by better evidence. In addition I would like to add that Manns' unvarnished candour, even in his polemics, arouses my human sympathy and that I find it far preferable to a certain apparent objectivity hiding covert attacks. What I have to say on the matter after studying the question yet again I have set down in a series of notes attached to the text.

Finally my judgement on the reunion plan of Fries and Rahner aroused a lively reaction. Interestingly enough from the Protestant side E. Herms indicated cautious agreement,[4] while on the Catholic side I was overwhelmingly greeted with abuse. Unfortunately I cannot evaluate here the wide-ranging debate that arose about the book by Fries and Rahner; a survey of this is offered by H. Fries in his postscript to the 1985 enlarged edition of the volume.[5] What is without a doubt the most important contribution to the dialogue has been provided by the Protestant systematic theologian from Munich, Eilert Herms, with his lecture, *Ökumene im Zeichen der Glaubensfreiheit. Bedenken anlässlich des Buches von H. Fries/K. Rahner, 'Einigung der Kirchen — reale Möglichkeit',*[6] and with his book, *Einheit der Christen in der Gemeinschaft der Kirchen.*[7] What Herms has presented at this high level of reflection demands a thorough investigation and debate, the significance of which extends far beyond the problems raised by what one might term the Rahner project. What is involved here is the fundamental question of the relationship between conscience and authority in the mediation of the Christian faith and thus the legitimization

[4] "Ökumenische Zeichen der Glaubensfreiheit" in *Una Sancta* 39 (1984), pp. 178–200 (the reference is to p. 200 note 29), and cf. his *Einheit der Christen in der Gemeinschaft der Kirchen,* Göttingen 1984, p. 47 note 2, pp. 184–185 note 7. A positive and sympathetic appreciation of my views is offered by O. Cullmann in his latest book, *Einheit durch Vielfalt,* Tübingen 1986, whose trains of thought I can to a considerable extent endorse.

[5] Expanded edition 1985, including *"Zustimmung und Kritik. Eine Bilanz",* pp. 157–189.

[6] Cf. note 4 above.

[7] Cf. note 4 above.

of its claim to truth, which is increasingly showing itself to be the fundamental question for the survival of contemporary Christianity. The fact that Herms has brought the question of the truth of the faith and of its claim to truth once again into the centre of theological reflection is in my eyes the real service of his book, and as a result it should not be put on one side after a brief debate, snowed under by short-lived ecumenical discussion papers, but must be the subject of further consideration on the basis of its fundamental intentions. H. Fries is no doubt himself aware that his responses to Herms do not provide the discussion that is needed.[8] Certainly his references to Herms' misunderstanding of the Catholic concept of revelation are useful, but they do not exhaust the problem.[9]

A more thorough dialogue with Herms thus remains a desideratum which can only be indicated, not met, here. In the context of this postscript an indication must suffice of the direction in which in my opinion the debate should move. Without a doubt Herms has laid bare the core of the reunion proposals of the Fries-Rahner book when he underlines Rahner's thesis of "epistemological tolerance" as their decisive point on which the whole plan depends. The Protestant scholar has summed the problem of this "tolerance" up in four questions, the unambiguous negation of which at the same time turns the Fries-Rahner project upside down. Here I shall simply mention the three points which in my opinion are what matters. First of all Herms denies that Reformed theology teaches what Rahner and Fries suppose it does on the status of the canon of scripture, of the apostolic creed and of the Nicene-Constantinopolitan creed.[10] I think that in this sense one must be still more general and say that the position of these texts in the structure of the act of faith is not the same for the Reformed understanding as Catholic doctrine presupposes. On the

---

[8] Fries, op. cit., pp. 178–189: valuable hints for a dialogue with Herms are provided by Schütte, op. cit., pp. 74–76, without him wanting to go in for a comprehensive debate.

[9] Fries, op. cit., pp. 182ff.

[10] Herms, op. cit., p. 136.

basis of my own knowledge of the Reformed understanding
of faith and revelation this view seems to me to be completely
obvious: the fact that the two Catholic ecumenists simply
ignored this fundamental question in their proposal was for
me one of the reasons why I described what they were up to as
a "forced march towards unity". In his second question
Herms states "that the Roman view of the infallibility . . . of
papal doctrinal decisions and the establishment of these
teachings as dogma is the integral element of a doctrine on
revelation, faith, the ministry of the Church and the unity of
the Church", which contradicts and is inconsistent with
Reformed theology.[11] In keeping with the logic of this
statement it is stated in the fourth question that "in a Church
whose life is oriented by the theological convictions of the
Reformation the decisions of office-bearers" cannot be
decisive "for the Church as a whole" and that in such a
Church public opinion is not decided by the Church's office-
bearers.[12]

It seems to me that here Herms on the one hand brings up
an urgent and legitimate question about the relationship of
authority and conscience in the question of truth, but on the
other hand distorts the Catholic Church's concept of
revelation and probably also defines the Reformed position
in a one-sided and extreme manner that can hardly be
justified by the entirety of Reformed traditions. According to
his conviction the canonical forms of Christian witness are to
be understood exclusively as the "form of human witness to
this thing", whereby a very different relationship to the bible
and to the apostolic and Nicene-Constantinopolitan creeds is
signalled than is presupposed by the Catholic faith.
According to Herms Reformed theology teaches "that the
truthfulness of all these propositions is made evident to and
bestowed on every one of the elect in an individual way—*ubi
et quando visum est Deo*".[13] Here his presentation of
Reformed theology comes into very close contact with what I
said in my interview about the fundamental distinction

[11] Ibid., p. 139.
[12] Ibid., p. 149.
[13] Ibid., p. 138.

between Luther and Catholic tradition. I stated that the doctrine of justification marked the real dividing point when it was taken in such a radical and profound manner as Luther had done; then the opposition to the Catholic conception of faith, the history of salvation, scripture and the Church became visible on this one point in the sense of a "radical personalization of the act of faith". Herms puts things this way: "It is not the doctrine of justification as such that forms the centre of the conflict but a quite definite version of the doctrine of justification, namely that which arises if one brings into play in it Luther's insight into the constitution of the objective status and certainty of faith by means of the self-presentation of the divine will in a free verification of the gospel handed on by the Church (and therefore Luther's doctrine of revelation and grace)."[14]

I would like to raise the question whether so extreme a personalization of the act of faith does in fact do justice to the totality of the Reformers' perceptions; whether such a total allocation to the merely human of word and sacrament and thereby also of the Church and its ministry is really their last word. Catholic theology knows itself to be on firm biblical ground when it relates God's enlightening and saving action not so exclusively to the individual and his or her conscience but is aware of God acting also through the body of Christ. My conviction is that nothing justifies us in allocating everything that is communal to the merely human and limiting God's own action only to the individual elect being inwardly moved by him. Quite the reverse: divine action is always both divine and human and therefore mediated through another human being (the God-man Jesus Christ and his bodiliness). The effect of his action consists precisely in the fact that what counts in the encounter with Jesus Christ is "I" but "no longer I" (Gal 2:20). Since Christ, *ubi et quando visum est Deo* is no longer some unknown somehow and somewhere but means Christ, and we cannot want to be more godly than God when he has linked his quality of not being at our disposal in this way with the body of Jesus Christ. Hence the first effect of this *ubi et quando visum est Deo* is that

---

[14] Ibid., pp. 139–140.

the human being is led out of his or her limited ego and obtains a new ego, a new subjectivity in community with him who suffered for us (the mystery of vicariousness), died and rose again. Thus all Christian faith is sharing in knowledge with him. The enlightenment consists in the fact that I am no longer alone with a distant God but that, living in and sharing in the life of the body of Christ, I myself touch the ground of all reality because this ground has become the ground of my own life. Enlightenment is at the same time salvation; because it changes me, I now see in a new way. And it changes me by giving me back my "I" in the "we" of the community of the saints.

With this, however, I now come to an important point where I again take issue with Herms. Faith, I said, is essentially sharing in faith with the Church as the new and greater "I". The "I" of "I believe" is not my old "I" shut in on itself; it is the "I" of the *anima ecclesiastica,* that means the "I" of the human being in whom the entire community of the Church expresses itself, with which he lives, which lives in him and which he lives. But this now also means that authority in the Church is not that of an absolute ruler, nor that of a democratic official. The same applies to it as applies to every individual: only to the extent that in fact it reflects the entirety of the true Church is it authority.

This means that the formulation of Herms' fourth question, according to which in the Catholic Church the decision of office-bearers on matters of faith is decisive for the Church as a whole and in it public opinion is decided by its office-bearers, is at the least extremely inexact and cannot be sustained at all in this form. Admittedly it was Rahner himself who provided him with these formulations. Herms re-shaped Rahner's ideas in an admittedly sharpened but in fact not simply inaccurate form: "The incorporation of Reformed Churches in the Roman Church comes about through the conversion of their leaders . . ., whom their congregations then obey."[15] Rahner would not talk of "conversion" here, nor of incorporation in the Roman Church, but in fact he puts ample stress on the docility of

---

[15] Ibid., p. 37.

congregations following the decision of their leaders. In his view, "while fully recognizing a not insignificant difference of congregational life between Catholic and Protestant congregations with regard to their relationship to the leadership of their Churches, in practice in the Protestant Churches congregations on the average usually demonstrate a docility towards Church leadership of the kind that is usual in the Roman Catholic Church", and hence as a consequence "one must not overestimate the danger of a rebellion 'from below' against the decisions of Church leadership in favour of reunion if those responsible for this leadership . . . exert themselves with sufficient zeal among members of their Churches to bring about an understanding of this decision . . ."[16]

This position I find completely intolerable. It is not only a Protestant theologian who must protest against it; a Catholic one cannot and should not accept it either. It reflects that misunderstanding of hierarchy springing from the Enlightenment, a misunderstanding which manipulates consciences in an impermissible way and noticeably threatens the internal cohesion of the Catholic Church. Hierarchy, we should recall, means not holy domination but holy origin. Hierarchical service and ministry is thus guarding an origin that is holy, and not making arbitrary dispositions and decisions.[17] The teaching office and indeed ministry in general in the Church is thus not a business of "leading" in the sense of the enlightened ruler who knows that he is in possession of better reason, translates it into regulations and counts on the obedience of his subjects, who have to accept his reason and its articulation as their divinely willed standard. Nor does hierarchical office correspond to a democratic authority in which individuals delegate their will to representatives and thereby declare that they agree that the will of the majority should be law. Even in the political field this delegation of one's will and being bound by the will of majority are not without

[16] Fries-Rahner, op. cit., p. 66.

[17] Certainly Rahner too ties the action of "Church leaders" to the Lord's command of unity, but given his epistemological scepticism there appears within this command what seems like almost unlimited room for the ecclesiological "voluntarism" that he had already postulated in the 1960s.

their problems, as is shown by the increasing desire for grassroots democracy. In any case there are limits to what can be delegated; no deputy or representative can vote against his or her conscience, and anyway decisions about certain fundamental values of a society cannot be made by voting. But in the Church, where it is really Church and not a body administering earthly things, it is a matter of those fundamental goods that are withdrawn from our vote because the decisive measure of themselves that they are is not something that we ourselves have discovered. For this reason the idea of a council of religions is an absurd and extravagant suggestion. Who could empower the delegates at such a council to decide by voting about the consciences of their faithful or indeed of all people who were in some way "religious"?

The fact that such nonsense could surface at all, we must acknowledge shamefacedly, is because among ourselves an idea of ministry as the domination of a ruler on the model of the Enlightenment and a corresponding conciliar idea have prevailed to a considerable extent. But a council is not a parliament which makes laws that "the congregations" then have to obey. It is a place of witness. Admittedly, to a certain extent it rests on the idea of representation. But this representation rests not on the delegation of people's wills but on the sacrament. To receive the "sacrament of order" means to represent the faith of the whole Church, the "holy origin", to be a witness of the faith of the Church. It is a form based on faith of being called to be a representative. But because this representation is sacramental it can only represent what is Church and cannot create what in the opinion of this person or that (or of the representative himself or herself) it ought to be. By its essence a sacrament involves the elimination of arbitrarily following one's own designs. To stand firm in the sacrament means to live on the basis of the new "I" we have talked of and thus truly to speak in the sense of the whole (and not of some average opinion). In practice this means that statements of belief that are "decided" at a council are not "decisions" in the usual sense. The moral unanimity that is essential for them is for the Church the expression of the fact that here the common faith of the Church is being stated. They do not create anything but simply articulate what already exists in the Church of the Lord, and therefore make it publicly binding as a mark by which the *anima ecclesiastica* can be known.

There is therefore the one faith of the Church in which and by which the faithful recognize themselves as members of the Church. And hence the Church has the right and the duty to say that anyone who does not share this faith does not belong to it. But that is something very different from the decision of a handful of leaders who declare something to be true and oblige the rest to accept it as such or at least not to speak against it. It must be admitted that the question of the mutual relationship between the "I" and the "we", between the evidence provided by the individual conscience and the joint evidence of the one faith which we can only receive by sharing in believing, has for too long not been satisfactorily explained. The problem that has been so much discussed of the relationship between the proclamation of the faith by the teaching authority and theological deliberation is merely an especially visible sector of this more general problem. Herms' book should be the occasion of considering the question afresh in its full extent.[18] But as far as things stand with Rahner the possibility of unity rests on nobody knowing any longer exactly whether he or she has correctly understood the Church's teaching (based on the bible), whether he or she has rightly grasped the other's theology. In the present "intellectual political situation" (what a linguistic monstrosity) all that can be stated is merely that we all have as our point of reference "always still clearly and tangibly . . . Jesus as our Christ". Thus there remains the "eschatological hope that the fact that our faith is the same will emerge

---

[18] I tried to develop some ideas on this with reference to Galatians 2:20 (I, but no longer I) in my Toronto lecture on the Church and theology which was published in 1986 in the *Internationale katholische Zeitschrift*. To my joy I learn from B. Hallensleben (op. cit., p. 238) that Cajetan also used this text to try to elucidate the problem of Christian existence. From the indissoluble community of Christians with Christ described in Galatians 2:20 "it follows that I can say in complete truth 'I am acting commendably, but not I but Christ effects the merit in me' . . . In this way the merit of eternal life is to be ascribed not so much to our works as much more to the works of Christ, the head, in us and through us".

оборот

despite the present (partial) incommensurability of our theologies".[19] If this is how things are, if in the general fog nobody can see the other and no one sees the truth, then the "epistemological tolerance" is displayed by the fact that no one contradicts anyone any more. The only thing that is clearly visible in the darkness of the tendencies of our civilization to diminish differences is Christ's command of unity which then becomes fundamentally the only at all clear component. The "authorities" are now there to bring this unity to realization, and since anyway nobody can judge his or her own thinking, let alone anybody else's, obedience to this instruction should not be too difficult.

But what kind of unity is it really? A formal unity without any clear content is fundamentally no unity at all, and a mere linking together of institutions is no value in itself. Unity conceived of in this way is based on common scepticism, not on common knowledge. It is based on capitulation before the possibility of approaching one another in the truth. The fact that a not inconsiderable number of Christians think in this way and that a portion of Church leadership acts on this basis is beyond doubt. But it is equally evident that this does not bring us any closer to a real unity. At this point I would like once again to take up the question of authority in the Church. An authority that serves the truth, as should be the case with a Church authority based on the sacrament, is an obedient authority. An authority based on scepticism becomes arbitrary and high-handed. And should one not add that often it is precisely those who in the wake of the Council see themselves as the spearhead of progress who take for granted the obedience of the faithful while themselves criticizing obedience and wish to use this obedience to make of the Church what seems useful to them?

Certainly Rahner has nothing to do with tendencies of this kind. But his idea of unity rests on a mixture of scepticism and authority which can all too easily lead in this direction. While fully recognizing his positive intentions we must therefore reject, as contradicting the real nature and essence

---

[19] Fries-Rahner, op. cit., p. 42.

of unity, his plan of an "epistemological tolerance" in the
present "intellectual political situation": on this I am in
agreement with E. Herms. As far as Herms' counter-proposal
is concerned I would like to single out merely one point: his
desire for a mutual renunciation of excommunication. Here a
distinction must first of all be made between the pattern of
excommunication in canon law and the theological data with
regard to the impossibility of eucharistic fellowship. The
category of excommunication in canon law includes along
with exclusion from communion a whole bundle of further
legal measures. According to the self-limitation of the new
code this category is an internal means of applying the law
within the Catholic Church; it affects merely those who as
Catholics separate themselves from their own Church and
does not refer to those who already at baptism are
incorporated into another Church community. On the other
hand the theological datum persists that no eucharistic
fellowship is possible between the Catholic Church and the
Churches of the Reformation. This is because communion in
the body of Christ is the bodily form of communion in the
truth, in the unity of faith. Sacrament and faith are
inseparable; if communion is not communion in faith then it
is nothing. If Herms should think that eucharistic fellowship
("fellowship at the Lord's table") is possible while at the
same time there is "contradiction and dissent" on essential
fundamental questions of faith, then this would show that his
understanding of the sacrament is fundamentally distinct
from that of the Catholic Church and that hence such
"fellowship" would not be fellowship in the same thing but
merely a sham.

The images I chose to use in my brief references to the
Rahner-Fries book have particularly been held against me as
hurtful and inaccurate. In my eyes neither the image of a
forced march nor that of marching in step has anything
hurtful in it.[20] But if metaphors obstruct dialogue I gladly

---

[20] I see in P. Manns, op. cit., p. 65 note 49, that in KNA ÖKI no. 5, 1:2, 1984, p. 5
H. Meyer compares R. Frieling with a show-jumper who rides the wrong way round
the course and misses the jumps. From this I deduce that the metaphor need not be
as groundless and hurtful as certain attacks have supposed.

withdraw them; in what is at issue I cannot change anything, and I hope that the reason for this has become more or less clear from what I have said above, that the unity Fries and Rahner propose has no content and that no authority has the right to demand the obedience that is here envisaged.

Against this Fries would probably object that it is not in any way a question of theological minimalism. "On the contrary; here a maximum is contemplated . . ."[21] This is indeed a truly remarkable assertion. The Lutheran confessional statements in any case contain substantially more — not just what is properly the heritage of the Reformation but also they go very much further in taking up and incorporating the faith of the early Church. It remains unclear what Church Fries and Rahner are really talking about; all that is clear is that their vision is essentially confined to the German-speaking world and only takes marginal account of the context of the world as a whole. Indeed, the Free Churches are explicitly excluded from the plan in the second edition.[22] But in this case it becomes all the more incomprehensible how reducing everything to the first two ecumenical councils can be a maximum. The attempt to shunt everything that has followed afterwards into the category of "epistemological tolerance" is precisely what I would label as "ecumenism in reverse": an attempt to freeze history at the year 400 A.D., to go back in history and then to start again from that point. This kind of going back is certainly impossible.

At the end there remains the question what we should do instead. Here I can only repeat what I said on this point in my interview in 1983. Our faith, hope and love must always be directed towards the great goal of complete unity. But at the same time we must have the humility to accept realistic intermediate goals: to strengthen our common witness of love in a world that needs it ever more desperately; to give joint witness to the fundamentals of the faith, to lose nothing of it and to try to be able to give this witness ever more comprehensively; not just to respect one another in our

---

[21] Fries, op. cit., p. 164
[22] Op. cit., p. 163.

separation but to love each other in the conviction that we need each other precisely in our separation, to receive from each other, to live for each other, to be Christians together. Separation, as long as the Lord allows it, can also be fruitful, can lead to a greater richness of faith and thus prepare the diverse but united Church which today we cannot yet imagine but in which nothing will be lost of the positive things that have grown in history, wherever they may be found. Perhaps we need separations in order to reach the complete fullness that the Lord awaits.

6

The progress of ecumenism*

Dear Professor Seckler,

You have invited me to outline my ideas about the progress of ecumenism for your journal. It is not easy for me to respond to so important a question given that my time is unfortunately all too limited and that I am therefore forced to respond extremely sketchily and unsatisfactorily. But on the other hand it is becoming more and more clear to me that we need new goals, and so despite all my hesitations I would prefer not to turn your invitation down.

First of all let me briefly glance back at the developments of the past twenty years, since it seems to me essential to fix where we are today if we are to look at tomorrow. The moment when the Second Vatican Council created new foundations for ecumenical activity in the Catholic Church was preceded by a lengthy process of joint struggle in which much matured that could now quickly be implemented. The speed with which so much that was new and hitherto unexpected suddenly became possible seemed to give ground for hope of a rapid and complete end to the division. But when everything that had become possible in this way was translated into official forms a kind of standstill had necessarily to occur. For those who had been aware of the ecumenical process from its beginnings or who had themselves contributed to it this moment had been foreseeable, since people knew where solutions were already in sight and where the frontiers had not yet opened up. But for outsiders on the other hand this must have been a

---

* In 1986 the *Tübinger Theologische Quartalschrift* devoted an issue under the editorship of Professor M. Seckler to the present state of the ecumenical movement, and I was invited to contribute to this. This letter is my attempt to respond to this invitation.

moment of great disappointment; the blame had unavoidably to be allocated, and it was easy to lay it at the door of the Church authorities.

Already soon after the first flush of conciliar vigour had subsided the counter-model of grassroots ecumenism surfaced which was to bring about unity from below if it was not to be had from above. What is correct about this idea is that the authorities in the Church cannot create anything that has not already matured in its life in the way of the insight and experience that comes from faith. But when this process of maturation was not meant but instead the dominant idea was the division of the Church into the grassroots Church and the official Church no new unity of any importance could grow. This kind of grassroots ecumenism ultimately produces only splinter-groups which divide communities and do not even sustain any more profound unity among themselves despite their joint propaganda throughout the world. For a time it could well appear as if the traditional ecclesiastical divisions were to be superseded by a new one and that in the future progressive committed Christians on one side would confront traditionalists on the other with both sides gaining their recruits from the various Churches existing up till now. This perspective gave birth to the proposal that the authorities should be left completely out of the ecumenical movement because a possible rapprochement or even reunion at this level would only strengthen the traditionalist wing of Christendom and would impede the formation of a progressive new Christianity.

Such ideas may not be quite dead yet today, but it does seem that they are now past their prime. Being a Christian in a way that essentially defines itself by criteria of commitment is too hazy and indistinct in its outlines to be able to bring about unity in the long term and consistent common life as a Church. People do not remain permanently in the Church because they find community celebrations or action groups there but because they hope for answers to what in their lives is outside their control, answers which are not invented by the parish clergy or other authorities but which come from a greater authority and are handled by the clergy in the spirit of trustees. Even today people are suffering, perhaps even more than formerly; an answer that simply comes out of the parish priest's head or from some ginger group doesn't satisfy them. Religion still always enters into people's lives especially at the point where their life is affected by what is beyond their control and that of everybody else; and then the only thing that helps is an answer that comes from this thing itself that is beyond their control. When parish priests or bishops no longer appear as advocates of this power that is outside their control too but instead merely have their own activities to offer, they turn into an official Church and thus become superfluous.

By this I mean to say that the stability of the phenomenon of religion comes from areas that are not comprehended by grassroots ecumenism and that the search for what is beyond our control also marks the boundary of all activity by the authorities in the Church. This means that neither an isolated grassroots nor an isolated authority comes into consideration as the subject of ecumenical activity; effective ecumenical action presupposes the inner unity of the authorities' action on the one hand and the Church's real life of faith on the other. At this point I see one of the fundamental errors of the Fries-Rahner project: Rahner's view is that Catholics would follow the authorities anyway and that this is provided for by tradition and structure. In practice however things would not be essentially different among the Protestants; if the authorities decreed reunion and campaigned for it sufficiently here too the congregations would not fail to follow. As far as I am concerned that is a form of ecumenism by the authorities that corresponds to neither the Catholic nor the Protestant understanding of the Church.

A unity negotiated by men and women could logically only be an affair *iuris humani*. It would not involve at all the theological unity intended by John 17 and as a result it would not be able to be a witness for the mystery of Jesus Christ but merely a token of the diplomatic skill and the ability to compromise of those conducting the negotiations. That is indeed something, but it does not involve at all the genuinely religious level which is what ecumenism is concerned with. Even theological agreed statements necessarily remain on the level of human (scholarly) insight, which can provide essential conditions for the act of faith but does not affect the act of faith itself as such. It seems important to me, therefore, looking towards the future, to recognize the limits of what one might term the "ecumenism of negotiation" and not to expect of it any more than it can provide: rapprochements in important human fields, but not unity itself. It seems to be that many disappointments could have been avoided if this had been clear from the start. But after the successes of the early period just after the Council many have understood ecumenism as a diplomatic task in political categories; just as one expects of good negotiators that after some time they will come to a joint agreement that is acceptable to everyone, so people thought they could expect this of the Church authorities in matters of ecumenism. But this was to expect too much of the ecumenical movement; what it was able to do after the Council depended on a process of maturation which it had not created but which it only needed to translate into the public order of the Church.

But if this is how things are, what should we do? What I find very helpful for this question is the slogan that Oscar Cullmann recently injected into the debate: unity through diversity. True, schism belongs to what is evil, especially when it leads to hostility and to the impoverishment of the Christian witness. But when the poison of hostility is slowly extracted from the schism and when as a result of mutual acceptance what emerges from the difference is no longer just impoverishment but a new wealth of listening and understanding, then it can be in transition towards being seen as a *felix culpa* even before it is completely healed. Towards the end of my years at Tübingen, Professor Seckler, you gave me to read a work prepared under your supervision which presented Augustine's interpretation of that mysterious phrase in Paul, "there must be factions" (1 Cor 11:19). It is not a question here of discussing the exegetical problem of interpreting this passage; it seems to me that the Fathers were not so wrong when they found a statement with more general implications in a remark with an originally very local reference, and even H. Schlier takes the view that as far as Paul was concerned it was a matter of an eschatological and dogmatic proposition.[1] If one may think in this direction, the exegetical conclusion derives its especial weight from the fact that in the bible δεῖ always refers in some way to an action of God's or expresses an eschatological necessity.[2] But this then means that, even if schisms are to begin with the work of men and women and their fault, nevertheless there is in them a dimension that corresponds to God's disposing. Hence it is only to a certain point that we can repair them through repentance and conversion; but it is only the God who judges and forgives who decides entirely on his own when the point is reached that we no longer need this split and that the "must" drops away.

Following the path indicated by Cullman we should therefore first try to find unity through diversity. That means to accept what is fruitful in these divisions, to take the poison out of it and to receive precisely the positive element from this diversity — naturally in the hope that finally the division will cease to be a division at all and is merely a polarity without opposition. But when this final stage is striven for too directly in a hectic do-it-yourself rush, then the division is deepened instead of being healed. May I give an empirical and practical example of what I mean? Was it not from many points of view a good thing for the Catholic Church in Germany and beyond its borders that Protestantism existed alongside with its liberality and its piety, with its conflicts and disunity and with its lofty spiritual claims? Certainly, in the times of the religious wars division was virtually merely a matter of mutual hostility; but increasingly a positive appreciation of the faith has grown on both sides since then that enables us to understand something of St Paul's mysterious "must". Putting things the other way round, could one really imagine a purely Protestant world? Or is not Protestantism in all its statements, precisely as protest, so completely related to Catholicism that it remains hardly conceivable without the latter?

From this would emerge a twofold direction for ecumenical

---

[1] Kittel, *Theological Dictionary of the New Testament,* vol. I, Grand Rapids p. 64, pp. 182–183.
[2] Thus for example Grundmann, op. cit., vol. II, pp 21–25.

activity. The first strand will and must continue to consist of us trying to find complete unity; to think up models of unity; to try to investigate obstacles to unity — not just in learned debates but above all in prayer and penance. Alongside this there should however be a second field of activity which would presuppose that we know neither the day nor the hour, nor are we able to determine, when and how unity will come into existence. For this what applies, really and in its full rigour, is Melanchthon's *ubi et quando visum est Deo*. In any case it should be clear that we do not create unity, no more than we bring about righteousness by means of our works, but that on the other hand we should not sit around twiddling our thumbs. Here it would therefore be a question of continually learning afresh from the other as other while respecting his or her otherness. As people who are divided we can also be one.

This kind of unity, for whose continuing growth we can and must exert ourselves without putting ourselves under the all too human pressure of having to succeed by reaching our goal, has a variety of approaches and therefore demands a variety of effort. First of all it is a question of discovering, discerning and acknowledging the various kinds of unity that already exist and that in truth are not inconsiderable. The fact that we jointly read the bible as the word of God, that we share the confession, shaped by the early councils in their reading of the bible, of God three in one and one in three, of Jesus Christ as true God and true man, of baptism and the forgiveness of sins, and hence that we share the same fundamental image of God as of man: this must continually be realized afresh, publicly acknowledged, and deepened in its implementation. We share too the fundamental form of Christian prayer and the essential ethical instruction of the Ten Commandments read in the light of the New Testament. Corresponding to this fundamental unity in what we confess should be a fundamental unity in what we do. It would therefore be a question of putting this existing unity to work, of making it actual and broadening it. This would naturally include a diversity of forms of encounter at all levels (ministers, theologians, lay people) and of joint action; all this must take shape in actual experiences and be developed further, as thank God already happens to a considerable extent.

Additional symbolic actions could and should be included in this effort towards unity through diversity so as to keep it continually before the minds of congregations. O. Cullmann's proposal of ecumenical collections should be recalled here. The Eastern Churches' custom of distributing blessed bread would suit the West well. Even when genuine eucharistic fellowship is not possible this is a real and physical way of being with each other in our differences and to "communicate"; to endure the thorn of difference and at the same time to transform division into mutual giving.

Also belonging to this unity through diversity is not to want to force anything on the other that still threatens him or her in his or her Christian identity. Catholics should not try to pressurize Protestants into recognizing the papacy and their understanding of the apostolic succession; the insertion of the word into the sphere of the sacrament and the order described by the sacrament clearly seems to Protestants an attack on the freedom of the word and the fact that it is not at our disposal, and we should respect this. In return Protestants should refrain from pressurizing Catholics towards intercommunion on the basis of their understanding of the Lord's Supper; for us the twofold mystery of the body of Christ — the body of Christ as the Church and the body of Christ as sacramental gift — is a single sacrament, and dissociating the bodiliness of the sacrament from the bodiliness of the Church means crushing both the Church and the sacrament underfoot. This kind of respect for what constitutes for both sides the "must" of the division does not delay unity; it is a fundamental pre-condition for it. This kind of respectful restraint before this "must" that is something we have not invented for ourselves will give rise to much more love and also much more closeness than would forceful pressure, which creates resistance and finally refusal. And this kind of respect will as a consequence not just not impede the search for more understanding precisely in these central areas but will have as its fruit a peaceful maturation and a joyful thankfulness for so much closeness despite the mysterious "must".

I can imagine that many will not be pleased with the concept sketched out here. But whatever one can say about it there is one objection to it which ought not to be raised, that this is a concept of stagnation and resignation or even a renunciation of ecumenism. It is quite simply the attempt to leave to God what is his business alone and to discover what then in all seriousness are our tasks. Among these tasks of ours belong doing and enduring, activity and patience. Anyone who deletes one of these pairs distorts the whole. If we tackle everything we have to do, then ecumenism will continue to be, and even more than hitherto, something that is very much alive and demanding. I am convinced that, freed from the pressure to do it ourselves and the overt and covert deadlines this sets, we shall approach each other more quickly and more profoundly than if we start to transform theology into diplomacy and faith into commitment.

I hope, Professor Seckler, that these lines will leave my idea of ecumenism a littler clearer, and I remain

Yours sincerely,

Joseph Cardinal Ratzinger

PART III

THE CHURCH AND POLITICS

SECTION I

FUNDAMENTAL QUESTIONS

7

Biblical aspects of the question
of faith and politics*

The epistle and gospel that we have just listened to have their origin in a situation in which Christians were not citizens of a state who were able to shape their own lives but the persecuted victims of a cruel dictatorship. They could not share in responsibility for their state but simply had to endure it. It was not granted to them to shape it as a Christian state; instead their task was to live as Christians despite it. The names of the emperors in whose reigns tradition dates these two passages are enough to cast light on the situation: they were Nero and Domitian. Thus the first letter of Peter describes Christians as strangers within this state (1:1) and the state itself as Babylon (5:13). By doing so it indicates very impressively the political position that Christians were in; it corresponded more or less to that of the Jews living in exile in Babylon who were not responsible citizens of that state but its subjects without any rights, and who thus had to learn how they might survive in it, not how they could build it up. Thus the political background of today's readings is fundamentally different from ours. Nevertheless they contain three important statements which are significant for political activity among Christians.

1) The state is not the whole of human existence and does not embrace the whole of human hope. Men and women and

---

* This is a homily that was delivered on 26 November 1981 in the course of a service for Catholic members of the Bundestag in the church of St Wynfrith (Boniface) in Bonn. The readings provided for the day by the lectionary were 1 Peter 1:3 – 7 and John 14:1 – 6. At first sight they seemed to be out of keeping with the subject, but on closer inspection they showed themselves to be unexpectedly fruitful.

147

their hopes extend beyond the thing that is the state and beyond the sphere of political activity. This does not only apply to a state that is Babylon but to any and every state. The state is not the totality: that takes the load off the politician's shoulders and at the same time opens up for him or her the path of rational politics. The Roman state was false and anti-Christian precisely because it wanted to be the totality of human capacity and hope. In that way it claimed what it could not achieve; and in that way it distorted and diminished men and women. Through the totalitarian lie it became demonic and tyrannical. Getting rid of the totality of the state has demythologized the state and thereby liberated men and women as well as politicians and politics.

But when Christian faith, faith in man's greater hope, decays and falls away, then the myth of the divine state rises up once again, because men and women cannot renounce the totality of hope. Even when such promises dress themselves up as progress and monopolize the concept of progress and of progressiveness, nevertheless considered historically they are a going back behind the Christian thing that is new, a turning back on the scale of history. And even when they proclaim as their goal the complete liberation of mankind and the elimination of all domination, they stand in contradiction to the truth of man and in contradiction to his or her freedom, because they force people into what they can achieve themselves. This kind of politics that declares the kingdom of God to be the result of politics and distorts faith into the universal primacy of the political is by its nature the politics of enslavement; it is mythological politics.

To this, faith opposes the standard of Christian reason, which recognizes what man is really capable of creating as the order of freedom and can be content with this because it knows that man's greater expectation lies hidden in God's hands. Rejecting the hope of faith is at the same time rejecting the standard of political reason. To renounce the mythical hopes of a society free of domination is not resignation but honesty that maintains men and women in hope. The mythical hope of a do-it-yourself paradise can only drive people into fear from which there is no escape: fear of the collapse of their promises and of the greater void that lurks behind it; fear of their own power and its cruelty.

So the first service that Christian faith performs for politics is that it liberates men and women from the irrationality of the political myths that are the real threat of our time. It is of course always difficult to adopt the sober approach that does what is possible and does not cry enthusiastically after the impossible; the voice of reason is not as loud as the cry of unreason. The cry for the large-scale has the whiff of morality; in contrast limiting oneself to what is possible seems to be renouncing the passion of morality and adopting the pragmatism of the faint-hearted. But in truth political morality consists precisely of resisting the seductive temptation of the big words by which humanity and its opportunities are gambled away. It is not the adventurous moralism that wants itself to do God's work that is moral, but the honesty that accepts the standards of man and in them does the work of man. It is not refusal to compromise but compromise that in political things is the true morality.

2) Although Christians were persecuted by this state, their attitude towards it was not fundamentally negative; instead they always recognized in it the state as state and tried to build it up as state within the framework of their possibilities, not to destroy it. Precisely because they knew they were living in "Babylon" the guidelines which Jeremiah had drawn up for those exiled there from Israel applied to them. The letter from the prophet handed down in Jeremiah 29 was in no way an instruction to act by way of political resistance, by destroying the slave state, however much one would have been able to understand this; it is rather an instruction to maintain and strengthen what is good. In this way it is an instruction for survival and at the same time for preparing what is better, what is new. To this extent this morality of the exile contains fundamental elements of a positive political ethos. Jeremiah urges the Jews not to persist in negative opposition but: "Build houses and live in them; plant gardens and eat their produce . . . Seek the welfare of the city where I have sent you into exile, and pray to the Lord on its behalf, for in its welfare you will find your welfare" (Jer 29:5,7). A similar warning is to be found in 1 Timothy, which is traditionally dated to the reign of Nero, where we read that prayers should be made "for all men, for

kings and all who are in high positions, that we may lead a quiet and peaceable life, godly and respectful in every way" (2:1–2). 1 Peter follows the same line with its warning: "Maintain good conduct among the Gentiles, so that in case they speak against you as wrong-doers, they may see your good deeds and glorify God on the day of visitation" (2:12). "Honour all men. Love the brotherhood. Fear God. Honour the emperor" (2:17). "But let none of you suffer as a murderer, or a thief, or a wrongdoer, or a mischiefmaker; yet if one suffers as a Christian, let him not be ashamed, but under that name let him glorify God" (4:15–16).

What does this mean? These Christians were not in any way a bunch of people fearful of and submissive to authority, people who were not aware that there can be a right and a duty of resistance on conscientious grounds: indeed the last sentence shows that they recognized the limits of the state and had not bowed to it when they ought not to because it was opposed to the will of God. It remains all the more important that nevertheless they tried not to destroy but to build this state up. Amorality was fought by morality, evil by a determination to persist in what was good, and not otherwise. Morality, doing good, is true resistance, and only what is good can be the preparation for a dramatic change to what is better. There are not two kinds of political morality, a morality of resistance and a morality of ruling. There is only one morality: morality as such, the morality of the divine commandments, which cannot be suspended for a period in order to bring about the transformation of things more quickly. One can only build things up by building them up, not by destroying them; that is the political ethics of the bible from Jeremiah to Peter and Paul. The Christian is always someone who seeks to maintain the state in the sense that he or she does the positive, the good, that holds states together. He or she is not afraid that thereby he or she is favouring the power of those who are evil, but instead is convinced that only strengthening what is good can ever dissolve what is evil and diminish the power both of evil and of evil people. Anyone who accepts the killing of the innocent or the destruction of other people's property cannot appeal to the faith. Against such a person 1 Peter is quite explicit:

"Let none of you suffer as a murderer, or a thief" (4:15); that was said by this letter against this kind of resistance. The true resistance, the Christian resistance that it demands happens when and only when the state demands the rejection of God and his commandments, when it demands what is evil, whereas in contrast it is always what is good that we are commanded to do.

3) From this follows a final point. Christian faith has destroyed the myth of the divine state, the myth of the state as paradise and a society without domination. In its place it has put the objectivity of reason. But this does not mean that it has produced a value-free objectivity, the objectivity of statistics and a certain kind of sociology. To the true objectivity of men and women belongs humanity, and to humanity belongs God. To genuine human reason belongs the morality that is fed by God's commandments. This morality is not some private affair; it has public significance. Without the good of being and doing good there can be no good politics. What the persecuted Church laid down for the Christian as the core of its political ethos must also be the core of any active Christian politics; it is only when good is done and recognized as good that a good human social existence can thrive. To bring to public acceptance as valid the standing of morality, the standing of God's commandments, must be the core of responsible political activity.

If we act in this way, then we should, in the midst of the confusions of difficult times, understand today's scriptural readings as addressed to us personally and as a reliable promise: "Let not your hearts be troubled" (Jn 14:1). "By God's power [you] are guarded through faith for a salvation ready to be revealed in the last time" (1 Pet 1:15). Amen.

8

Theology and the Church's political stance

The subject of theology and the Church's political stance presupposes first of all a clarification of the question of what is to be understood by theology and what by the Church's political stance. Only when these two have been defined at least in broad outlines can the "and" be defined which is probably this paper's real concern.

What is theology?

Let us start then by asking what theology is. The answer should first of all be in terms of intellectual history, that theology is a specifically Christian phenomenon which derives from the peculiar structure of the act of faith involved in Christianity: the special development that European civilization has undergone among the civilizations of the world and the special place it has gained among them are closely connected with the structure that prevails here. To go into greater detail, theology necessarily results from the fusion of biblical faith and Greek rationality on which even the historical Christianity to be found in the New Testament already rests. When the gospel according to St John describes Christ as the logos, this fusion come very clearly to light. The passage is expressing the conviction that in Christian faith what is rational, basic reason itself comes to light and is indeed trying to say that the foundation of being is itself reason and that reason does not represent an accidental by-product from the ocean of the irrational from which everything really came. The fundamental Christian act thus hides a twofold statement:

1) In Christian faith reason comes to light; faith precisely as faith wants reason.

2) Through Christian faith reason comes to light; reason presupposes faith as its environment.

This creates a relationship of tension which ultimately lies behind the "and" of our subject; on this basis it must belong to the nature and essence of Christian faith to seek its own reason and in that reason itself, the rationality of the real. But in return it places the task on reason, as far as its search is concerned, to recognize in faith the condition for its own effectiveness to be possible and not to push its absoluteness to the point of dissolving its own foundation, for that would mean confusing itself with the divine reason and thus surrendering the communication with the divine reason from which it lives. This kind of self-limitation of human reason may strike the contemporary reader as pre-critical. But that it is ultimately indispensable at least as a structural model has been shown by Horkheimer and Adorno with their analysis of the dialectic of the Enlightenment: enlightenment lives from the idea of the absoluteness, or we can well say the divinity, of the truth. If it no longer recognizes this condition for itself and pushes its own absoluteness beyond this presupposed absoluteness of truth, then by internal logic it returns to the justification of the irrational and turns reason itself into an irrational accident.[1] To provide evidence of this one does not need to point to thinkers who have declared freedom and human dignity to be out-dated concepts and have explicitly put the irrational above the rational or have given the two equal standing. In quite general terms, when the big bang counts as the absolute beginning of the universe reason is no longer the standard and foundation of reality but the irrational; even reason is then only a by-product of the irrational, the product of "chance and necessity", indeed, the result of a mistake, and to that extent itself too

---

[1] Cf. R. Spaemann, "Die christliche Religion und das Ende des modernen Bewusstseins", in *Internationale katholishhe Zeitschrift* 8 (1979), pp. 268ff.; A. Görres, *Kennt die Psychologie den Menschen?*, Munich 1978, pp. 21ff.

something ultimately irrational.[2] It cannot then be seen why one should see in it of all things an enduring standard, a final court of appeal; since reason itself is irrational, the irrational in all its forms can claim the same rights alongside reason and with reason.

But let us return to theology. It rests on the presupposition, itself a matter of faith, that what is believed, the basis and foundation of everything, is reasonable and is indeed reason itself. Hence it belongs to faith to seek to understand its foundation and its content, and it is precisely this undertaking that we call theology: more precisely we talk of theology when this undertaking takes place in an organized manner and under commonly recognized and well-founded rules that we describe as its method. This means that theology takes up the fundamental question of Greek philosophy with which the human mind entered on a new stage of its history: the question of truth itself, of being itself. Christian theology does not just interpret texts; it asks about truth itself and it sees man (and woman) as capable of truth. I thus think Martin Kriele is right when he says that Christian theology, if it is functioning correctly, is to be seen as a force for enlightenment.[3]

Certainly what this shows at once are the problems connected with the concept of enlightenment. The further the Enlightenment progressed historically, the more it fell victim

---

[2] M. Kriele, *Befreiung und politische Aufklärung,* Freiburg 1980, pp. 248f.: "The idea that even before the big bang the logos existed from which everything came into being and without which nothing came into being, and that in some way this logos has its effects on human life — this or a similar assumption is today as it was before the minimum condition for respect for people. In the understanding of the political enlightenment 'human dignity' is a metaphysical concept. It becomes meaningless under the presupposition that man is 'merely' the result of accidental evolution." Cf. on the other hand the radically anti-metaphysical stance to be found in Jacques Monod, *Chance and Necessity: An Essay on the Natural Philosophy of Modern Biology,* translated by Austryn Wainhouse, London, 1972 (French original, *Le hasard et la nécessité,* Paris 1970), p. 114: "Even today a good many distinguished minds seem unable to accept or even to understand that from a source of noise natural selection could quite unaided have drawn all the music of the biosphere." On the emergence of life and of man cf. p. 137: "Our number came up in the Monte Carlo game."

[3] M. Kriele, op. cit.: cf. "Politische Aufklärung gegen neuen Dogmatismus? Ein Gespräch mit Professor M. Kriele", in *Herder-Korrespondenz* 34 (1980), pp. 120 – 127.

to a narrowing down of the concept of reason: what is reasonable is what can be reproduced. This means that reason becomes positivist. It thereby limits itself to what can be repeated experimentally; but this has the consequence that it renounces its original question, "What is this?", and replaces it by the pragmatic question "How does this function?" Once again this means that, under the pressure of its standards of certainty, reason renounces the question of truth and investigates only that of feasibility. Thereby it has fundamentally abdicated as reason.[4]

This is precisely the point the development has reached for some time, and it is this that is tearing the university apart from within. The university arose because faith declared the search for truth to be possible and compelled this search, which then for its part demanded an expansion of its field into all the spheres of human knowledge and thus produced the various faculties, which were all held together in the diversity of their objects of study by being jointly oriented towards the question of truth; and the ultimate possibility of investigating this question they knew to be preserved in the faculty of theology. Because human knowledge was based on ultimate unity those who knew and those who were seeking to know could unite in the university of learners and teachers. The university is a product of the mandate of truth to be found in the Christian act of faith; when this context and connection is completely dissolved, there arises a crisis of the university that involves its foundations. The first stage of such a dissolution is to begin with when the question of truth disappears from the university as an unscientific question. The university falls under the law of positivism and thus becomes a conglomeration of technical departments in which the various specializations of positivist reason and functional thinking are further developed and make the greatest claims for themselves.

---

[4] Cf. for the problems of modern scientific thought K. Hübner, *Kritik der wissenschaftlichen Vernunft,* Freiburg 1978. Important as an attempt to overcome positivism is Karl R. Popper, *Objective Knowledge: An Evolutionary Approach,* Oxford 1972. On rationality and religion see R. Schaeffler, *Religion und kritisches Bewusstsein,* Freiburg 1973. The standpoint of positivist thought is formulated afresh with crystalline clarity by Jacques Monod, op, cit., pp. 30 – 31. But Monod is honest and brings out the agony to which thought is condemned by such a ban on questions as appears imperative to him.

This was the situation of the German universities from the end of the war up till 1968. What is common to the individual departmental undertakings in this situation is not just the positivist limitation of reason, the ban on the question of truth. Given this kind of orientation of the university the charge of departmental lunacy is not totally uncalled for, because the positivist fundamental principle compels positivist compartmentalization and excludes as alien to its method the profounder question of the origin and purpose of the whole. To this extent the explosion of 1968 was not simply unwarranted but unavoidable on the basis of what was at stake. Contrary to appearances Marxist ideology, whose various different variants provided the criticism, remains ultimately inherent in the system.[5] As materialism it necessarily rejects the primacy of the logos: in the beginning stands not reason but the irrational; reason as one of the development products of the irrational is ultimately itself something irrational. This means that things as irrational objects have no truth; only man can make truth, which is a human construct, and that means that in reality there is no truth. There are only human constructs, that is, the necessary bias of reason which recognizes in advance the force of development, anticipates it and thereby raises up the pressure towards freedom. Positivism can indeed be transcended on the basis of these presuppositions by instances of the bestowal of meaning which can then be represented as moral because they anticipate the law of development; from this depends the fascination of these attitudes and also the inevitable inferiority of all bourgeois arguments and analyses rooted in positivism. But what unites the different specializations in this case and raises them up once again to become a university is factional constraint, and hence the university as a locus of freedom for enlightenment is not restored but finally negated.

---

[5] R. Spaemann, *Einsprüche. Christliche Reden,* Einsiedeln 1977, p. 8: "Among its roles this civilization also supplies the role of opposition, the role of criticism and of resistance that changes the system. Its official version is today Marxism. Its goal is all the same none other in reality than the perfection of that functional system of technical rationality."

Let us return to theology. If in a university constituted on positivist lines it is naïve enough not just to explain the historical conditions in which John could say: "In the beginning was the logos" but believes this statement, regards it as truth and on this basis enquires further after the truth itself, then it appears opposed to the system and does not fit into the self-understanding of a modern university. So it seems reasonable for it to align itself with the prevailing conditions. This is easier than it may seem to an outsider. Theology can quite simply, instead of seeking truth itself in its authoritative texts, explain the historical conditions in which these texts arose, try to reconstruct their original significance by using historical methods, and compare them critically with the interpretations which have come into being during the course of their history. That means that it can withdraw into an absolute compartmental professionalism and thus show itself to be fully adapted to the canon of positivist reason. It thus becomes of equal status to the other disciplines of learning. The only thing is that the special task that originally was placed on it and on philosophy now falls by the wayside: the question about the whole, transcending the separate disciplines, that is now no longer asked. In such a situation it is likely that even theology students become satiated with the forced professionalism of their teachers, see more true theology in the bias of reason for the better world of the future than in the clarification of historical or structural states of affairs, and understand theology as a practical science in the sense of this kind of option for a future world. The idea that orthopraxis precedes orthodoxy has its origin here; what is true must arise by means of a human construct for which a practical philosophy works out the instructions for action. Hence it is no accident that the student uprisings in Germany in 1968 largely began in the theological faculties because it was in them that the crisis of positivist professionalism was most keenly felt, and their confessional dimension, stripped of its claim to truth, could effortlessly be translated into a partisanship for a better world, a partisanship that at last was once again understandable.

The Church and theology

At this point the transition from theology to politics becomes visible, as does the internal principle of what is termed political theology. At the same time we come up against the phenomenon of the Church, which so far has not yet been explicitly dealt with. The Church must of course appear as an obstacle to the future everywhere that the question of truth is understood either as pre-critical naïveté or as bourgeois illusion. But from our considerations it has also become clear that in the first case people are left at the mercy of anonymous interests and in the second are delivered over to factional constraints, and so this accusation should not frighten us. In order to provide at least an outline of the Church's understanding of itself we must return once again to our starting-point, the description of the Christian act of faith. We said that faith demands and reveals reason, understands itself as the environment of reason, so that faith is not correct if the insights to which it leads are not at least rudimentarily reasonable, while on the other hand reason cuts the ground from beneath its feet if it does away with faith. Such statements do not presuppose an abstract reason which operates as it were floating freely without being conditioned by historical and social factors; this concept of reason can rightly be criticized as a bourgeois fiction. Rather what is presupposed is that reason needs historical and social conditions of life in order to be able to be effective as reason. Hence the community of faith, which is called the Church, belongs to the Christian concept of faith and of reason; according to this the Church is the environment in which living in keeping with the faith is possible as a community act and is also the historical condition for reason to be able to pose the question made possible by faith and to maintain its claim to truth. On the one hand this question of reason can only be asked as a community question, in the context of a community that guarantees the rationality of reason; on the other hand it must be placed by such a community within the personal responsibility of the person asking the question and be borne by this responsibility.[6]

[6] Cf. J. Pieper, *Buchstabierübungen,* Munich 1980, pp. 32ff.

With this we come to the central problem of this essay. Critics of the new right hold against the Church that its relationship to science and learning is precisely the same as with Marxism: knowledge is linked to party doctrine. The tension between the Church's teaching authority and theological science accordingly has two different points of origin. The first is a tension that stems from the option for a Christianity understood as Marxism, as this has recently been formulated by Ernesto Cardenal, who sees two Churches as existing today: one which is an instrument of liberation and which, in keeping with the humanist impulses of Marxism, seeks to bring the society of the future into being—the kingdom of God, in Cardenal's view; the other that maintains society as it has existed up till now and is in reaction against this new Church. Here the tension is less one between the teaching authority and theology as one between two different realizations of the Church in which admittedly the teaching authority appears in some respects as the core of the reactionary concept of the Church. The other kind of tension between theology and the teaching authority rests on the train of thought portrayed above: the teaching authority appears as a party organ which aims to bind learning to an authority alien to it, to the "orthodoxy" of its party line.

That the teaching authority can come in danger of behaving like a party organ cannot be doubted. But that structurally it is something of this kind and thus an instrument of party constraint that is alien to learning must be disputed. The difference between the structure of a party constituted on ideological grounds and the Church lies precisely in the question of truth. Materialism, as we have already seen, presupposes that what we have at the beginning is not reason but the irrational—matter. Consequently reason is the product of the irrational: reason does not precede man but only comes into being as a human construct— "orthodoxy" can always be only the product of orthopraxis even if the blueprint of theory must squeeze in ahead of practice. This means that truth is absorbed in the construct of the party and is totally dependent on it. The fundamental conviction of Christian faith on the contrary is that at the beginning we have reason and with it truth; it brings forth man and human reason as capable of truth. Man's relationship to truth is first of all essentially receptive and not productive. The community of the Church is admittedly necessary as the historical condition for the activity of reason, but the Church does not coincide with the truth. It is not the constructor of truth but is constructed by it and is the place where it is perceived. Truth therefore remains essentially independent of the Church and the Church is ordered towards it as a means. For this reason there is here a genuine "and"—theology *and* the Church's teaching authority as realities that are ordered to each other. Hence it is the Church's function to delineate the boundary where theology dissolves its own environment, the Church, and thus in the dialectic of enlightenment does away with the conditions for enlightenment. But it is not its function to prescribe for theology beyond the basic structure of the faith what its content and method should be. One must admit that, because this specific mutual relationship between the Church and theology is alien to both the positivist and the Marxist cast of mind and thus to the two fundamental attitudes predominant today, the danger from both sides is very great of failing to achieve this relationship; on the other hand the contrast to these two modern positions can contribute towards what is specific in the Christian position being first properly recognized.

The concept of the Church's political stance

With this we come to the final point of our considerations. After clarifying what theology is and what the Church is politically in relation to theology this seeks to describe how theology and the Church's political stance are related to each other. But first of all we must take a clearer look at the relationship of the Church to the political sphere. For this Christ's words remain fundamental: "Render therefore to Caesar the things that are Caesar's, and to God the things that are God's" (Mt 22:21). This saying opened up a new section in the history of the relationship between politics and religion.[7] Until then the general rule was that politics itself was the sacral. Admittedly the later ancient world knew free religious groups, what are termed the mystery cults, whose attraction depended on the decline of the state religion. But tolerance with regard to them rested on the presupposition that the state was recognized as the bearer of a supreme sacrality. It safeguarded the ethical binding force of its laws and with this the human guarantee of its cohesion by these laws and in them the state itself appearing as the expression of a sacral, divine and not purely human will; because they are divine they must continue unquestionably and unconditionally to bind men and women.

This equation of the state's claim on man with the sacral claim of the universal divine will itself was cut in two by the saying of Jesus we have quoted above. At the same time the whole idea of the state as cherished by the ancient world was called into question, and it is completely understandable that in this challenge to its totality the state of the ancient world saw an attack on the foundations of its existence which it avenged with the death penalty: if Jesus's saying was valid the Roman state could not in fact continue as it had done up till then. At the same time it must be said that it is precisely this separation of the authority of the state and sacral authority, the new dualism that this contains, that represents the origin and the permanent foundation of the western idea of freedom. From now on there were two societies related to each other but not identical with each other, neither of which had this character of totality. The state is no longer itself the bearer of a religious authority that reaches into the ultimate depths of conscience, but for its moral basis refers beyond itself to another community. This community in its turn, the Church, understands itself as a final moral authority which however depends on voluntary adherence and is entitled only to spiritual but not to civil penalties, precisely because it does not have the status the state has of being accepted by all as something given in advance. Thus each of these communities

---

[7] Cf. for this entire section A.A.I. Ehrhardt, *Politische Metaphysik von Solon bis Augustin,* three volumes, Tübingen 1959 – 1969, especially volume 2, *Die christliche Revolution,* 1959.

is circumscribed in its radius, and on the balance of this relation depends freedom. This is not in any way to dispute the fact that this balance has often enough been disturbed, that in the middle ages and in the early modern period things often reached the point of Church and state in fact blending into one another in a way that falsified the faith's claim to truth and turned it into a compulsion so that it became a caricature of what was really intended. But even in the darkest periods the pattern of freedom presented in the fundamental evidences of the faith remained an authority which could be appealed to against the blending together of civil society and the community of faith, an authority to which the conscience could refer and from which the impulse towards the dissolution of total authority could emerge.[8] The modern idea of freedom is thus a legitimate product of the Christian environment; it could not have developed anywhere else. Indeed, one must add that it cannot be separated from this Christian environment and transplanted into any other system, as is shown very clearly today in the renaissance of Islam; the attempt to graft on to Islamic societies what are termed western standards cut loose from their Christian foundations misunderstands the internal logic of Islam as well as the historical logic to which these western standards belong, and hence this attempt was condemned to fail in this form. The construction of society in Islam is theocratic, and therefore monist and not dualist; dualism, which is the precondition for freedom, presupposes for its part the logic of the Christian thing. In practice this means that it is only where the duality of Church and state, of the sacral and the political authority, remains maintained in some form or another that the fundamental pre-condition exists for freedom. Where the Church itself becomes the state freedom becomes lost. But also when the Church is done away with as a public and publicly relevant authority, then too freedom is extinguished, because there the state once again claims completely for itself the justification of morality; in the

---

[8] For the patterns and problems of the historical development important material is to be found in U. Duchrow, *Christenheit und Weltverantwortung*, Stuttgart 1970; documents in H. Rahner, *Kirche und Staat im Frühen Christentum*, Munich 1961.

profane post-Christian world it does not admittedly do this in the form of a sacral authority but as an ideological authority —that means that the state becomes the party, and since there can no longer be any other authority of the same rank it once again becomes total itself. The ideological state is totalitarian; it must become ideological if it is not balanced by a free but publicly recognized authority of conscience. When this kind of duality does not exist the totalitarian system is unavoidable.

With this the fundamental task of the Church's political stance, as I understand it, has been defined; its aim must be to maintain this balance of a dual system as the foundation of freedom. Hence the Church must make claims and demands on public law and cannot simply retreat into the private sphere. Hence it must also take care on the other hand that Church and state remain separated and that belonging to the Church clearly retains its voluntary character.

The Church's political stance and theology

This also defines in its fundamental outlines the relationship of the Church's political stance and theology. The Church's political stance must not be directed simply at the Church's power; according to what has been said this can become a direct contradiction of the Church's true nature and would consequently go directly against the moral content of the Church's political stance. It is guided rather by theological perception and not simply by the idea of increasing influence and power. It must incidentally, following our considerations so far, take care for the safeguarding of the dual structure with regard to theology; the Church's ministry should not become a central committee of the party in relation to theology, a body that scrutinizes the party's ideology of the strategy of gaining power. As we have established, the Church understands itself rather as the actual environment of reason in its search for meaning. In keeping with this it must on the one hand warn reason against an abstract independence that becomes fictitious, but on the other hand it must respect the proper responsibility of reason asking questions within the environment of faith. Just as in the field of the relationship of Church and state it is here also a question of safeguarding the duality as a fruitful functional relationship. Just as in that case two fundamental distortions of this relationship are possible. One is to be found when the Church's ministry cuts away the autonomy of theology and leaves it merely the task of looking for proofs of what the teaching authority has proposed; theology in that case is degraded to the function of a party ideology. But another distortion occurs when theology dissolves the Church or only accepts it as a supportive organization without spiritual content. Then it no longer reflects the spiritual basis of a living community; in this case its active agent is merely the private reason of the individual scholar, and that means, as has already been shown, that it becomes either positivist or ideological. But then it ceases to be theology. That means that by making itself completely autonomous it attains not some higher level but its destruction as theology. Whenever one of these two voices, that of the Church's ministry or that of theology, loses its autonomy then the other side also loses its essential content.

In concordats this particular relationship is translated into the legal form of the *nihil obstat*. As representative of the Church's ministry the bishop does not take a positive part in choosing the occupant of a professorial chair, but he has the negative function of a right of objection, whereby the freedom of theology on the one hand and its link to the Church on the other is in my opinion expressed with complete accuracy. If I have been right in what I said earlier about the significance of theology for the existence of the university and if for its part theology cannot exist without reference to the Church, then such an order of things ultimately serves the university as such and as a whole. Of its essence this relationship of tension will always be critical. But as long as it is critical it is also alive; this critical liveliness is ultimately what the relationship of the Church's political stance and theology is concerned with.

9

Conscience in its age*

In his *Conversations with Hitler* Hermann Rauschning, president of the senate of the Free City of Danzig (Gdańsk) in 1933 and 1934, reports the dictator saying the following to him: "I liberate man from the constraint of a spirit become an end in itself; from the filthy and degrading torments inflicted on himself by a chimera called conscience and morality, and from the claims of a freedom and personal autonomy that only very few can ever be up to."[1] For this man conscience was a chimera from which man must be liberated; the freedom he promised would be freedom from conscience. It fits in with this that Goering told the same author: "I have no conscience. My conscience is called Adolf Hitler."[2] The destruction of the conscience is the real precondition for totalitarian obedience and totalitarian domination. Where conscience prevails there is a barrier against the domination of human orders and human whim, something sacred that must remain inviolable and that in an ultimate sovereignty evades control not only by oneself but by every external agency. Only the absoluteness of conscience is the complete antithesis to tyranny; only the recognition of its inviolability protects human beings from each other and from themselves; only its rule guarantees freedom.

Here objections can be raised from very different quarters. A first and rather superficial objection would dispute the contemporary relevance of such a statement. While this might have its significance in the struggle against Hitler's

---

* A lecture given to the Reinhold-Schneider-Gesellschaft.

[1] Quoted from T. Schieder, *Hermann Rauschnings 'Gespräche mit Hitler' als Geschichtsquelle*, Opladen 1972, p. 19, note 25. Schieder offers a thorough analysis of the historical reliability of the details Rauschning provides.

[2] Ibid., p. 31; for the question of the authenticity of the remark p. 31 note, p. 35 and p. 19, note 25.

dictatorship, are we not oppressed today by quite different problems? Today must not social duty instead of individual freedom, structural instead of personal liberation be in the forefront of the question? Certainly the focuses of the struggle for man can change and very different tasks come to the fore according to the characteristics of the age; but in this it remains true that the contemporary relevance of a subject cannot offer a criterion for measuring its importance on the human scale and that at the same time what is truly human always remains of contemporary relevance in a profounder sense. Even if it is not in the foreground of a historical scene, it belongs to the decisive powers of the human drama, and to forget it must have a lethal effect, whichever act of the drama one is involved in. Dictatorship, the enslavement of man under the pretext of liberating him, is always a danger that lies in wait for man, and the anatomy of totalitarianism and of its opposite thus belongs among the permanent tasks of reflection on what is human in man.

Beyond this I am bold enough to assert that the temptation we are exposed to today, however different the labels and the colours may be, shows for those who look more deeply a frightening similarity, indeed unity, with what apparently lies behind us in the past. In this context another reference to Rauschning is needed. In 1938 this man who had seen the demon face to face, and who for a time had believed him before he understood the terrible thing that was afoot, diagnosed National Socialism, in a book that is still of significance, as the revolution of nihilism. "In its active and leading circles this movement is completely lacking in requirements and programme, ready for action, in its best core troops instinctive, in its guiding élite very deliberate, cold and cunning," he writes. "There was and is no aim that Naziism would not be ready at any time to surrender or to adopt for the same of the movement." For a revolution of this kind there are no firm aims of foreign policy. As there are none of economic or domestic policy. The total pulverization of what had hitherto been the components of order is rather the only thing that characterizes the

"doctrineless nihilistic revolution in Germany".[3] Of course
even a doctrineless nihilism contains in its own way a
doctrine, and to that extent these statements are open to
criticism. But its basic content comprises very exactly what
really happened then and thereby exposes a false
interpretation which visibly has a disastrous effect: the nature
of the revolution that took place then is only partly
comprehended by the concepts "Fascism" and
"nationalism" but to a more important extent concealed and
misjudged. In the mental climate of the time Hitler's
revolution made use of the nationalism of the bourgeoisie,
which at the same time he fanatically hated and wished to
destroy, and also of its order, which seemed to him like the
real antithesis of his will. To this extent it is a historical
perversion if one uses the slogan "law and order" to taunt
the right with being fascist and Hitlerian in order to cover
with this taunting precisely that revolution of nihilism which
stands in the true succession to the disaster of 1933. Anyone
who looks more closely and who does not let himself or
herself be blinded by phrases will discover sufficient
similarities between the disaster of that time and the forces
that today proclaim as salvation revolution in itself, the
denial of order in itself. The link between this nihilism and
the social idea, and with our shock at the misery suffered by
millions of men and women in this world, is no less deceitful
than the link between the nihilism of that time and the
national idea.

Only someone who is blind or who finds it convenient to be
blind can overlook the fact that the threat of totalitarianism
is a question of our age. Hence the men who at that time
stood out against totalitarian "liberation" in obedience to
conscience in freedom of conscience are today once again of
fresh importance to us. Is conscience really a power we can
count on? Must we not arm ourselves with more substantial
weapons? In his novel about Las Casas Reinhold Schneider
has given an impressive portrayal of the mystery of
conscience in the nameless girl of the Lucayos who slowly

[3] Ibid., p. 33; cf. H. Rauschning, *Die Revolution des Nihilismus*, Zürich, 1938,
new abridged edition edited by Golo Mann, Zürich 1964. Cf. also the remark of
Hitler's quoted by Schieder, p. 18, about the need "to bring up a violently active,
intrepid and brutal youth".

makes the conscienceless Spanish adventurer Bernardino understand the mystery of suffering and re-awakens the soul that has died in him by enabling him to become a sympathizer, one who shares in suffering.[4] This fragile young being who has no power left other than that of suffering embodies what conscience is among the adventurers for whom the only things that count are gold and the sword, hard economic or military power. She stands there, the fragile Lucaya, like a nobody, and that is how conscience stands in the world up to the present hour: a powerless girl abandoned to an early death over against the colossi of economic and political interests. Is it not sheer lunacy to count on this young girl conscience when one sees what really counts in the world and what alone counts in it? Is it not a vain and senseless reverie to look up to the witnesses of conscience in the face of the threats of today when all they can have to contribute is suffering? Should one then—and this is the objection that will be raised against us—conduct politics with poetry and use poetry to solve the problems of the age?

The nature and meaning of conscience

But a yet more difficult objection emerges. What is it really, conscience?[5] Does it even exist? Or is it not simply a superego which has been moved inwards and which transforms the taboos of one's education into divine commandments and thus makes them untransgressable? Do not finally those in power use the idea of conscience to shift

---

[4] I quote the novel *Las Casas vor Karl V. Szenen aus der Konquistadorenzeit* from the 1968 Ullstein paperback edition. The story of Lucaya is to be found on pp. 81–94. P. 81: " 'My soul?', he asked, 'I don't know if it was still my soul. Perhaps it had lived for many years in another being and had only been given back to me on its death.' " For an interpretation of the whole of Reinhold Schneider's work cf. Hans-Urs von Balthasar, *Reinhold Schneider. Sein Weg und sein Werk*, Cologne 1953.

[5] For the question of the nature of conscience, which cannot be analysed in detail here, see especially J. Stelzenberger, *Das Gewissen. Besinnliches zur Klarstellung eines Begriffs*, Paderborn 1961; *Das Gewissen. Studien aus dem C. G. Jung-Institut Zürich*, vol. VII, Zürich 1958, especially the contribution by H. Zbinden, "Das Gewissen in unserer Zeit", pp. 9–51. Cf. also J. Messner, "Moral in der säkularisierten Gesellschaft", in *Internationale katholische Zeitschrift* 2 (1972), pp. 137–158.

their power into the hearts of those they shamelessly exploit by drumming all their claims into their victims' heads until the latter come to hear them as the "voice of God" from inside themselves? Then would not Hitler have been right after all in saying that conscience is a form of slavery from which before all else man must be liberated? But, we must now ask, what direction remains for the person who has liberated himself or herself from his or her conscience? What has he or she really been liberated for? Is he or she no longer bound by respect for the humanity of the other person when the higher interest of the society of the future demands that he or she should disregard it? Can crime therefore—murder, for example—become a legitimate means of bringing the future about?

It is not easy to answer all these questions. Certainly under the idea of conscience there can sneak in the canonization of a superego which prevents people from becoming themselves; the absolute call on the person to become responsible is then overlaid by a structure of conventions that is wrongly presented as the voice of God when in truth it is only the voice of the past, fear of which is blocking the present. Conscience can also become an alibi for the fact that one has let oneself be carried away and cannot be told anything, when one's defiant inability to correct oneself is justified by loyalty to one's inner voice. Conscience then becomes the principle of subjective obstinacy established as an absolute, just as in the other case it becomes the principle of the ego losing its autonomy by surrendering to the ideas of other people or an alien ego. To this extent the concept of conscience needs continual refining, and laying claim or appealing to conscience stands in need of a cautious honesty that is aware that one abuses something that is great when one rashly calls it into play. Someone who talks all too easily of conscience arouses suspicions similar to those aroused by the person who drags the holy name of God into anything and everything and thus serves idols rather than God.

But the vulnerability of conscience, the possibility of its being abused, cannot destroy its greatness. Reinhold Schneider has said: "What is conscience if not the knowledge of responsibility for the whole of creation and before him who has made it?" To put it quite simply, conscience means to recognize man—oneself and others—as creation and to respect the creator in him or her. This defines the limits of any power and at the same time indicates its direction. To this extent insistence on the powerlessness of conscience remains the fundamental pre-condition and the inmost core of every true restraint on power. When this inmost core is not maintained then fundamentally one can no longer talk of restraint on power but rather only of a balance of interests in which man and human society are reduced to the pattern of selection: what is good is what succeeds and survives, and to exist means to succeed and survive. Man lives no longer as creation but as the product of selection, and the power he or she sets out to restrain becomes his or her only criterion. He or she is destroyed in his or her humanity. That is why we need people who make a point of standing out alongside the poor fragile girl conscience, who embody the power of powerlessness and protest against the exploitation of human beings in no other way than by sharing in the suffering of this tormented being, man, by placing themselves on the side of suffering. For that reason Reinhold Schneider's sonnets were a power, "poetry" was a power, which the dictators feared as a weapon and before which they had to tremble. For reasons of conscience Schneider suffered from the abuse of power. Suffering for the sake of conscience is virtually the formula of his existence. Only suffering, one could say: what's the use of that? But ultimately injustice can only be overcome by suffering, by the voluntary suffering of those who remain true to their conscience and thus in their suffering and in their whole existence bear real witness to the end of all power. Slowly we are beginning to realize once again what it means that the salvation of the world, the overcoming of power, is the suffering of a hanged man, that it is precisely where power comes to an end in suffering that the salvation of men and women begins.

Las Casas and the problem of conscience

I would like to take this fundamental idea that the core of the control and limitation of power that is needed in this world is the courage to follow one's conscience and to try to develop it by using as an example the Las Casas material dealt with by Schneider. But first of all let us look briefly at the historical background. With the discovery of America Christian Europe was faced anew with the question of the rights of man as man; in the course of the Crusades and the expanding contacts with the Arab world it had admittedly arisen with increasing urgency from the thirteenth century onwards, but it only gained its full intensity thanks to the powerlessness of the newly discovered peoples when faced with the weapons of the Spaniards. Up till now the problems of the limits of power had only emerged as to a considerable extent an internal Christian one in the counterplay of *sacerdotium* and *imperium.* With these two entities two powers, both of which were by their intention absolute, clashed in the Christian world: as Christian it seemed totally subordinate to the *sacerdotium,* as secular totally subordinate to the *imperium,* as Christian and secular, that is in the congruence of world and Church, it put to both the question of their self-limitation. But now there emerged what to a considerable extent was a new problem. Christian faith understood itself as absolute, as the revelation of the one truth that saves man; it knew of original sin by which human reason is clouded over, only to be made clear once again by faith and restored to itself. According to this it was only in faith that reason could find the foundations of real justice, and it could not really recognize structures of justice outside the faith as true justice; this in any case was what Augustine seemed to be saying in *The City of God,* in which he refused to allow heathen states that did not know God and thus neglected an essential part of true justice the characteristic of justice and defined them in practice as mere coalitions of interests which as such fulfilled a partial function of maintaining the peace and thereby gained their legitimacy as far as he was concerned.[6] But now the question arises: what

[6] For the problems connected with these developments cf. U. Duchrow, *Christenheit und Weltverantwortung,* Stuttgart 1970.

criteria and what possibilities for the limitation of power exist
when in the encounter between two peoples awareness of the
superiority of the only binding truth is linked with superiority
of weapons? Do the missions and colonialism together form
the hybrid that created the misery of the third world? Where
could the means of correction arise here? Reinhold
Schneider's answer in his novel is that the means of
correction can only emerge from faith itself — in the
conscience that suffers and struggles and that is in fact
aroused by this faith. The only thing that justifies this faith as
truth is that on the basis of its founding principle it may not
be a multiplication of power but the summons that awakens
the conscience that limits power and protects the powerless. It
is here that it has its absoluteness, in the protection of the
other as creature.

Let us look once again at the findings of history. Did this
conscience exist at all? Was it a real power or was there only
that false absoluteness of faith in which it functions as the
ideology of power instead of proclaiming the absoluteness of
the creator in the absolute dignity of the powerless? In 1552,
in his *Brevissima Relación de la destrucción des las Indias
Occidentales,* Las Casas wrote the most terrible
condemnation of the powerlessness of conscience and of the
brutality of power without conscience that we know. We are
aware today that this work depends to a considerable extent
on very dubious sources, that it is "extemely one-sided and
often exaggerated and distorted"; that it keeps silent about
the atrocities on the other side, such as that the Aztecs were in
the habit of sacrificing twenty thousand human hearts at a
single religious service.[7] Nevertheless there remains a
monstrous charge against the Spanish conquistadores who
unscrupulously enslaved and robbed people and by their
brutal exploitation of them as a work-force condemned
whole tribes to extinction. There remains the fact that
conscience really was there just like a weeping Lucaya who
could only watch the monstrous things going on, weeping and

---

[7] On the question of Las Casas cf. most recently G. Kahle, *Bartolomé de Las
Casas,* Cologne/Opladen 1968, especially here pp. 18 and 32; B. M. Bierbaum, *Las
Casas und seine Sendung,* Mainz 1968.

lost in unspeakable pain. Yet there was this conscience and Las Casas is by no means the only witness to it; the trail of conscience leads from the first laws of Queen Isabella, who declared all Indians free subjects of the crown and forbade their enslavement, by way of the laws of Burgos of 1512 to the "new laws" of 1542 which were decisively influenced by Las Casas and which tried to bring about the comprehensive liberation of and complete protection for the Indians; the prescription that they should with all possible care and love "be instructed in our holy Catholic faith" did not aim at dominating them but at putting them on the same level and withdrawing them from the arbitrary whims of those in power.[8]

The fact that here too success remained relatively modest does not alter the fact that conscience was fundamentally recognized as a limit of power and that thereby an attempt was made to allow faith to become effective as a political force without transforming it into yet another element of power among others. What must remain characteristic of it is precisely that its power lies in suffering, that it is the power of the crucified one; it is only in this way that it can be prevented from opening up for its part a new form of enslavement. It is only as the power of the cross that faith redeems; its mystery lies in its powerlessness, and in this world it must remain powerless in order to be itself. I think it is only from this perspective that the New Testament's stance on the problem of political power can be correctly understood. I shall only give a brief comment on this. Anyone who reads the sermon on the mount, anyone who takes up the New Testament with a view to the political pressures and difficulties of our time and Christians' responsibility for them, is for the most part disappointed. The whole thing seems to be an escape into an apolitical inwardness. There is hardly any talk of shaping the world, rather of a loyalty that seems to us like criminal passivity and an authoritarian mentality; whether one thinks of Romans 13:1–7 or 1 Peter 2:13–25, in every case the key word is ὑποτάσσειν, subordination, patience, obedience—in

---

[8] Kahle, pp. 10ff., 17–18; J. Höffner, *Christentum und Menschenwürde. Das Anliegen der spanischen Kolonialethik im Goldenen Zeitalter*, Trier 1947.

the case of 1 Peter with regard to the example of the suffering Christ. And even Jesus's only saying about the state, Mark 12:17 ("Render to Caesar the things that are Caesar's and to God the things that are God's"), remains fixed in a fundamental attitude of loyalty. In fact Jesus was no revolutionary, and anyone who asserts otherwise is falsifying history. It is also correct that as a result of its situation the New Testament did not feel itself called to develop a political ethics for Christians in a positive and detailed manner; here one can make no progress with mere biblical fundamentalism. The New Testament was written out of the minority situation of the slowly growing Christian Church and is thus ordered towards safeguarding what is specifically Christian in the midst of Christians's political impotence, not towards the ordering of a Christian power. Nevertheless it contains the decisive point which continually remains the basic principle. In his saying about rendering unto Caesar that which is Caesar's and unto God that which is God's Jesus separates the power of the emperor and the power of God. He removes the *ius sacrum* from the *ius publicum* and thereby breaks up the fundamental constitution of the ancient world and indeed of the pre-Christian world as a whole. By separating the *ius sacrum* from the emperor's *ius publicum* he created the space of freedom of conscience where every power ends, even that of the Roman God-emperor, who thereby becomes a purely human emperor and changes into the beast of the Apocalypse when he nevertheless wants to remain God and denies the inviolable space of the conscience. To this extent this saying sets limits to every earthly power, and proclaims the freedom of the person that transcends all political systems. For this limitation Jesus went to his death; he bore witness to the limitation of power in his suffering. Christianity begins not with a revolutionary but with a martyr.[9] The growth of freedom that mankind owes to the martyrs is infinitely greater than that which it could be given by revolutionaries.

---

[9] On Mark 12:17 and the way this saying was handled in the political catechesis of the early Church cf. once again U. Duchrow, op. cit., pp. 137 – 180. For the entire problem see the exact presentation by O. Cullmann, *Jesus und die Revolutionären seiner Zeit*, Tübingen 1970.

In his novel about Las Casas Reinhold Schneider's basic subject of the relationship between power and conscience is given a particularly impressive form. Alongside the Lucaya Las Casas himself and Charles V appear as living representations of what conscience is; all three together represent its function at different levels and they orchestrate the subject throughout its entire range. Without a doubt it is symbolized in its purest form by the girl Lucaya. In the humility of her suffering and in the simplicity of her faith conscience exists virtually in its pure untroubled nature. The people of the Lucayos to whom she belongs and whom she embodies are portrayed as follows by the knight Bernardino: "They were so defenceless and innocent as if Adam's sin had never fallen on them."[10] The islands where they lived meant for them the world of men and women. They believed that they were bordered by the world of spirits where the dead lived. When the Spaniards reached them all they could imagine was that these aliens came from beyond the world of men and women, from the land of the spirits. That was why they followed them full of innocent trust, because they expected to be brought to the souls of their ancestors by these strangers. On this Bernardino remarked: "And I must recall today how pure the conscience must have been of these people who were so very glad to look forward to being reunited with the dead, while we . . . perhaps had to be afraid of such a reunion, because then many hidden sins would become manifest and we would not dare to look those near to us in the eye."[11] People who live in family neighbourliness with the eternal, whose world stands open into the other world, whose standard of judgement is merely co-operation with what is to come and thus is conscience, encounter the brutal power that knows no conscience and has lost its soul. They think they are reaching heaven and land in hell. In my view this very scene shows how profoundly Reinhold Schneider had come to know and to suffer the way human existence and the world of experience is poised over the abyss long before he wrote *Winter in Wien*. Here reality is not

[10] Schneider, op. cit., p. 81.
[11] Ibid., p. 85.

smoothed over with edifying apologetics; here we do not have the world of Job's rationalizing friends who have a pious refrain for everything and an explanation for everything. Here what rings out is the cry of Job himself: people think they are going to heaven and are led into hell. Reality as it is strikes faith in the face and no *deus ex machina* arises to put things right. All that remains is the "muffled moaning and screaming" of the mass of humanity:[12] the silent weeping of the deceived woman and the face of the crucified. There remains the suffering of this woman who has suffered just as much over the conqueror as over her tortured brothers. For her he in his blindness is no less pitiful than they are in their torment, even if he himself does not notice how miserable his madness has made him, how much he stands in need of redemption in order to become himself once again. It seems to me that this mysterious figure of a woman expresses most of all in the entire novel what Schneider noticeably experienced as his own task and his own fate. It was not granted to him to become involved on the field of power. All that remained for him was to be the voice of conscience, to withstand the sin and guilt of the age in suffering, and through his suffering to authenticate the call of conscience.

Las Casas embodies a second possibility, how conscience can become mission. Alongside the suffering conscience he represents the prophetic conscience which shakes the power of the powerful, which raises the rights of those deprived of their rights, places himself calmly between the thrones and does not cease to disturb the rest of those whose power is at the expense of the rights of others.[13] Las Casas himself had been a soldier and *encomendero*; even after he was ordained to the priesthood he had been far more concerned about his income than about the Indians entrusted to him. Then something happened that is encountered more than once in

[12] Ibid., p. 92: "We were not afraid of the mass of humanity below decks, and just like my companions of previous voyages I was used to hearing the muffled moaning and screaming from beneath me: it affected me just as little as the lowing of cattle in their stalls. The idea that I was listening to the voice of my guilt did not enter my mind."

[13] Hans-Urs von Balthasar, op. cit., pp. 177–178, is insistent on this: "The saint not as the guiding spirit of a state but as the conscience of the king: that would be the realization of the transcendent ethics that does not have double standards."

the lives of saints: he suddenly recognized that a particular saying of scripture that affected his situation was intended quite literally and was meant to be taken literally by him. He reads Sirach 34:21 – 22 and knows that it concerns him: "The bread of the needy is the life of the poor; whoever deprives them of it is a man of blood. To take away a neighbour's living is to murder him; to deprive an employee of his wages is to shed blood."[14] From then on Las Casas becomes the guilty conscience of the powerful, hated, cursed, but no longer to be brought to silence. This is part of the real greatness of Christian faith: that it is able to give conscience its voice; that it relentlessly opposes the world that the faithful have established for themselves and founded with faith; that the prophetic "no" dwells in it; in general that it arouses prophets, people who are not the voice of an interest but the voice of conscience against other interests. Las Casas thus becomes at the same time a witness to the sovereignty of law: "Law does not need any human witness; it stands above man, not in man. But when people are not in agreement they can ask their conscience for counsel; and if they do so without hatred or zeal their conscience will help them."[15]

In the figure of the emperor Charles V we encounter a third possibility: the conscience of the man or woman on whom power is bestowed and who must try to exercise power responsibly. The scene where on a chilly evening the friar meets the tired emperor who has on his desk only a copy of the *Imitation of Christ* is extremely impressive. Its decisive key words·are "conscience" and "cross". In a prophetic reproach to his own age Schneider portrays a ruler who wishes not to conquer but to reconcile; a ruler who is ready to jettison the greatness that is characterized by the burden of sin and guilt and who recognizes true greatness in responsibility for men and women. He portrays a man of power who bears power as a burden and suffering and hence is able to lead power towards its true meaning.[16] This idea

---

[14] Cf. G. Kahle, op. cit., pp. 13ff.

[15] Schneider, op. cit., p. 153 (the speech of Las Casas to Bernardino).

[16] There are some fine remarks about the connection between power and the ability to suffer according to Luther which touch on what is said here to be found in Duchrow, op. cit., pp. 547 and 552.

reaches its full intensity with the bestowal of a Mexican bishopric on Las Casas; the prophet must take over power and thereby enters on his severest test: whether under the sway of power he remains loyal to the prophetic calling. Power as suffering and thereby as power that has been healed and made holy: in this vision the first and the third characters are intertwined. The absolute monarch lives under the restraint of power imposed by conscience, without which any restraint on power would be impotent.

Only power that comes out of suffering can be power for healing and salvation; power shows its greatness in the renunciation of power. A remarkable parallel to these ideas is to be found in André Malraux's description of his last conversations with de Gaulle. These dialogues circle continuously around de Gaulle's central subject of France and greatness, and they show how the idea of greatness had at the end changed for this remarkable ruler of our century. Asked what he would have said at the Invalides to commemorate the bicentenary of Napoleon's birth, de Gaulle answered: "He left France smaller than he had found her, agreed; but that is not the way a nation is conditioned. For France he had to exist . . ."[17] On this Malraux comments that de Gaulle did not think of France in terms of strength: "He thought Stalin's remark, 'France has fewer divisions in line than the Lubin government', idiotic." Still less did he think in terms of winning or losing territories. When he decided in favour of the independence of Algeria, "he had chosen the soul of France above everything else, and first of all against himself."[18] Malraux must have been certain of his interlocutor's agreement when he remarked to him that France only found its own soul when it found it for others: "the Crusades, and the Revolution much more than Napoleon."[19] The balance of these conversations overshadowed by a characteristic melancholy can be recognized quite clearly: the greatness the general could give his country consisted in the fact that he left it smaller, that he gave away

[17] André Malraux, *Fallen Oaks: Conversations with de Gaulle*, London 1972, p. 46.
[18] Ibid., pp. 46–47.
[19] Ibid., p. 62.

an empire that stretched round the world. This greatness did not come about in the vain attempt to become once again a great power on the old pattern, but in the renunciation he taught himself and his nation. At the end the general measured himself no longer against Napoleon the conqueror but against the banished emperor and his saying that greatness is sad. Apart from the ambiguity that naturally still remains lurking in this saying it must mean that power attains greatness when it lets itself be moved by conscience. That is Reinhold Schneider's legacy to this age; that is the opportunity and the task of Christian faith in the midst of the conflict of powers in which we stand today.

SECTION II

ASPECTS OF THE CONCEPT OF FREEDOM:
CHURCH — STATE — ESCHATON

10

Freedom and constraint in the Church

Freedom has become almost a magic word. The cry for freedom to be heard throughout the entire world comes out of a situation in which men and women may have sampled the taste of freedom but at the same time feel that this freedom is threatened and hedged in on all sides. It may seem strange that this description applies precisely to those societies of the West that with good reason are able to call themselves "free"; this already indicates something of the complex of problems connected with the concept of freedom and something of its unfathomability. It must in fact be admitted that to a considerable extent man has shed the ties of custom and tradition that in the class-organized society of former times often predetermined the possibility of shaping his or her existence. But while in this field people have attained a freedom of movement that hitherto was hardly imaginable, technological civilization, with its centralization of services and the anonymity of its organization, has created pressures that were formerly unknown, from fixing the angle of roofs to regulating tombstones, from traffic regulations to the general organization of education which embraces teacher and pupil in a network of legal prescriptions that arises from observing citizens' rights to freedom. It can thus be doubted whether the modern history of freedom has really brought about a considerable increase in freedom or whether what has happened is simply that the sphere of freedom and the sphere of constraint have shifted. In any case the plethora of prescriptions that reach into every aspect of everyday life has given rise to a curious feeling of being hemmed in, a surfeit of institutionally organized freedom and a cry for a better, a radical, an anarchistic freedom.

Yet another observation immediately imposes itself. Formerly an institution was to a considerable extent represented by individuals. Limitations on freedom could be traced back to the arbitrary whim of individuals. What was needed was to limit the power of these individuals by countervailing institutions and by sharing responsibility more widely. Once this happened the institutions appear as embodiments of grey anonymity, as a faceless and indeterminate power, as Kafka presented them in the black visions of his novels *The Trial* and *The Castle.* So it is not surprising that the institution has come generally to be perceived as the opposite of freedom and that people want to combat the organization of freedom in order finally to reach freedom itself.

1. *The concept "freedom" in recent intellectual history*

This first quite unsystematic attempt to cite a few observations in connection with the idea of freedom indicates the initial task demanded by any treatment of the subject of freedom and constraint in the Church. We have to clarify what is to be understood by freedom. What kind of freedom can man expect? In what way can he attain it? At the same time it should have become clear that this question cannot be dealt with in the abstract. It owes its actual shape to the new period of history opened up by the Enlightenment, a period aiming in a special way at being a history of freedom in which it first comes to light what freedom is. Only now, with their emancipation from the compulsions of nature and of superstition, do men and women begin to become themselves the agents of history. It is only now that they need no longer accept history as an unalterable fate but can guide their own destiny and thus shape history into a process of liberation. In fact in the history of the last two hundred years the concept of freedom has been thoroughly examined with regard to its various different objects. So one can and must try to study the question of what freedom is and what it cannot be in the panorama of this history.

a) The starting-point in the fundamental principle of the Enlightenment

The first step was the Enlightenment's motto *sapere aude,* dare to use your reason.[1] Man wished no longer to persist in the stage of being a child but to come of age. He or she no longer submitted simply to authority and tradition but used his or her reason himself or herself. Freedom emerges here as liberation from the power of tradition to lay down norms; it is no longer the will and insight of someone else that can oblige one but instead it is only one's own insight that shows one's will the way. Rationality is at the same time self-determination which seeks to redeem one from the alien determination imposed by authority. It seems important to me to discern that in no way was this a question of simply replacing obligation by a lack of any obligation or constraint. Rather it was a question of shaking off the alien obligation and replacing it by rational obligation, in other words by the constraint that follows insight. It seemed to be something taken for granted that rationality imposes obligations and that irrationality did not offer any alternative to it. To this extent one can say in the spirit of the Enlightenment that freedom is constraint, in other words the obligatory nature of truth when it is understood; it has nothing to do with a purely arbitrary whim.[2]

The difficulty begins when the social dimension of freedom has to be dealt with. The traditions from which reason offered emancipation had in fact also been the tried and tested methods for regulating the ways in which human beings shared their lives; on their maintenance depended the co-operation of individuals within the organism of the social body. They prescribed the roles in which being human was divided up and understood and in which it could meaningfully be lived. In contrast the fundamental idea of

---

[1] Cf. Immanuel Kant, "Beantwortung der Frage: Was ist Aufklärung?", in *Berlinische Monatschrift* 4 (1784), pp. 481 – 494: "Enlightenment is man's leaving the immaturity for which he is himself responsible. . .*Sapere aude* — have the courage to serve your *own* reason — is therefore the watchword of enlightenment."
[2] For a comprehensive survey of the development of the modern concept of freedom cf. R. Spaemann in J. Ritter (ed.), *Historisches Wörterbuch der Philosophie,* vol. II, pp. 1088 – 1098.

the Enlightenment was quite simple: that in place of inherited social rules insight must take over, that the rational society would be a society of rational beings. But at the same time it was of course obvious that in the meantime not everybody had yet reached the stage of insight. So the enlightened Monarch took over the task of implementing the rule of reason and in this knew himself to be an organ of freedom, even if to begin with he had to promote its ends with compulsion. Here a paradoxical situation arose. It was the Enlightenment that first did away with the old freedoms of the different classes, the manifold ways in which society was formerly shaped and organized with their pockets of freedom, and was aware of itself in this destruction of these freedoms that had evolved as the executor of the higher freedom that bestowed higher insight. The strange ambiguity of all the processes of freedom that would repeatedly be demonstrated in the course of future history becomes here for the first time unmistakably clear.

b) Freedom through institutions

In the development that followed two contrary evolutions of the fundamental idea of the Enlightenment can be observed. On the one hand there is the development leading to the democratic constitutional state.[3] It starts from the idea that all citizens should be free but that they are free if they participate in the exercise of power. Then the state is their state and power is exercised not over them but by them, since their will has some influence on the general will. The citizens are no longer simply ruled, but here too the transition has been made from determination by someone else to self-determination. But one's own will can only be effective through sharing in the general will; one's own freedom operates by sharing in the common freedom and is of course also limited by this. In actuality this system depends on the

---

[3] On this cf. the mass of material in the article on "Democracy" by C. Meier, R. Kornscheck, H. Maier and W. Conze in *Historisches Lexikon zur politisch-sozialen Sprache in Deutschland,* 1973, pp. 821 – 898; H. Maier, *Revolution und Kirche. Zur Frühgeschichte der christlichen Demokratie,* Munich 1973, and his *Kirche und Gesellschaft,* Munich 1972.

separation of powers, which is meant to effect the division, limitation and control of power. A major element in this is the system of representation, which includes the periodic transfer of power. An essential element is the inviolability of the law, the independence of the administration of justice from the organs of the exercise of power. The reliability and impartiality of the law should be the really distinctive mark of this form of state. To an even greater extent than sharing in power by affecting the formation of the will of the whole it is this that protects people from capricious despotism, gives them equal rights alongside the powerful, and thereby gives them freedom. Freedom is above all freedom from capricious despotism and the guarantee of justice without respect for persons. What it means is that it is not power but justice that affords protection. Its effect is that every human being through being human is recognized and in fact accepted as the agent of justice.

If one considers this type of organization of human affairs it is clear that here too freedom includes constraint, in this case constraint through the regulations that by their constraint protect and guarantee freedom. The participation in power of every citizen does not mean anyone can at any time do just what he or she wants. It is rather only to be maintained by the delegation of his or her political will to corresponding bodies, by the recognition of the division of power that is also the limitation of power, and by the recognition of the law that is established by the will of the majority. Freedom thus exists through a system of manifold constraints and obligations, and it is precisely these constraints and obligations which are themselves the system of freedom. It is clear that in the working of all this out in actual practice questions must arise, especially if one understands freedom as a process the dynamics of which always tends towards more freedom, towards "more democracy". A fundamental question for the democratic system is whether the will of the majority can and should do anything it likes. Can it declare anything it likes to be law that then is binding on everyone, or does reason stand above the majority so that something that is directed against reason cannot really become law? But who is to say what is reason?

Must one simply presuppose that the majority also incorporates more reason? Ultimately the democratic system can only function if certain fundamental values—let us call them human rights—are recognized as valid by everyone and are withdrawn from the competence of the majority. To put it another way, the democratic system of the limitation and division of power does not function on its own as a purely formal system. It cannot be applied in a complete absence of values, but presupposes an ethos which is jointly accepted and maintained, although its rational basis cannot be established absolutely conclusively. Democracy cannot function without values and thus cannot be neutral with regard to values. The formal element of its institutions is linked to the material element of an ethos that belongs to the Socratic and Christian tradition. Behind its formal obligations one comes across the more profound element of this moral obligation and constraint that the state must presuppose but cannot itself justify and thereby cannot itself guarantee. Here the question arises of an authority of ethical legitimation: the existence of the state points beyond itself and becomes a question concerning a different kind of society.

All this shows the fragility of the extremely subtle balance of freedoms that is attempted in an enlightened democracy. The institutions of freedom can in actual life easily be experienced as institutions of the lack of freedom, and they are of course always in danger of contradicting their own purpose and justification. The mechanisms of the transfer of power can become alienated. The party system seems imperative to allow the process of forming the general will to be focused, but its dangers cannot be overlooked. Elections are the decisive means for everyone being able to share power, but it is once again obvious that the methods of publicity and behind these the financial resources that direct this publicity can overlay self-determination by a variety of other forms of determination. The most fragile is the whole complex of the values that really sustain democracy. What must one protect for freedom to exist? Where must one leave things open because constraint would be unsuitable? Developments over recent decades have increasingly understood the right to be able to say and show anything and everything in the media as the real right of freedom and have alongside this denounced as mere taboos values of ethical tradition, particularly those in the field of marriage and the family. But in reality does this not mean that the right of a small group is given more and more privileges over against the right and dignity of the many? Is it not the creation of a monopoly which is exercised by a few, which necessarily goes on shifting in one direction, and which thereby constricts freedom of opinion because one particular position increasingly understands and establishes itself as the only correct one?

c) Freedom through the logic of history

This phenomenon of crisis in the organization of democratic freedom leads us to the second path taken by the modern development we have mentioned. What I have in mind is Hegel's conception which found the form in which it affected history through Marx and in Marxism. Hegel understood history as a whole as the history of freedom which takes its course dialectically by means also of the opposites of freedom. Following his line one has to say that anyone who places himself or herself on the side of the logic of history serves freedom. Action directed against this logic is action contrary to freedom because it is opposed to the process of freedom. Karl Marx brought into fully effective play the dogmatic concept of freedom that is indicated here. For him too what applied was that anyone who followed the gradient of history which with inner necessity was pressing on towards the classless society was acting in accordance with freedom. Agreeing to this necessity was acting for freedom.

But with Marx this takes on a decisively practical character which has been brought forcefully to our notice. This is because he prescribed for these ideas the political, pedagogical and psychological means needed for them to be dispensed. The bearer of future history is the proletariat, the bearer of the logic of history is therefore the party of the proletariat, the Communist party. So the history of freedom is identical with the history of the party; it is history biased in favour of the party. In practical terms this means that someone who acts in the sense of party logic, and only someone who does so, acts in keeping with freedom. If the logic of the party demands imprisonment and terror even this is obviously action in keeping with freedom because it forms part of the logic that will lead to freedom. In *The First Circle* Alexander Solzhenitsyn has presented these links vividly and shatteringly in the form of the veteran Communist Lev Rubin who maintains his faith in the party even in prison. Such faith forces him against his will to recognize in the organs of the party apparatus "the positive forces of history". From this there follows for him that anyone who undermines them is "standing in the way of progress and must be swept aside".[4]

An example from the western world is provided by Ernesto Cardenal, who in 1978 criticized his own book on Cuba dating from 1972. At that time he had already started from the conviction that anyone who wanted to be a true Christian today must also be a Marxist. At that time he already believed he had discovered the congruence of the kingdom of God with Castro's system. But nevertheless he still indulged in a little criticism of the realities he encountered on the island. In 1978 he remarked self-critically that it was only gradually that he became a party man; adherence to the party is the decisive viewpoint and only the person who is absolutely a party man or woman is liberated.

A quite definite understanding of human nature belongs to this biased interpretation of the idea of freedom. In the present age this understanding has a continually stronger influence on defining the image of true human education and thanks to this "education for freedom" is beginning to become a kind of general intellectual property far beyond party circles. While the decision to accept the discipline of obligation to the party is difficult, it is that much easier to assent to its understanding of human nature which to begin with appears to be the logical completion of the Enlightenment. To educate people to hold definite values seems like an enslavement of their nature; indeed, education in general is violation by the domination of authority and

---

[4] Alexander Solzhenitsyn, *The First Circle*, London 1968, paperback edition 1970, chapter 33, pp. 234–239 (the quotation is from p. 236). Cf. also chapters 8, pp. 48–54, 60, pp. 457–466, and 66, pp. 494–504. (References are to the paperback edition).

tradition. Only one single kind of education seems to be suitable and seems to be really an education for freedom: being brought up to rebel against all existing values and making men and women absolutely free so that they can then "creatively" construct themselves. A greater effect than the philosophy of Marx may well be given here by the ideas of Sartre, whose thinking to begin with seemed to be diametrically opposed to that of Marx but then in a curious way became linked with Marxism. For Sartre man is pure existence without essence. There is no certainty about what he or she is or how he or she should be. One must discover anew what it is to be human from the nothingness of an empty freedom. The idea of freedom is here pushed to its ultimate radical position, no longer merely emancipation from tradition and authority but emancipated from the idea of the creation of man, emancipation from his or her own nature and essence, a state of complete indeterminancy which is open to anything. But it is precisely this freedom that seems at the same time to be hell: to be free means to be damned.[5] So the radical idea of freedom turns into party loyalty which takes the place of the lost idea of human nature and is meant to give man footing and direction.

2. *The modern concept of freedom in the life of the Church*

a) Towards a definition of freedom

One could now ask what all this has really got to do with the subject of freedom and constraint in the Church. I think there are two ways in which it is important for this subject: first, because only in this admittedly very rough sketch of recent intellectual history could the various different aspects and dimensions of the concept of freedom come to light; secondly, because all these different views have their effect on the complex of problems to be found within the Church and leave their mark on conflicts in the contemporary Church. It would be premature to want to try to formulate a definition

[5] On this cf. J. Pieper, "Kreatürlichkeit und menschliche Natur. Ammerkungen zum philosophischen Ansatz von Jean-Paul Sartre", in his Über die Schwierigkeit heute zu glauben, Munich 1974, pp. 304–321.

of freedom at this point in our considerations. But this much has nevertheless become clear, that constraint and obligation belong to the essential form of human freedom. No kind of realization for freedom can escape this. Further, it is certain that indeterminacy does not form the essential nature of human freedom, even if to begin with the longing for freedom seems spontaneously to venture in this direction. Freedom must be defined positively if it is to be positive. According to our reflections so far it should be sought perhaps in the direction of self-possession, as a possibility of self-realization, of realizing one's own essential nature and one's potentialities. It means that man is the bearer of rights; the more completely he or she possesses his or her rights and can observe them the more does freedom become a reality. But rights can only exist where law exists, and hence freedom is bound to the existence of law; law is not the opposite pole to freedom but its pre-condition and its content, if also perhaps not on its own its entire content. Anyone who desires freedom must therefore strive not for lawlessness but for good law, law on a human scale as the law of freedom.

b) How the modern understanding of freedom is applied in the Church

With this we come to the reflection of these modern problems in the life of the Church. If in its first stage the Enlightenment means emancipation from tradition and authority, then this automatically calls the Church into question, since authority and tradition are constitutive for it. One belongs to the Church through faith, not through the unaided perception of one's reason. To this extent the Church seems on the basis of its fundamental principle to be in conflict with the world that has resulted from the Enlightenment and with its idea of freedom. The fundamental problem that we touch on here of the limits of the modern age and the appropriateness of faith for human nature does not need to be dealt with in this context; I wanted merely to indicate it as the comprehensive background to our considerations. It is obvious that the two ways we have mentioned in which the modern history of freedom finds realization share to a substantial extent in marking the life of the Church today. The Church has a constitution which follows from its own nature and hence is not identical with any political constitution. On the other hand it is completely logical that in the actual patterns of Church life a certain correspondence should always occur with the political forms and structures that exist at any particular time. Hence it would be surprising if the model of the democratic constitutional state were not applied to the Church too and the attempt undertaken to "democratize" the Church. This is today the actual way in which the conflict over freedom and constraint in the Church takes place. Because of its nature and its origin it should be understandable that one cannot simply turn the Church into a copy of a democratic constitutional state. But the question arises all the more forcefully: which democratic institutions can one transfer to the Church? Which are unsuitable for the embodiment of Church life and why are they so?

If one looks more closely, one can discern in the current dispute about freedom in the Church the overlapping of different tendencies which often interpenetrate and combine with each other in a curious way. While in the political field suspicion of the democratic constitutional state and doubts about its method of guaranteeing freedom often occur, in the sphere of the Church one often encounters what is virtually a naïve and credulous erection into a dogma of the formal structural elements of democracy. Not a few are of the opinion that the Church will remain an authoritarian society untouched by the Enlightenment so long as it has not reconstructed all its institutions according to this pattern. The idea of freedom is placed totally in the sphere of formal functioning; freedom coincides with the functionalism that consists of activating the democratic structures known from their political use in the state. The fact that the formal nature of structures is only a secondary vehicle of freedom as against the primary one of guaranteeing people's essential rights and quality of life is lost from sight; the question why the Church exists as a particular and different society and whether the same formal means fit in with the specific nature of its values is not asked, and hence the individual quality of the Church by which its structures are to be determined is left out of view. Beyond this it belongs to the nature of the democratic constitution that the modalities of the specifically political sphere do not present any universal pattern and should not be transferred to many other fields, such as to that of the administration of justice or that of education.

When the formal aspect of democratic freedom is elevated into a universal model what is at work is in reality a concept of freedom that presses beyond the constitutional state and its balance of freedoms. This becomes especially clear when the slogan "more democracy" occurs; here the constitutional form of the constraints and obligations that lead to freedom are seen merely as a stage on the way to man's complete liberation which is meant finally to lead to freedom from all institutions. The concept of grassroots democracy that belongs here seems especially suitable for transfer to the Church because it appears to correspond in its inner nature with the idea of the congregation and thus of the structure of the people of God that is based on the local Church. Satiety with the anonymity of large-scale societies makes its contribution to let the idea of the self-determining small community seem the solution and on this basis to present the Church as an oasis of freedom. The universal Church and its sacramental structure now become the official Church which belongs, along with all other political, social and economic large-scale structures, to the powers that block freedom, while Christianity in the sense of Jesus is only to be found in the congregation and the congregation forms the clear and understandable framework in which everyone can share in everything and so freedom is realized.

I think that in this return to the idea of the congregation there are very positive elements which are able to make Christian faith alive and relevant. Social responsibility for one another and for the cause of the faith, experience of actual co-operation on the basis of belief, an oasis of brotherliness and sisterliness and of closeness in the midst of a world of anonymous pressures: these are values in which Christian freedom can express itself and dedicate itself directly to people. But when the element of the congregation is isolated and separated off from the broad stream of the sacramental community of the entire Church the freedom of the congregation evaporates into play-acting and becomes void. The autonomous congregation degenerates into mere social work or a leisure association; the activity of worship becomes irrational or merely a celebration of community spirit. It becomes clear once again that acting on one's own is not as such yet freedom.

Because the unreality of this kind of retreat can never remain hidden for long, there is in the Church too the shift to the radical idea of freedom as it was finally created by Marx out of the history of the prophetic promises. I have already mentioned Ernesto Cardenal. Along with many others he stands for the idea that one must strive for a more complete freedom than that of democracy and the Church as they are constituted, the freedom of the kingdom of God, and that this can and must be brought about by political means. That the Christian does not regard democracy as the last word in human freedom is of course correct; the Christian is in fact looking for the higher and more comprehensive freedom of the children of God in the kingdom of God. But he or she regards it as an error to want to place this freedom in the political sphere and thus to force the being man into the space of politics; that curtails the breadth of his or her being, deprives him or her of its loftiness, and therefore destroys his or her freedom. This means levelling the Church down to the sphere of the political, suffocating what is specific in its nature, and thus not only filling in an area of freedom but also its source.[6]

3. Remarks about the biblical concept of freedom

With all this we have admittedly still not yet said positively how freedom and constraint in the Church are related to each other, even if in the mirror of contemporary disputes the answers can gradually begin to be discerned. To explain the matter suitably one would need really to give a comprehensive presentation of the origin and meaning of

---

[6] On the questions raised here cf. the fundamental work of G. Fersard, *Chrétiens marxistes et théologie de la libération,* Paris/Namur 1978.

being a Christian. One would have to show how Christian faith can put forward the claim to be man's and woman's true liberation; one would have to make clear how this liberation is presented in actuality in the Church's sacramental form. One would have to investigate the meaning of authority and tradition in the Church and their relationship to Christian freedom. All this would far exceed the space of a single lecture which anyway can only really show the size of the task indicated by our subject. Meanwhile in order to avoid our conclusions with regard to the actual shape of freedom and constraint in the Church of today appearing too positivist, I would like at least briefly to analyse the significance of two fundamental biblical concepts which belong to the range of questions we are considering: ἐλευθερία (freedom) and the active concept related to it of παρρησία (outspokenness, frankness).

The researches of Nestle and E. Coreth[7] have shown that ἐλευθερία belongs to a different dimension of thought from our word freedom. With this term the Greeks did not in any way express the idea of freedom of choice and therefore did not express the possibility of people doing or allowing what they wanted. ἐλευθερία is rather, as the opposite of the concept of life as a slave, the expression for the status of full membership with full rights of the relevant social structure, the family or the state.[8] It means the full possession of rights, belonging fully, being at home, and so, on the basis of sharing fully in the community's life and responsibility, full rights to share in determining how the community's fate is to be shaped. The

---

[7] D. Nestle, *Eleutheria. Studien zum Wesen der Freiheit bei den Griechen und im Neuen Testament. Teil 1: Die Griechen,* Tübingen 1967; E. Coreth, "Zur Problemgeschichte menschlicher Freiheit", in *Zeitschrift für katholische Theologie* 94 (1972), pp. 258–289, especially pp. 264–265 and 268–269. A brief compendium of the material is to be found in D. Nestle s.v. *Freiheit* in *Reallexikon für Antike und Christentum* vol. VIII, pp. 269–306; cf. also H. Schlier s.v. ἐλεύθερος in Kittel, *Theological Dictionary of the New Testament,* 1964ff., vol. II, pp. 487–502.

[8] Cf. H. Schlier in Kittel, vol. II, p. 485: "In these lines [Pindar, Pyth. I:61–62] the νόμοι are mentioned along with ἐλευθερία. This gives us the limit within which freedom is to be sought and given, namely, the νόμοι and therefore the essence of the νόμος of the polity". On this Nestle (*Reallexikon,* vol. VIII, p. 278) says about the Roman Republic's concept of freedom: "*Libertas* has its essence in the trinity of *ius, leges, res publica* . . .".

free man is the person who is at home, who really belongs to the house. Freedom has to do with being at home. Freedom is identical with the possession of rights, with a quality of life; a consequence of this is sharing in determining the community's fate, a right which arises from membership, and the other forms of activity as against the slave, who is allotted "servile work" while the free man cultivate leisure and suitable arts.

This fundamental idea was taken over into biblical usage, even if the context in which the word appears necessarily led to the idea gaining a quite new depth. If we consider the allegory of Sarah and Hagar in Galatians 4:21 – 31 this will become quite clear.[9] The free person is the one born of Abraham's freeborn wife Sarah and hence has the right of inheritance in the house. The serf is the one born of the slave-woman and therefore does not really belong to the house but only lives there for a time. The difference between free and unfree does not consist at first in differences in what they are allowed to do: "I mean that the heir, as long as he is a child, is no better than a slave, though he is the owner of all the estate" (Gal 4:1). The difference consists first of all in status, in the kind of membership included in the right of inheritance, the right of settlement and the right of possession. To be free means to be the heir, that is, to be oneself the possessor; freedom is identical to the status of son (Gal 4:5). It is only from this original difference of being that there then follows at a given time a different manner of acting.[10] Because this is so it is for Paul no contradiction but a logical consequence when he says: "For you were called to freedom, brethren; only do not use your freedom as an opportunity for the flesh, but through love be servants of one another" (Gal 5:13). An equally logical component of this concept of freedom is when he says: "Fulfil the law of Christ" (Gal 6:2).

The freedom of Christians accordingly means first of all that they, the baptized, have been made full citizens of the

---

[9] For interpretation cf. H. Schlier, *Der Brief an die Galater*, Göttingen [12]1962; F. Mussner, *Der Galaterbrief,* Freiburg 1974, pp. 316 – 334.

[10] On this cf. H. Schlier's interpretation of Gal. 3:27, op. cit., p. 173: "[The putting on of Christ] is therefore not the expression of an ethical relationship but of a relationship of being with Christ. It marks the start of [jointly] sharing in Christ's being . . .".

people of God from a status of being aliens and now belong
to "the Israel of God" (Gal 6:16) with unrestricted civil
rights. This being taken up into the citizenship of Israel
coincides with the moment when the educational laws of
childhood no longer apply (Gal 4:4) and from when as a
result the only thing that applies for everyone is the law of the
Son, the law of Christ (Gal 6:2). This follows from their
status of being, in other words from the fact that by the Spirit
of Christ they are given a share of Jesus Christ's own status
of being. They are πνευματικοί, spiritual (Gal 6:1). To live
the law of Christ therefore means to live according to the
status of being of a spiritual person, in the manner of the
Spirit. That includes the crucifixion of the flesh "with its
passions and desires" (Gal 5:24); what this excludes is
indicated by Paul in a catalogue of fifteen vices which, he
notes, could be extended (Gal 5:19 – 21). Undemanding,
therefore, is something this freedom is not, nor is it a matter
of doing what you want. Its obligations extend to the point
that it can be called "crucifixion".

So we can try to make at least an attempt at a biblical
definition of freedom. Considered biblically freedom is
something other than indeterminacy. It is participation, and
indeed not just participation in some particular social
structure but participation in being itself. It means to be the
possessor and not the subject of being. Only on this basis can
indeed God be defined as freedom in person, because he is
the totality of the possession of being. We can pick up an
earlier formulation and say that freedom is identical with
exaltation of being, which admittedly only makes sense if
exaltation of being is really exaltation: the gift of life and
being given in love. Hence the education of freedom is being
led into this exaltation of being, being brought up for being,
being brought up for love, and thus being led into θείωσις, into
being made divine. "Being like God" is doubtless also the
goal of radical emancipatory theories of education which
have in their sights an unrestricted god-like freedom that has
everything at its disposal. The goal is right: it is only the
image of God that is wrong. Being like God means being like
the trinitarian God. The education of love as education of
θείωσις is necessarily the education of the cross, which does

not for nothing form the key concept of the Pauline doctrine of freedom.[11]

With this we come to the application of freedom is παρρησία. This term, which is best translated as "frankness", also comes from the political vocabulary of the Greeks. There it means "the right of the free man to say everything publicly"; παρρησία counted as "the sign of true democracy".[12] The free man has the right to say everything publicly, or, to put it the other way round, the right to say everything belongs to the person who is free. It presupposes the quality of being free, namely the responsibility of the free person. Because the free person is himself or herself the heir and possessor, he or she speaks in the responsibility of someone who does not wish to destroy what is his or her own. The right of freedom flows from the responsibility of freedom. Anyone who wishes to speak freely will therefore first ask himself or herself if he or she is a free man or woman. In 1 Thessalonians 2:1 − 12 Paul based himself on the term παρρησία to develop something like a Christian rhetoric, a rhetoric of freedom as against the rhetoric of slavery, and thus provided a Christian and Church interpretation of a characteristic

---

[11] In this context I would like to indicate a moving modern testimony of the experience of freedom. Sheila Cassidy reports of her experience in a Chilean gaol: 'We [she, a Christian, and the women imprisoned with her, many of them unbelievers and Marxists] discussed the whole concept of freedom and came to the conclusion that the freedom of the spirit that we had was a very real thing and that, although we were surrounded by ten foot walls, barbed wire and men with machine guns, really we were quite free. It was the people who held us prisoner who were enslaved'." This experience she found summed up in Lovelace's lines "To Althea from Prison":

> If I have freedom in my love
> And in my soul am free,
> Angels alone, that soar above,
> Enjoy such liberty.

Sheila Cassidy, "Beten in Bedrängnis" ("Prayer in Prison"), in *Geist und Leben* 53 (1980), pp. 81 − 91: the quotation is from p. 89. Something very similar is to be found in Solzhenitsyn, *The First Circle* (note 4 above), e.g. p. 107 (chapter 17): "You can tell old You-know-who—up there—that you only have power over people so long as you don't take *everything* away from them. But when you've robbed a man of *everything* he's no longer in your power—he's free again."

[12] H. Schlier, *Der Apostel und seine Gemeinde. Auslegung des ersten Briefes an die Thessalonicher*, Freiburg 1972, p. 29, and his article on παρρησία in Kittel, *Theological Dictionary of the New Testament*, vol. V, pp. 871 − 886.

fundamental right of freedom. For him the rhetoric of the ancient world has three distinguishing marks: flattery, covetousness, and thirst for glory. It curries favour with its audience and wants to win it over to the speaker's side. It is publicity for itself. As such its aim is above all to bring in material gains; it is intent on having more. In the Bible covetousness appears as "one of the chief vices". It is therefore connected with the concept of impurity, and as something that makes one impure in the sight of God and blocks communication with him it is identified with idolatry (Col 3:5, Eph 5:5).[13] The destruction of being which occurs in the domination of having becomes even clearer in the third distinguishing mark, thirst for glory. It could better be translated as the domination of appearance: people act no longer for reality but for opinion, and they no longer judge their actions according to what they are really worth but according to how they are valued in public opinion. Appearance oppresses being and becomes the standard that is valid in all circumstances. People live for appearances and thus their life becomes a sham. The Bible rightly sees in this the embodiment of slavery, of unfreedom. To turn things round, this is why freedom has to do with truth. "Truth and freedom, freedom and truth belong together. The courage born of freedom does not exist where truth does not exist, and truth only appears thanks to the courage born of freedom."[14] The apostle's frankness consists of saying the truth to a world dominated by appearance, even though this involves him in conflict (1 Thess 2:2). The free courage of the free man presupposes above all freedom of itself, "a state of being set free from oneself, because he has committed himself to the word of the gospel".[15] It thus becomes clear that freedom begins first in man's being in order then to take actual shape in the rights of freedom for action. But, when the basis of being is lacking, these rights in the sphere of action become empty and threaten to turn into their opposite.

---

[13] Schlier, *Der Apostel,* p. 112 note 44.
[14] Ibid., p. 31.
[15] Ibid., p. 30.

From this there follows once again that freedom can only be maintained by an education for freedom, that is by a meaningful network of obligations and constraints aimed at freedom.

4. Final conclusions on the subject of freedom and constraint in the Church

In practice what follows from all this for the question of freedom and constraint in the Church? Even this question far exceeds the scope of a paper setting out a basic principle. I can only try to conclude with one observation. In contrast to modern constitutions the 1917 code of canon law does not mention the basic right of freedom. It talks of the freedom of the Church (canons 2333, 2334, 2336 § 1) but not of the freedom of the Christian. But throughout it includes material which can be directed towards the idea of the Christian's rights of freedom. It would probably be sensible to present this kind of interconnection in the revision of the Church's code so as to make it clear from a technical legal point of view too how the legally protected right of freedom is perceived in the way the Church is organized. In this what should of course not be concealed is that the Christian concept of freedom extends into the theology of man being made in the image of God and with this into the theology of the cross, that is into an area beyond the scope of the Church legislator. The following data could probably provide the right direction for efforts to codify in legal terms the Christian concept of freedom:

1) Freedom is first of all a status of being and is characterized positively by the existence of rights. Rights presuppose law and gain reality only in the context of the binding nature of law. Law in its turn presupposes ethos and indeed, in the ultimate assent of being, faith.

2) In the Church it is a matter of freedom in the profoundest sense of that word, of opening up the possibility of sharing in the divine being. The fundamental organization of the Church's freedom must therefore be to ensure that faith and sacrament, in which this sharing in the divine being

is mediated, are accessible without diminution or adulteration. The fundamental right of the Christian is the right to the whole faith. The fundamental obligation that flows from this is the obligation of everyone, but especially the Church's ministers, to the totality of the unadulterated faith. This is the only way to safeguard the fundamental right of the faithful to receive the faith, to celebrate the liturgy of faith, and not to be handed over to the mercy of ministers' private opinions.

3) All remaining freedoms in the Church are directed towards and subordinate to this fundamental freedom. Ultimately it will be a question of making active and fervent participation in the Church's life of faith possible in the most comprehensive and varied way possible without letting this turn into compulsion towards congregational activity. The diversity of spiritual plans and forms of life must be given ample space the common criterion of the faith. Corresponding to this diversity of forms of life the breadth of ways of thinking must have room in their relationship to the faith of the Church. In this context the correct balance between the freedom of theology and the unity of the faith belongs always to the particularly important tasks of shaping the life of the Church, because on the one hand what is at stake is the fundamental right of the faithful to the unadulterated faith, on the other hand the legal right of making the faith present in the thought and speech of a particular epoch.

4) With regard to the world the Church must defend the right to freedom of belief in a double sense: in the first place as the right freely to be able to choose one's faith in the sense of what the Second Vatican Council said about religious freedom; in the second place positively as the right to believe and to live as a believing Christian. Belonging to this context is also the classical subject of *libertas ecclesiae,* the right of the Church to be the Church and to live in its own way. The right to believe is the real core of human freedom; when this right is lacking the loss of all further rights of freedom follows after with inner logic. At the same time this right is the real gift of freedom that Christian faith has brought into the world. It was the first to break the identification of state

and religion and thus to remove from the state its claim to totality; by differentiating faith from the sphere of the state it gave man the right to keep secluded and reserved his or her own being with God and in the face of God, a seclusion in which God calls him or her with a name that no-one else knows (Rev 2:17). Freedom of conscience is the core of all freedom.

5) In conscience the synthesis of our subject finally becomes visible. It is the locus of man's most inward obligation and for that very reason also the locus of his or her true freedom.

11

A Christian orientation
in a pluralistic democracy?

THE INDISPENSABILITY OF CHRISTIANITY IN THE MODERN AGE

On my walks through the older parts of Rome it is not just the traces of past ages that the tourist keeps a look-out for that strike me. On the walls of the houses I read the changing slogans that — sometimes only in chalk, sometimes written up in thick paint — mirror the spirit of the moment. Events from the world of football play a great part in this and often reach almost a poetic level, such as when Roma's winning the Italian championship evokes the cry: "Roma, you are like first love", or with somewhat gentler affection the words are written up: "Thanks, Roma". More lasting and emphatic are the political slogans. In the narrow Borgo that is nearest to me I read: "True socialism is anarchy". A few steps further on there follows the defiant cry: "Baader lives". Round the corner I find the statement: "Anarchy is freedom in equality". It seems relatively harmless when round the corner once again in the street running parallel those in power are described as thieves because of the continual rise in prices. A few steps further on angry seriousness returns with the words: "Neither Christ nor Marx — the people's struggle". The comment on the wall opposite runs: "Fighting is good even if one dies in it".

Of course one should not overestimate such graffiti. Their emotion often gets lost in words and not infrequently is mere imitation. Nevertheless they are not simply of no importance. If after the war the message of democracy was taken up among us almost with a religious emotion and with the moral zeal of the pupil who is eager to learn and who has finally found the correct solution for his or her sums, so today the disquiet is all the greater the more exaggeratedly one took the democratic promises then. To see the extent of the problem one must place alongside the doubt that is affecting belief in the democratic constitution in our own country the hypocrisy which has meanwhile gained prescriptive rights in the judgement of public opinion on world politics. Criticism of undemocratic goings on in third world countries falls silent when a Communist régime has established itself there. "For the victory of the Vietnamese people" was written up in large red letters on the walls of the refectory of our Regensburg university when the Vietnamese war reached its end. Today one will look for inscriptions of this kind in vain. Vietnam, like other countries that have turned Marxist, is no longer a subject of public discussion. One does not criticize third world countries with Marxist governments. Apparently in the opinion of western politics they have reached a state of order that should not be disturbed. All the more zealously one recommends for states that are hovering between dictatorship and democracy Marxist ideas of liberation that one would not like to see applied in one's own country at all. The fact that young people should have such schizophrenic ideas should not really surprise anyone. It is only logical that the emotional appeal of such ideas of freedom should seize hold of them with their desire for the absolute and that they should want to apply them in their own field.

But what has all this got to do with our subject? What becomes clear from this is that pluralist democracy is never simply made secure. It does not of itself remain the kind of thing that unites its citizens in a fundamental assent to the state they have in common. Even when it is run fairly well, as despite everything has been the case with us over the past thirty years, it does not automatically bring forth the conviction that with all its shortcomings it is the best form of state. It is not only economic crises that can bring it to collapse; the pounding of intellectual waves can also wash away the ground on which it stands. With an eye to such facts Ernst-Wolfgang Böckenförde has put forward the thesis that today's liberal and secularized state is no longer a *societas perfecta:* "For its foundation and maintenance it depends on other powers and forces", or to put it another way it lives on the basis of presuppositions "which it cannot guarantee itself''.[1] This means there is an element which is indispensable for pluralist democracy but which is not native to the political field. My subject suggests forcefully the idea of Christianity, and I do not deny that I shall come to it. But we should not fall back on this answer quite so easily, especially as the negative effects of the Christian approach even in the most recent political history should not be overlooked. Hence it seems to me that it is necessary first of all to investigate the most important element of the contemporary threat to democracy. This should be followed by a self-criticism of the Christian approach in its political effects. Then finally it makes sense to ask about its positive significance and indeed its indispensability.

1. The three roots of the present threat to democracy

What threatens democracy today? I see three main tendencies that lead or could lead to the denial of democracy. First there is the inability to come to terms with the imperfection of human affairs. The longing for the absolute in history is the enemy of the good in it. Manès Sperber talks of a passion that arises from revulsion at what exists.[2] This revulsion for what exists is on the increase today, and with it goes delight in anarchy from the conviction that the ideal world must exist somewhere. Today no-one may want to subscribe to the Enlightenment's belief in progress any more, but a kind of profane Messianism has penetrated deep into the general consciousness. Ernesto Cardenal's saying ''I believe in history'' expresses many people's secret creed. Somehow Hegel's idea that history itself will finally bring about the great synthesis has anchored itself in the general consciousness. The idea that the whole of history up till now has been a history of the lack of freedom and that now at last and soon the just society can and must be built is spread in a multitude of slogans among atheists as among Christians

[1] E.-W. Böchenförder, *Staat — Gesellschaft — Kirche*, Freiburg 1982 (part 15 of Böchle, Kaufmann et al., *Christlicher Glaube in moderner Gesellschaft*), p. 67.
[2] Quoted by K. Löw, *Warum fasziniert der Kommunismus?*, Cologne 1981, p. 87; for the whole question see R. Spaemann, *Zur Kritik der politschen Utopie*, Stuttgart 1977.

today and extends as far as bishops' statements and texts used in worship. The mystique of the *Reich* that marked the period between the wars and then came to such a macabre end is recurring in a peculiar way. Once again people prefer to talk simply of "the kingdom" instead of "the kingdom of God"—*das Reich* instead of *das Reich Gottes*—as if of something for which we are working, which we are building, which thanks to our efforts has become tangibly close. The "kingdom" or the "new society" has become a kind of moralism that replaces political and economic argument. That we are working for a new world that will finally and definitely be a better world has long since become something taken for granted. What is philosophically and politically dubious about this kind of imminent eschatology becomes clear, in my view, from considering three main aspects of this idea.

a) In society that has been liberated the good no longer depends on the ethical efforts of the people responsible for this society but is simply and irrevocably provided in advance through its structures. The myth of the liberated society depends on this idea, since ethical behaviour is always at risk, is never perfect, and must always be striven for anew. Hence a state that depends on ethical behaviour, that is on freedom, is never finished, never quite just, never secure. It is as imperfect as man himself. For this very reason the "liberated society" must be independent of ethical behaviour. Its freedom and its justice must as it were be provided by its structures; indeed, ethical behaviour has in general been shifted from people on to structures. Present structures are sinful, future structures will be just, one must simply think them out and build them like one builds pieces of equipment, and then they will be there. For this reason sin becomes social sin, structural sin, and should be labelled as such. For this reason in turn salvation depends on the analysis of structures and the political and economic activity that follows from this. It is not the ethical principles and behaviour that carry the structures but the structures that carry the ethical principles and behaviour, because the latter are fragile whereas the structures count as what is firm and secure. In this reversal that lies at the root of the myth of a better world I see the real essence and nature of materialism, which does not simply consist of the denial of an area of reality but at its most profound a programme concerned with the understanding of human nature, a programme which is necessarily connected with a particular theory about how individual areas of reality are related to each other. The assertion that mind is merely the product of material developments and not the origin of matter corresponds to the theory that ethical principles and behaviour are produced by the economy and that it is not the economy that is ultimately characterized by fundamental human decisions. But if one sees the presuppositions and the consequences of what seems such a wonderful relief for man from the burdens of his changeability, then one recognizes that this relief — "liberation" — depends on the abdication of ethical principles and behaviour, that is on the abdication of responsibility and freedom, on the abdication of conscience. Hence this kind of "kingdom" is a picture puzzle with which we are duped by the Antichrist; this kind of liberated society presupposes perfect tyranny. I think we must today make it categorically clear to ourselves once again that neither reason nor faith ever promises us that there will ever be a perfect world. It does not exist. Continually expecting it, making play with its possibility or nearness, is the most serious threat and danger to our politics and to our society, because from this there necessarily comes enthusiasm bent on anarchy. For the continued existence of pluralist democracy, in other words for the continued existence of a humanly possible measure of justice, it is urgently necessary to learn once again the courage to accept imperfection and the recognition that human affairs are always at risk. Only those political programmes are moral that arouse this courage. This means that the kind of apparently moral appeal that will only be satisfied with perfection is immoral. An examination of conscience will in this context be necessary with regard to moral sermons delivered by those belonging to or close to the Church in cases when their exaggerated demands and hopes have encouraged the flight from morality to utopia.

b) There are yet other roots to the attempt to make morality, with its shortcomings and risks, superfluous through the as it were mechanical safeguard of a correctly established society. These are to be found in the one-sidedness of the modern concept of reason as it was first clearly formulated by Francis Bacon and then came ever more strongly to predominate in the nineteenth century. According to this it is only quantitative reason, the reason of calculation and experiment, that is seen as reason at all, and all the rest as the non-rational that must slowly be overcome and at the same time brought over into the field of "exact" knowledge. The goal with Bacon as with Comte — to name only two programmatic thinkers — is that finally what will be reached will be a physics of human affairs.[3] In this context Martin Kriele talks of a reversal of the relationship between science and practical reason, of a reduction of ethics and politics to physics.[4] Using a terminology that has not yet been perfected and to that extent is in need of criticism, Romano Guardini repeatedly drew attention to the same set of data and characterized it as the fateful problem of European politics. He talks of the logical and the non-logical not being recognized in their unity of opposition. Rather to be more correct one had to say that the logical was reduced to a certain kind of rationality and that everything else was pushed aside into the category of the non-logical. "For this reason", he went on, "there is not yet any Europe in the proper sense but instead the various intellectual and human spheres, despite all efforts at organization, remain disunited in hostile juxtaposition."[5]

We can therefore establish that the rejection of morality in favour of technology does not depend primarily on flight from the troublesomeness of morality at all but on the suspicion that it is not rational. It cannot be deduced rationally in the same way as how a piece of equipment functions. But if this has now been elevated to become the

---

[3] On Bacon see M. Kriele, *Befreiung und politische Aufklärung,* Freiburg 1980, pp. 78–82; on Comte Henri de Lubac, *The Drama of Atheist Humanism,* London 1949, pp. 77–159. For the whole complex of problems raised here see J. H. Tenbruck, *Die unbewältigten Sozialwissenschaften oder Die Abschaffung des Menschen,* Graz 1984, especially pp. 230–243.

[4] Op. cit., p. 76.

[5] Romano Guardini, *Religiöse Gestalten in Dostojewskijs Werk,* Munich 1977, p. 427.

criterion of what is rational then the various classical expressions of morality can only be allocated to the sphere of the irrational. Meanwhile attempts to present morality too with precision are on the increase. In one form or another it is then brought back to the pattern of calculation, to calculating the relationship of favourable and unfavourable outcomes of an action. But this means to reject morality as such. The categories of what is good in itself and what is evil in itself exist no longer, and all there is is a balancing of advantages and disadvantages. Things are not changed by the fact that we are assured that in general matters will stay at the level of proverbial wisdom.

With this, law has the ground cut from under its feet. I cannot resist quoting here an example from the way justice is administered in Munich, an example that for me makes frighteningly clear the process whereby our law has been losing its legal substance. At least twice recently charges that religion was being slandered were rejected on ground that public peace was not endangered by the events which gave rise to the charges. I am not concerned here with the question whether these charges were in fact justified, merely with the reason why they were rejected. In fact this reason contains an incitement to the law of the jungle. If those who were offended had made a move to unleash public disorder in their cause, then the case would have had to be considered seriously: that is what this amounts to. But this means that one is no longer in the business of protecting those things that enjoy legal protection but is merely concerned to prevent opposing interests clashing with each other. This is admittedly logical if morality as such is no longer recognized as something deserving the protection of the law because it is seen as a matter of subjective preference which can only become a matter for legal action if the public peace is in danger. A consequence of this invalidation of the moral reason is that law can no longer be referred to a fundamental image of justice but becomes merely the mirror of whatever happen to be the predominant views and opinions. But in this case everyone is aware that justice cannot be built in this kind of way. Escape to an ideologically established pattern of justice which apparently derives from a scientifically assured interpretation of history thus becomes almost inevitable. Hence the question of re-establishing a fundamental moral consensus in our society is at the same time a question of the survival of our society and of the state.

c) Allow me to add yet a third point of view which embraces and extends the two preceding ones. Once again I shall try to illustrate it by means of an example. Recently I was able to ask a friend from East Germany what in his opinion lay behind the recent increase in pressure to leave that country and move to the West, whether essentially the driving motive was the resistance of conscience against ideology. He said there were a variety of reasons for this state of affairs and they certainly included the one I had mentioned. But what was by no means an infrequent reason was something quite different. They had persistently hammered into people's minds the idea that this life was the only one there was and that people could not expect any happiness other than whatever joy they had at present. In these circumstances life under socialism appeared so grey, so boring and so empty that one had to escape and seek real life somewhere else. This kind of escape, this kind of "dropping out" exists to a great extent in the West too, since ultimately all its diversions and sensations are vain when they claim to be the whole. The loss of transcendence evokes the flight into utopia. I am convinced that the destruction of transcendence is the actual amputation of human beings from which all other sicknesses flow. Robbed of their real greatness they can only find escape in illusory hopes. Beyond this it also indicates and confirms that constriction of reason which is no longer able to perceive what are actually human affairs as rational. Marx taught us that we must depart from transcendence so that mankind, saved from false consolations, may at last build the perfect world. Today we know that man needs transcendence so that he may shape his world that will always be imperfect in such a way that people can live in it in a manner in keeping with human dignity.

If we bring together our reflections so far, Böchenförde's thesis that the modern state is a *societas imperfecta* has at any rate been emphatically corroborated; imperfect not only in the sense that its institutes always remain as imperfect as its denizens, but also in the other sense that it needs forces from outside itself in order to be able to survive itself. Where are these forces that are indispensable for it?

2. *Self-criticism of the political effects of Christianity*

A first glance at Christianity as a possible source of this kind of force or power is not exactly encouraging. To this extent Christian self-criticism is indispensable for the person who wants to see in it what can come to the rescue. There is a thesis that Marxism can only gain a foothold where Christianity has previously superseded traditional religions. Christianity apparently has to precede in order that Marxist logic can find a *point d'appui.* I do not know how far this thesis can be sustained empirically. But all the same it does not come out of thin air. Alongside the classic left-wing criticism of the Christian idea of the state the criticism of the new right has meanwhile appeared, and one will have to do battle with both. In addition this criticism has a long history. Augustine's *The City of God* is an answer to the assertion of conservative Roman criticism that Christianity had a destructive effect on the state. Even then there was nothing new in that; the Roman empire's persecution of Christians rested on the argument that Christianity was fundamentally the same as anarchism. I would like to outline the critical questions that are to be directed at Christianity as a political force in the light both of its history and of its present state on the basis of three points of view.

a) Christianity's Messianic dynamism is directed at the absolute goal of the "kingdom". It thereby includes the temptation to leap-frog the limited and imperfect sphere of the nature of the earthly state and to ignore or fight the state. The epistles of the New Testament are continually marked by the struggle with this kind of misunderstanding of Christian hope. The temptation of anarchy has certainly existed in all ages independent of Christianity in particular. But anarchy as the object of an apparently rational political philosophy and programme in fact only became possible from the triple root of Jewish Messianism, Christian millennarianism, and the modern idea of progress nourished by technology.[6]

b) A second element through which Christianity can have a disruptive effect on the ethical principles and behaviour that form the state is its rejection of justice from works and the criterion thereby set up of holiness from grace alone. This can lead to a relativization of ethics and an inability to compromise that destroy the humility of what is imperfect on the basic of which, as we saw, human life in common depends. This is the question at issue in the dispute over the political significance of the sermon on the mount. The same complex of problems is clearly to be found in Augustine's work on the two cities and their membership. The *civitas Dei* cannot become an empirical state, as Augustine clearly saw in contrast to his later interpreters; in this sense it remains non-empirical. For its part the state can always be only a *civitas terrena*. Although attempts can be spotted in Augustine to make this a morally neutral concept, its relationship to the state of the devil remains very close; at all events a genuinely positive foundation for the earthly state is not considered more closely.[7] Similar questions, even if arising from different circumstances, must be directed at Luther's doctrine of the two kingdoms.[8] In contrast Catholic theology has since the later Middle Ages, with the acceptance of Aristotle and his idea of natural law, found its way to a positive concept of the profane non-Messianic state. But it then frequently loaded the idea of natural law with so much Christian ballast that the necessary readiness to compromise got lost and the state could not be accepted within the limits essential to it of its profane nature. Too much was fought for and as a result the way to what was possible and necessary was blocked.

c) Connected with this is a third thing. Christian faith exploded the ancient world's idea of tolerance because it would not let itself be included in the pantheon that formed

[6] Cf. H. Kuhn, *Der Staat,* Munich 1967, pp. 80 – 81, 98 – 99, and elsewhere.

[7] I have tried to present a comprehensive account of my interpretation of Augustine's *City of God* in my short book *Die Einheit der Nationen,* Salzburg 1971, pp. 69 – 106.

[8] From the immense wealth of literature on this subject I would like to mention just one work that I have found particularly illuminating, U. Duchrow, *Christenheit und Weltverantwortung. Traditionsgeschichtliche und systematische Struktur der Zweireichenlehre,* Stuttgart 1970, pp. 437 – 573.

the sphere of religious live-and-let-live in its exchange and its mutual recognition of gods. From a legal point of view it could not therefore be admitted to enjoy religious tolerance because it refused to let itself be allotted to the sphere of private law where arbitrary forms of religion had their place. This allocation to private law was not possible for the faith of Christians because public law was the law of the gods. In the face of this Christian monotheism could not withdraw into private law; that would have destroyed it as monotheism in its claim to truth. It must publicly claim legal validity at least negatively; it must demand the right to reject the religious character of the currently valid public law. In this sense, however small the number of its adherents may have been at first, Christianity from the start laid a claim to public legal status and placed itself on a legal level comparable to that of the state. For this reason the figure of the martyr is to be found in the innermost structure of Christianity.[9] In this is to be found its greatness as the adversary of any and every totalitarianism on the part of the state. But in this too can be found the danger of theocratic exaggeration. Connected with this is the fact that Christianity's claim to truth can rise to the point of political intolerance and has done so more than once.

To this extent the law of what is imperfect and threatened applies just as much to Christianity as a reality lived by men and women. Its positive political effect is not guaranteed automatically. This is precisely not something it has been promised, and Churchmen must at all times remember this in their political activities. But this does not alter the fact that the state remains a *societas imperfecta* and that it now calls for the other component that is able to supplement it and to open up for it the moral forces that it cannot create out of its own resources. Where will it find these moral forces? If one enumerates the possibilities that exist in the world and looks out for other possible solutions there are only two alternatives on offer outside Christianity: the attempt to return to pre-Christian ideas, such as a purified

---

[9] One of the lasting achievements of E. Peterson is to have brought out these connections with great vividness: cf. especially his *Theologische Traktate*, Munich 1951.

Aristotelianism; or taking up non-European cultures on the one hand and Islam on the other. But the reconstruction of the pre-Christian world remains an abstraction that is incapable of realization. Philosophies of life produced from a test-tube, an exercise that is now frequently undertaken, are artificial products which ultimately are incapable of realization. Jaspers had the idea that in his existential philosophy he had found a universal model which could take the place of a Christianity condemned to particularity.[10] Today there are no longer all that many who are even aware of his philosophy. However interesting such experiments in the realm of ideas may be, one does not get very far with undertakings of this kind which lack the vital spark of organic historical reality. Islam has again come to the fore as an alternative to forms of the state based on Christianity, and we must certainly study it much more attentively than we have done so far. But it is quite obviously exactly the opposite model to pluralist democracy and cannot therefore become its foundational force. The fact remains that this democracy is a product of the fusion of the Greek and the Christian heritage and can therefore only survive in this basic context.[11] If we do not grasp this once again and learn in keeping with this to live democracy on the basis of Christianity and Christianity on the basis of the free democratic state we shall certainly gamble democracy away.

---

[10] Cf. H. Saner, *Karl Jaspers in Selbstzeugnissen und Bilddokumenten,* Hamburg 1970, pp. 103 – 110, as well as the as yet unpublished Regensburg dissertation by J. Zöhrer, *Der Glaube an die Freiheit und der historische Jesus. Eine Untersuchung der Philosophie Karl Jaspers' unter christologischem Aspekt* (1982), chapter 5.

[11] To be more precise it should be added here that democracy in our contemporary understanding of the concept does not have automatically to spring from this root and has not automatically done so but in fact was first formed under the particular conditions of the American Congregationalist pattern, in other words apart from the classic European traditions of the Church-state relations that have developed here. To the extent the assertion that the Enlightenment led to democracy has only very limited application, as Hannah Arendt showed in her book *On Revolution* (London 1962). Still less was the European Reformation with its ideas of a state Church able to open the way to it. But all this should not cloud our awareness of the existence of fundamental democratic elements in pre-revolutionary Christian society. For a concise historical survey readers are referred to the study by G. Bien and H. Maier in J. Ritter (ed.), *Historisches Wörterbuch der Philosophie,* vol. II, Basle/Stuttgart 1972, pp. 50 – 55, with detailed bibliography. An important work on the subject is H. Maier, *Katholizismus und Demokratie,* Freiburg 1983.

3. *The indispensability of Christianity in the modern world*

The question thus remains: how can we correctly take up the self-criticism of Christianity that has just been sketched out? How can Christianity become a positive force for the political world without becoming turned into a political instrument and without on the other hand grabbing the political world for itself? Following the pattern I have followed in expounding the criticism of Christianity's political role I would like in this final section similarly to sketch the answer to these questions under three heads.

a) In contrast to its deformations Christianity has not established Messianism in the political sphere. Quite the contrary; from the start it insisted on leaving the political world in the sphere of rationality and ethical principles. It taught and made possible the acceptance of what is imperfect. To put it another way, the New Testament is aware of political ethics but not of political theology. It is precisely in this distinction that there runs the dividing line which Jesus himself and then very emphatically the apostles in their letters drew between Christianity and fanaticism. However fragmentary and occasional the various utterances of the New Testament on political matters may be in detail, they are totally united and clear in this basic decision: whether one thinks of the account of Jesus's temptations with their political implications, of the story of the tribute money that is Caesar's, of the political admonitions in the letters of Peter and Paul, or even of the book of Revelation that in many ways is so very different, there is always a rejection of the enthusiasm that seeks to elevate the kingdom of God into a political programme.[12] What always applies is that politics is not the sphere of theology but of ethics, which admittedly can only be given a rational basis in theology. Precisely in this way the New Testament remains loyal to its rejection of justice through works, since political theology in liberate human beings and human affairs from the outside,

---

[12] Worth noting in this context is Ernst Käsemann's interpretation of Romans 13:1 – 7 in Ernst Käsemann, *Commentary on Romans,* London 1980, pp. 350 – 359.

on the basis of what is quantitative and feasible, must of its nature come to nothing. On principle it means the subordination of the spiritual to the quantitative, the subordination of freedom to constraint. Liberation from morality can of its nature be merely liberation into tyranny. In keeping with all this it is no solution either to force morality into the sphere of the subjective and thus formally to do away with it as a publicly effective force. Just as little is it a solution to transform morality into calculation, because thereby it is once again done away with as morality.[13] There is no way out of the conclusion that we must return once again to a greater scope for reason, that we must learn to appreciate moral reason once again as reason. For the nature of the state this means that society is never finished but must always be built up again anew on the basis of conscience and can only be made secure on this basis. This means moreover that the fundamental action for the development and survival of a just society is moral education in which human beings learn how to use their freedom. The Greeks were absolutely right when they made education the key concept of their doctrine of salvation and saw in education the counter-force to barbarism. When morality is declared to be superfluous corruption becomes taken for granted, and corruption corrodes states just as much as individuals.

But ethics does not provide its own rational foundation. Even the ethics of the Enlightenment which still holds our states together lives on the after-effects of Christianity, which provided it with the foundations of its rationality and its internal cohesion. When the Christian foundations are removed completely nothing holds together any more. We see this today in the gradual dissolution of marriage as the basic form of co-operation between the sexes, a dissolution which is followed by the de-grading of sexuality to a kind of easily obtainable source of pleasure. The conflict of the generations with each other, the conflict of the sexes with each other, the splitting apart of mind and matter follows as a necessary

---

[13] For the problems that arise here I refer readers to J. Finnis, *Fundamentals of Ethics,* Georgetown University Press 1983.

consequence. We see the same process of dissolution in attitudes to life. If a kind of agreement is reached that babies presumed to be handicapped should be aborted to spare them and others the burden of their existence, what contempt for all the handicapped this is. What they are being told is that they only exist because science has not yet progressed sufficiently far. One could continue along these lines. What is essential is that reason shut in on itself does not remain reasonable or rational, just as the state that aims at being perfect becomes tyrannical. Reason needs revelation in order to be able to be effective as reason. The connection between the state and its Christian foundations is imperative precisely if it is to remain the state and be pluralist.

c) Here we touch on the neuralgic point in the relationship between Christianity and pluralist democracy. Nobody among us disputes the right of Christianity, just like that of the widest variety of social groups, to cultivate its moral concepts and develop its forms of life, that is, to work and be effective as one social force among others. But this retreat into the private sphere, this categorization in the pantheon of all possible value systems contradicts faith's claim to truth which is as such a claim to public validity. In this context Robert Spaemann speaks of the Christian Churches' fatal tendency to understand themselves as part of the ensemble of "social forces", a tendency which automatically involves a recantation of their claim to truth and thus eliminates precisely what the Church is all about and what makes it "valuable" for the state. As against this Spaemann holds that the Church should not withdraw into representing a "religious need" but must understand itself "as the place of an absolute public validity surpassing the state under the legitimizing claim of God", while he is aware that this understanding of itself can find no adequate representation in the sphere of state law.[14] We are faced with a dilemma. If the Church gives this claim up it no longer achieves for the state what the latter needs of it. But when the state accepts this

[14] See R. Spaemann's introduction to P. Koslowski, *Gesellschaft und Staat. Ein unvermeidlicher Dualismus,* Stuttgart 1982, p. xvii, and also Koslowski himself especially pp. 301–302.

claim it ceases to be pluralist and both state and Church are lost.

Particularly in the Church of the West there has been a fight throughout all the centuries over the balance between these two extreme possibilities. On this balance depends the freedom of the Church and the freedom of the state. According to the historical situation the danger is greater of transgressing in the direction of one pole or the other. In the present cultural situation as a whole the theocratic danger is small; it appears most prominently when the misalliance between Christianity and Marxism evokes the pretence of a kingdom of God to be created politically. But in general it is clear in the contemporary world that the faith's claim to public validity should not impair the state's pluralism and religious tolerance. But a complete neutrality with regard to values on the part of the state cannot be deduced from this. The state must recognize that a basic framework of values with a Christian foundation is the precondition for its existence. It must in this sense as it were simply recognize its historical place, the ground from which it cannot completely free itself without collapsing. It must learn that there is a continued existence of truth which is not subject to consensus but which precedes it and makes it possible.[15]

Let me conclude by presenting an example in which the whole drama of the matter becomes clear. The battle over crosses in the schools which is being fought in Poland today and which was fought by our parents in Germany in the period of the Third Reich is completely symptomatic. For parents in Poland, as at that time for ours, the cross in the schools is the sign of a last bit of freedom which they do not want to allow the totalitarian state to take. It is the guarantee of a humanity in the eradication of which they see a claim to dispose freely of human beings, a process which is no longer subject to the criterion of the cross and thus is no longer subject to any criterion at all. They are fighting for the public validity of Christianity and they are thus fighting for the fundamental persistence of humanity and of human criteria

[15] Cf. K. Forster, *Glaube und Kirche im Dailog mit der Welt von heute*, vol. II, Würzburg 1982, especially pp. 344–350.

which the state too needs. When we no longer have the power to understand and to maintain such symbols in their indispensability Christianity makes itself dispensable. But this does not mean that the state thereby becomes more pluralist and freer; instead it loses its foundation. The state needs public symbols of what sustains it. Feast days and holy days as public demarcations of time belong to this category too.

Hence Christianity must insist on these kinds of public symbols of its humanity. But it can admittedly only insist on them if it is sustained by the force of public conviction. That is what is demanded of us. If we are not convinced and cannot convince others we have no right to demand public recognition. We are then dispensable, and we must admit it. But with our own lack of conviction we take away from society what objectively speaking is indispensable for it: the spiritual foundations of its humanity and its freedom. The only power which enables Christianity to appear publicly in the best light is ultimately the power of its inner truth. This power, however, is as indispensable today as it ever has been, because human beings cannot survive without truth. That is the sure hope of Christianity. That is the enormous demand it makes on every single one of us.

12

Europe:
A heritage with obligations
for Christians

In the varied history of the idea and the reality of Europe it is characteristic that the thought of Europe always arose emphatically when danger threatened "the nations to be united under this collective concept".[1] This did not happen for the first time in our own age when in view of the destruction that had been caused in the European world after both world wars the question of the West and of the restoration of a united Europe became pressing. Heinz Gollwitzer has shown that the shift of the word Europe from educated to popular speech that took place as early as the start of the modern period was not just a consequence of the extensive effect of humanist ideas with their roots in the ancient world but is also to be seen as a reaction to the threat from the Turks.[2] Europe experiences what it is itself most clearly when it is explicitly confronted with its exact opposite. The quickest way of approaching the nature of something is by first establishing what it is not. The problem of contemporary debates about Europe and also of the political conflict about Europe consists to a considerable extent in the fact that it remains unclear what is now really meant or intended by Europe. Is it more than a somewhat nebulous romantic dream? Is it more than a community of the political and economic interests of powers that formerly dominated the world and have now been pushed to the margin? What is

---

[1] H. Gollwitzer s.v. "Europa" and "Abendland" in J. Ritter (ed.), *Historisches Wörterbuch der Philosophie,* vol. II, Basle/Stuttgart 1972, p. 826.
[2] Ibid.

really meant by Europe must probably lie between nebulous idealism and a merely pragmatic community of interests. Only if it is more than either of these can it in the long term represent a goal that is at one and the same time real and ideal for political action characterized by morality. Mere realism without moral idealism to give it shape yields nothing; but mere idealism without any actual political content remains ineffective and vain. Thus a first thesis to form the basis of this paper could be that only if the concept "Europe represents a synthesis of political realism and moral idealism can it become a force that will leave its mark on the future.

So we must look for a concept of Europe that fulfills these demands. As to method, on the basis of the history of the idea and the reality of Europe the way has presented itself of first enquiring into the counter-images of what Europe is not. In a second section I would then like to try to formulate the positive components of the concept of Europe. The third section's aim is to define quite briefly the tasks faced by those who want Europe.

I: COUNTER-IMAGES TO EUROPE

If we begin by ascertaining the counter-images to what on the basis of history and of the ethical approach maintained in it must be called Europe, I see three of these in particular which express a distinct historical difference with respect to the historical dynamism of the European thing. As the first there is throughout the world today a strong psychological and political trend that would like to move back behind the European element in history. It wants as it were to purify history from the impact of this European element, which is seen as alienation from what is one's own, or simply as the original sin of history, as the reason for the life-endangering crisis in which mankind stands today. As the second there is a trend which wants as it were to escape from European history into the future and to continue its own direction of movement in such a way that the link it contains with what is given in advance is dissolved. As the third there is a trend which combines both directions of movement with each other and thereby aims at the strongest blend of realism and ideal impetus; in this way it becomes the strongest counter-proposal to Europe.

In what follows I would like to try briefly to outline these three trends which I believe can mark the boundaries of the concept "Europe".

1. Back behind Europe

From the end of the ancient world until far into the early modern period Islam turned out to be Europe's real opponent. The contrast between Europe and Asia, between Erebos (evening) and Orient, which is to be found as early as the sixth century BC in Hecataeus of Miletus and was not intended purely geographically,[3] continues to have a different effect in this confrontation. Already in its emergence Islam is to a certain extent a reversion to a monotheism which does not accept the Christian transition to God made man and which likewise shuts itself off from Greek rationality and its civilization which became a component part of Christian monotheism via the idea of God becoming man. It can of course be objected to this that in the course of history there were continually approaches in Islam to the intellectual world of Greece; but they never lasted. What this is saying above all is that the separation of faith and law, of religion and tribal law was not completed in Islam and cannot be completed without affecting its very core. To put it another way, faith presents itself in the form of a more or less archaic system of forms of life governed by civil and penal law. It may not be defined nationally, but it is defined in a legal system which fixes it ethnically and culturally and at the same time sets limits to rationality at the point where the Christian synthesis sees the existence of the sphere of reason.[4]

---

[3] H. Treidler s.v. "Europe" in *Der kleine Pauly, Lexikon der Antike*, vol. II, p. 448.
[4] Cf. for example the presentation by Ringgren-Ström, *Die Religionen der Völker*, Stuttgart 1959, pp. 98 – 142.

From the eighteenth century on Islam noticeably lost political and moral influence of its own and from the nineteenth century on came more and more within the domination of European legal systems, which therefore regarded themselves as potentially universal because as the law of the Enlightenment they had freed themselves from the Christian foundation and now came forward as purely the law of reason. But wherever Islam is or becomes alive as faith it is precisely for this reason that these legal systems must be felt to be Godless and opposed to the faith. In view of the unity of the ethnic and religious elements they seem like an attack that is both ethnic and religious, as alienation not only from what is one's own but from what is real; both together trigger the violence of the counter-reaction we can observe today.

There are certainly many reasons why this tendency should emerge more strongly today, but they cannot be dealt with in detail here. Above all there is on the one hand the fact that the Arab world has grown stronger politically and economically, on the other the crisis in which the European law of reason has found itself after having totally renounced its religious foundations and threatening to turn in fact into a domination of anarchy. At a time when Europe is calling into question or eliminating its own spiritual foundations, is dividing itself from its own history and declaring this to be a cesspool, the answer of a non-European culture can only be radical reaction and a move back behind the encounter with Christian values.

Incidentally, I regard this reaction on the part of the Islamic world to be only the most visible and politically the most effective part of a movement that is active in many variants and that is powerfully at work at the core of the European consciousness itself. The work of Lévi-Strauss, to name only one example, expresses for its part within the European mind the longing once again to leave the Christian domestication behind itself precisely as domestication, as a form of slavery in contrast to which the *monde sauvage* appears as the better world.[5] Admittedly on another level, but

[5] A critical discussion of this is provided by a work by my pupil B. Adoukonou, *Jalons pour une théologie Africaine,* Paris.

in many respects related to it structurally, is the cruellest and most frightening form of going back behind Christianity: what Germany experienced during the first half of the present century and demonstrated in front of the rest of mankind. According to its fundamental tendency National Socialism was a rejection of Christianity as alienation from the beauties of Germanic savagery, and the longing to return behind this Jewish-Christian "alienation" into this kind of savagery, which was celebrated as the genuine civilization.[6]

2. Escape into the future

A second antithesis to what appears historically and morally as Europe has, in complete contrast to what has been described above, developed from the nature of the European spirit itself and must probably today be characterized as the dominant element in the political thinking of what is called the Western world. For Europe what is characteristic is the separation of faith and law, a separation that has its roots and justification in Christianity; this involves the rationality of law and its relative autonomy vis-à-vis the religious sphere but also the duality of state and Church. Politics may be subject to ethical norms that have their roots and justification in religion, but is not understood theocratically.

This independence on the part of reason has in the modern period led even more rapidly to its total emancipation and to the absolute autonomy of reason. With this reason takes on the form of the positive reason in the sense of Auguste Comte, something whose only criterion is what can be verified experimentally. The radical effect of this is that the entire sphere of values, the entire sphere of what is "above us", drops out of the sphere of reason, and the only binding criterion of reason and thus of man politically as well as individually becomes what is "below him", that is the experimentally available mechanical forces of nature. God may not be rejected as such, but he belongs to the sphere of what is purely private, what is subjective. In an extremely

[6] On this cf. for example R. Baumgartner, *Weltanschauungskampf im Dritten Reich*, Mainz 1977.

problematical essay full of thought-provoking questions Friedrich Wilhelm Bracht tried to present 1789 as the real turning-point when God ceased to be the public supreme good, with first of all the nation taking his place, then in 1848 the proletariat or world revolution. Of the modern consumer society one must say: "Their god is the belly" (Phil 3:19).[7] But in a society in which God is no longer the common and public supreme good but is relegated to the private sphere God's status is changed even for the individual. I would describe as post-European a society in which the movement sketched out above has reached its full measure. In it what constituted Europe as a spiritual reality has been abandoned. In this sense the present societies of the West seem to me already to a considerable extent to be post-European societies which admittedly live on the continuing effect of the European heritage and to that extent are still European. The plurality of values that is legitimate and European is visibly intensified towards a pluralism from which are more and more excluded the establishment of any moral basis of law and the establishment of any public basis of the sacred, of respect for God as something that is also a social value. To ask about this already seems to a considerable extent like an offence against tolerance and against a society that has its roots and justification in reason alone. But my conviction is that a society in which this radically is the case cannot in the long term remain a society based on law. It will open itself up to tyranny once it is sufficiently exhausted by anarchy. In a clear-sighted analysis of the problem of law which he undertakes in the course of his exposition of the trial of Jesus Rudolf Bultmann coined a phrase that is well worth considering: "An unchristian state is possible on principle, but not an atheistic state."[8] Today western societies are on the point of undergoing this experience. The Islamic reaction to Europe, as already indicated, is extremely closely connected with this.

---

[7] F. W. Bracht, "Die Abkehr von Gott in der Politik", in *Zeitbühne* 8 (1979), pp. 4 – 14, 41 – 48. I regard neither Bracht's political nor his ecclesiastical ideas as acceptable, but the question of the position of God in public awareness deserves attention, even if one cannot otherwise follow Bracht's line.

[8] R. Bultmann, *The Gospel of John: A Commentary*, Oxford 1971, pp. 660 – 661.

3. Marxism

The two tendencies described above find themselves strangely connected in Marxism, the third and the most impressive form of deviation from Europe's historic form. On the one hand Marxism is a return behind Christian faith in the salvation begun in Christ to the still completely open structure of hope to be found in Israel. But it does not do this in the sense of becoming anchored in the latter's great religious heritage; all it draws from it is religious dynamism and the entire force of a hope that transcends the rational, but then adopts as its instrument the reason of the modern age that has been completely emancipated from metaphysical links of any and every kind. It sees its supreme good in the world revolution, which means in the complete rejection of the world so far; as the negation of the negation the world that has to be created anew must be complete positivity. In the connection of the two counter-movements with the European idea Marxism shows itself to be the most radical antithesis not only to Christianity as such but also to the form of history as shaped by Christianity. What has happened up till now counts simply as of no value and for this very reason the revolution counts simply as what is of value. The fact that what has happened up till now has its essential place in the now understood process of history does not change the fact that only its being overcome can be progressive behaviour leads history towards its goal. In this way Marxism is the product of Europe but at the same time the most decisive rejection of Europe in the sense of that inner identity that has formed it in its history.

II: POSITIVE COMPONENTS OF THE CONCEPT OF EUROPE

In this second section I shall try to give a positive outline of what Europe is. I would like to do this on the basis of the history of the meaning of the term "Europe", a history in which the internal stratification of the complex structure Europe becomes visible. Four such strata seem to me to be recognizable.

1. The Greek heritage

As a word, as a geographical concept and as an intellectual concept Europe is a Greek formation. The very word itself is indicative. It probably goes back to the common Semitic term for evening (*ereb*) and thus refers to the fateful encounter of the Semitic and the Western mind which belongs to the essence of what is European.[9] Geographically the area denoted by Europe gradually enlarged itself. At first it included only the area covered by Thessaly, Macedonia, and Attica, but as early as Herodotus with the division into the three continents of Europe, Asia, and Libya it stood for one of the three great geographical and cultural zones which came into contact with each other in the Mediterranean basin.[10]

Europe thus seems to be constituted first of all by the Greek spirit. If it were to forget its Greek heritage it could no longer be Europe. The myth of Europa does indeed point to the sphere of the chthonic religions of the underworld and of the circle of Minoan religion, but the shaping of Europe depends on the overcoming of chthonic religion by the Apollonian form. What Greece means as a heritage that imposes its obligations is difficult to describe in detail. I would see the central element in what Helmut Kuhn has called the Socratic difference: the difference between the good and goods, therefore that difference in which at the same time the right of conscience and the mutual relationship of reason and religion are also to be found.[11]

The Greek heritage can also be summed up from another point of view that is somewhat more comprehensible for us. Granted all the differences between the meaning of the term then and what is meant by it today, democracy is the discovery that it made that is valid through the ages; and, as Plato worked out, democracy is by its nature linked to *eunomia,* to the validity of good law, and can only remain democracy in such a relationship.[12] Democracy in this way is

---

[9] Treidler, op. cit., (note 3 above), p. 448.
[10] Ibid.
[11] H. Kuhn, *Der Staat,* Munich 1967, pp. 25 – 26.
[12] Cf. C. Meier s.v. "Demokratie" in *Geschichtliche Grundbegriffe. Historisches Lexikon zur politisch-sozialen Sprache in Deutschland,* Stuttgart 1973, pp. 829ff.

never the mere domination of majorities, and the mechanism whereby majorities are provided must be guided by the common rule of *nomos,* of what internally is law, that is under the rule of values that form a binding presupposition for the majority too.

2. The Christian heritage

The second layer of the concept of Europe becomes visible in the well-known episode recorded in Acts 16:6 – 10. According to this extremely curious and dramatic tale the spirit of Jesus stopped St Paul from continuing his missionary journey inside Asia. Instead at night a vision of a Macedonian appeared to him and besought him: "Come over to Macedonia and help us." The text goes on: "And when he had seen the vision, immediately we sought to go on into Macedonia, concluding that God had called us to preach the gospel to them." This may admittedly only be portrayed in this way in Acts, but in my view it has a broader basis in the New Testament. What this passage is saying coincides in my opinion in its inner meaning with a saying in the gospel according to St John that occurs in a significant place. Before the passion, after Jesus's entry into Jerusalem, at the moment when the talk is of the fulfilment of Jesus's glorification, the Greeks make their request: "Sir, we wish to see Jesus" (Jn 12:21). Bishop Graber has pointed out that in Luke's account of Pentecost (Acts 2:9 – 11) only Asiatics are named at first in the enumeration of the peoples representing the world. It is only towards the very end that the Romans who are present are mentioned.[13] The point of origin of the gospel is therefore to be found in the East. Like John and the entire New Testament, Luke emphasizes the root of Israel: salvation is from the Jews (Jn 4:22). But Luke adds to this a way that opens a new door. The way described by Acts is as a whole a way from Jerusalem to Rome, the way to the heathen by whom Jerusalem is destroyed and who nevertheless accept it into themselves in a new manner.

[13] R. Graber, *Ein Bischof spricht über Europa,* Regensburg 1978, pp. 10 – 11 and 22 – 23. Here too there is a reference to the connection with John 12:21.

According to this Christianity is the synthesis mediated in Jesus Christ between the faith of Israel and the Greek spirit. Wilhelm Kamlah has put this very impressively.[14] Europe depends on this synthesis. The attempt of the Renaissance to provide a pure distillation of the Greek thing by removing the Christian element and to present it once again as what is purely Greek is as pointless and nonsensical as the more recent attempt at a de-Hellenized Christianity. In my view Europe in the narrower sense arose through this synthesis and is based on it.

3. The Latin heritage

A third layer of the concept is seen in the fact that in the sixth century Gaul was understood under the term Europe and that the Carolingian empire then made the claim to be Europe and to exhaust the content of this term.[15] In the further course of development this never completely accepted identification was relaxed still further. An equation between the *imperium sacrum* of the later middle ages and Europe did not take place. The concept of Europe was wider than that of the Holy Roman Empire, which knew itself to be the Christian transformation of the *imperium romanum*. Europe however now became congruent with the West, and that meant with the area of Latin civilization and the Latin Church; this Latin area embraced not only the peoples speaking Romance languages but also those speaking Teutonic and Anglo-Saxon languages and a part of those talking Slav languages, above all Poland. The *Res publica christiana* which the Christian West knew itself to be was not any politically constituted structure but a real and living totality in the unity of civilization, in "legal systems that transcended tribes and nations, in councils, in the establishment of universities, in the establishment and spread of religious orders, and in the circulation of the spiritual life of the Church with Rome as the ventricle of the heart".[16]

---

[14] W. Kamlah, *Christentum und Geschichtlichkeit*, Stuttgart 1951.
[15] Gollwitzer, op. cit., (note 1 above), p. 826.
[16] Ibid., p. 825.

The mediaeval *Res publica christiana* cannot be restored, and to restore it as such is not a possible goal. History does not go backwards. A future Europe will also have to include within itself the fourth dimension, that of the modern age, and above all will have to transcend the too narrow framework of the West, of the Latin world, and bear within itself or at least be open to the Greek world and the world of the Christian East. But again there cannot be a Europe that would rid itself of the Latin heritage, of the heritage of the Christian West in the sense that has been described. If this were to happen one could no longer talk of Europe; it would mean saying goodbye to Europe.

4. The heritage of the modern period

The fourth layer of what constitutes Europe is the indispensable contribution made by the spirit of the modern age. Admittedly the ambivalence that lurks within individual stages here perhaps becomes most strongly discernible. But this should in no way lead to a rejection of the modern age, a temptation that was to be encountered both in the nineteenth century in romantic nostalgia for the middle ages and in the Catholic sphere in the period between the two world wars.

As a positive characteristic of the modern age I count the fact that the separation of faith and law, which was if anything concealed in the *Res publica christiana* of the middle ages, was now carried through consistently with the result that freedom of belief gradually obtained a clear shape in the distinctions of civil law and that the internal claims of faith were distinguished in this way from the fundamental claims of ethical principles on which law is founded. What for the Christian view of the world are the fundamental humane values make possible, in a fruitful dualism of state and Church, the free humane society in which the right of conscience and with it the fundamental human rights are secured. In it different expressions of Christian faith can co-exist and make room for different political positions which however are linked by a central canon of values whose binding power is at the same time the protection of the greatest possible freedom.

As we know from our own experience, this is an ideal portrayal of the modern age as it would like to see itself but has never actually been in practice. The ambivalence of the modern age rests on the fact that it noticeably misjudged the roots and the living foundation of the idea of freedom and pushed towards an emancipation of reason that fundamentally contradicted the essential nature of human reason as a non-divine reason and for that reason must itself become irrational. What it is wrong to see as the exemplar of the modern age is that reason that has become completely autonomous, that knows only itself and has thus become blind and so becomes inhumane and hostile to creation in the destruction of its rational basis. This kind of autonomy of reason may be the product of the European spirit but at the same time according to its nature it should be seen as post-European, indeed as anti-European, as the inner destruction of what is not only constitutive for Europe but is in general the precondition of a humane society. So what must be adopted from the modern age as essential and indispensable dimensions of the European idea are the relative separation of state and Church, freedom of conscience, human rights and the independent responsibility of reason, while at the same time as against its radicalization what must be firmly held on to is the foundation of reason in respect for God and for the fundamental ethical values that come from the Christian faith.

III: THESES FOR A FUTURE EUROPE

From what has been said so far it becomes clear that not every form of political or economic union that happens in Europe signifies as such a European future. The mere centralization of economic or legislative powers can also lead to a speeded-up disintegration of Europe if it amounted to a technocracy whose sole criterion lay in the increase of consumption. But on the other hand in a larger context such institutions have their value as a means of overcoming the worship of the nation and as segments of a peaceful organization for the joint sharing of the good things of this world. Its fundamental law ought then of course not to be an extension of the group egoism of the rich nations keen to defend their own interests. Joint wealth must be understood as joint responsibility for the world as a whole, and in this sense Europe must be an open system even in its economic mechanisms. In place of the idea of world domination and the annexation of the other parts of the world as colonies there must appear the idea of the open society and of mutual responsibility. This fundamental orientation which emerges from the concept of the European thing that has been worked out so far can be developed in four theses on the basis of the four dimensions of the European idea that I have tried to sketch out.

First thesis: What is constitutive for Europe right from its beginnings in Hellas is the internal relationship of democracy and *eunomia,* of law that is not open to manipulation.

In contrast to the domination of parties or the party and dictatorship as the domination of arbitrary whim, Europe has respected the domination of reason and freedom, which can only enjoy permanent existence as the rule of law. The limitation of power, the control of power and the transparency of power are constitutive of the European community. The presupposition behind all this is the possibility of manipulating the law, the idea that it has its own inviolable space. The precondition for this in turn is what the Greeks called *eunomia,* that is the dependence of the law on moral criteria. Hence I regard it as antidemocratic to turn "law and order" into terms of abuse. Every dictatorship starts with the denunciation of law. Plato demands our agreement over the point that it is less a question of working out a certain kind of mechanism for forming a majority than of working out the most secure way of realizing within existing possibilities the content of the mechanisms of democracy, in other words the control of power by law, the inviolability of law as far as power is concerned, and the deriving by law of its norms from ethics. Anyone who fights for Europe is to this extent fighting for democracy but in its indissoluble link with *eunomia* in terms of the concept sketched out above.

Second thesis: If *eunomia* is the precondition for democracy to be capable of living as the antithesis to tyranny and mob-rule, then a fundamental precondition for *eunomia* once again is shared respect, binding on public law, for moral values and for God.

Once again I recall Bultmann's important statement: "An unchristian state is possible on principle, but not an atheistic state" — at least not as one that remains permanently a state based on law. Part of this is that God is not completely banished to the private sphere but is publicly recognized as the highest value. This includes — and I would want to lay decided emphasis on this — tolerance and space for atheists and should have nothing to do with compulsion in matters of faith. It is only that matters ought to be the other way round from what they are beginning to become. Atheism is beginning to be the fundamental public dogma and faith is tolerated as a private opinion, which means that ultimately in its essence it is not tolerated. This kind of private tolerance was accorded to faith by ancient Rome: sacrificing to the emperor was meant to be merely the concession that it did not present any public claim and in any case did not present any fundamental claim.

I am convinced that in the long run there is no chance of the survival of the state under the rule of law when subjected to an atheist dogma on its way to its radical extreme and that here there is a need for fundamental reflection — as a question of survival. Similarly I venture to assert that democracy is only capable of functioning when conscience is functioning and that this latter has nothing to say if it is not guided and influenced by the fundamental moral values of Christianity, values which are capable of realization even in the absence of any specific acknowledgement of Christianity and indeed in the context of non-Christian religion.

Third thesis: Rejection of the dogma of atheism as the precondition of public law and the formation of the state and a similarly publicly acknowledged respect for God as the foundation of ethics and law mean the rejection both of the nation and of world revolution as the supreme good.

Nationalism has not only *de facto* brought Europe to the edge of destruction; it contradicts what Europe is spiritually and politically according to its nature, even if it has dominated the most recent decades of European history. Hence supranational political, economic and legal institutions are necessary, though these cannot have the aim of building up a super-nation but on the contrary should restore to Europe's individual regions in a strengthened form their own character and importance. Regional, national and supranational institutions should interact in such a way that centralism and particularism are equally excluded. Above all non-state cultural and religious institutions and forces should once again bring to life a great measure of open exchange and unity in diversity.

In the universities, religious orders and councils the middle ages knew European institutions as an actual non-state reality that was effective precisely for this reason. I recall that Anselm came from Aosta in Italy, was an abbot in Brittany and became Archbishop of Canterbury in England, that Albert the Great came from Germany and could teach just as well in Paris as in Cologne and could be Bishop of Regensburg, that Thomas Aquinas taught in Naples as well as in Paris and Cologne, and that Duns Scotus taught in England as well as in Paris and Cologne, to name only a few examples. This kind of thing must regain its strength; if these cultural unities do not become decisively stronger as living non-state realities then in my view the purely state and economic mechanisms cannot ultimately lead to anything positive. From this point of view Christian ecumenism has a European significance too. Just as nationalism stands against Europe's future, so Marxism too, at least in its pure form, contradicts the essential nature of the European idea. Its rejection of history, which as a whole is down-graded to become merely the pre-history of the world yet to be created, its methods and its goals lead to a tyrannical society in which law and ethics are capable of being manipulated and freedom is therefore turned into its opposite.

Fourth thesis: For Europe the recognition and safeguarding of freedom of conscience, human rights, freedom of science and scholarship, and on this basis human society based on freedom must be constitutive.

These achievements of the modern age are to be safeguarded and developed without falling away into the abyss of a reason without transcendence that destroys its own freedom from within. It is by these criteria that the Christian will measure the policies and politics of Europe and it is on their basis that he or she will accomplish his or her political task.

13

Eschatology and Utopia

The phrase "eschatology and utopia" links together concepts that by origin and content are very far apart; the only thing that seems to link them together is the reference to a conceivable future better world and the stimulus of hope that arises from this. The task of comparing the two that is posed by our subject thus demands first of all a clarification of the precise content of the two terms. In this endeavour I depend to a considerable extent on the work of Wilhelm Kamlah, who has already investigated the content of our two concepts in his study of utopia, eschatology, and historical teleology.[1]

In keeping with this the first thing to be established is that as a literary and philosophical genre utopia had its origins in the humanist philosophy of the Renaissance with Thomas More as its first classic representative. Utopia became a form of political philosophy that can more exactly be characterized as Platonism with Christian elements. It can also be asserted that utopia takes up once again the undertaking that occupied Plato with his construction of the ideal state. This makes clear the presuppositions and aims of utopia in its classic form. In this stricter sense it is not linked to a philosophy of history; it is not animated by the idea of a dynamic progress of history whose subsequent goals are sketched out in anticipation in utopia and thus at the same time brought closer to realization. Ernst Bloch's understanding of utopia as the revolutionary goad that unremittingly drives the process of history forward must on this basis be criticized as conceptually inexact; in the subsequent course of these considerations we shall see where this model may more suitably be fitted in from the point of

[1] W. Kamlah, *Utopie, Eschatologie, Geschichtsteleologie. Kritische Undersuchungen zum Ursprung und zum futurischen Denken der Neuzeit,* Mannheim 1969.

view of intellectual history and conceptual accuracy. Let us repeat, utopia rests on the foundation not of a dynamic philosophy of history but on the foundation of Platonic ontology. [2] Kamlah defines the fundamental idea of utopia in its classic form as follows: it is "the rational construction of the optimal *institutions* of a community that make a happy life possible" and that are "held up as a critical mirror before existing abuses".[3] In this definition an important dimension is neglected: with More the talk is of *instituta et mores,* and therefore institutions are dealt with not as self-sufficient regulatory mechanisms but are seen only in the closest connection with the ethics that sustains them, which means with a tradition of human responsibility; what this means can be recognized very clearly from de Tocqueville's presentation of democracy in America. But for the moment this connection is not the aim of our question. What is important for our building up of the concept and thus for the organization of its intellectual elements is first of all that utopia is not understood as a future reality but is related to the actual state in something of the same way as pure mathematical models are to their empirical realization. The construction of a utopia thus means for the actual state roughly the same as the meaning of mathematical operations in relation to our understanding of reality; here the ideal standard of law, of justice, is formulated in as pure a form as possible so as to obtain through this theoretical experiment critical standards for political reality. The aim is not the establishment of a utopia in the future but to measure politics here and now against the highest standards and thus to achieve the optimal approximation of the state to the norm of

---

[2] Admittedly the boundary cannot be drawn completely strictly from a historical point of view. The classification would be difficult as early as Campanella's *Civitas Solis* (cf. Kamlah, op. cit., p. 32): things first start moving properly in the eighteenth century, among other things in pietism (cf. ibid., pp. 19 and 32 – 33). For this reason strict conceptual distinctions as are attempted here following Kamlah remain problematical in view of the fluid connections with factual reality: not the least is the fact that the definition essayed here on the basis of the word's origin is opposed by a contrary usage that has meanwhile become deep-rooted. For this reason in what follows I put the word utopia in quotation marks when it is used in the technical sense defined here in contrast to this ordinary usage.

[3] Kamlah, op. cit., p. 23, cf. p. 18.

justice. To sum up, utopia is thus political philosophy as the operation of the practical reason within the framework of ontological thinking.

In contrast to this eschatology is a statement of faith: on the basis of achnowledgement of the resurrection of Jesus Christ it proclaims the resurrection of the dead, life eternal and the kingdom of God. I would not however go along with Kamlah in making eschatology simply identical with the proclamation of this statement of faith.[4] Eschatology is rather a product of the fusion of Christian faith with the Greek search for the *logos,* the reason that holds things together; it means the endeavour to think out the inner logic of the statements of Christian faith about eternal life, to feel how this logic works on the basis of the internal unity of the entirety of the Christian message about God, the world and man, and in this way to fit its content in with the idea of man as a meaningful entity. This search for a logic of faith which enabled the Fathers of the Church to describe faith as a philosophy, that is as a meaningful all-embracing view of reality,[5] certainly modifies the radical opposition of utopia which arises if like Kamlah one sets the two concepts in opposition to each other as the rational construction of institutions and the proclamation of the end of all distress.[6] Nevertheless there does remain to begin with a difference that is so great that it hardly seems possible to establish a meaningful connection between the two. Utopia evokes human action guided by the practical reason; eschatology is directed towards the receptive patience of faith. The difference would in fact be unbridgeable *if* faith and reason, receiving and acting were impenetrable with regard to each

---

[4] Ibid., p. 26: "In the proclamation of eschatology it is not just hope that is expressed but people are urged to hope . . . The proclamation of this end . . ., that is eschatology."

[5] Cf. among others J. Leclerq, "Pour l'histoire de l'expression 'Philosophie chrétienne' ", in *Mélanges de science religieuse* 9 (1952), pp. 221 – 226; Hans-Urs von Balthasar, "Philosophie, Christentum, Mönchtum", in his *Sponsa Verbi. Skizzen zur Theologie II,* Einsiedeln 1961, pp. 349 – 387. Instructive also is E. R. Curtius, "Zur Geschichte des Wortes Philosophie im Mittelalter", in *Romanische Forschungen. Zeitschrift für romanische Sprachen und Literatur* 57 (1943), pp. 290 – 309.

[6] Kamlah, op. cit., p. 26.

other. So the decisive question for our subject is whether the eschatological message which sees man primarily in the passivity of the person who receives gifts can also become a practical statement, that is one related to action, and whether it can do this in such a way that it enters into relation with man's practical reason. Since a statement that confined man to the strictest passivity would remain without actual content for its recipient, it would thereby become in fact meaningless and would hence not persist in the long term. For this reason alone the search must from the start be undertaken for the practical meaning of the eschatological proclamation. This means that from the start eschatology has been pressing towards an "and", as is to be found in the way our subject is formulated. In this, so it seems to me, four basic types can be demonstrated of a synthesis with models of action, and these types stand in different relationships to our subject.

1. The chiliastic model

The most noticeable is the attempt that has entered history under the label chiliasm or millenarianism. As is known, the term is derived from chapter 20 of Revelation, where the thousand-year reign of Christ and the saints on earth before the end of the world is proclaimed. Objectively what is understood by this is an idea that rests on the foundation of eschatology and thus of the expectation of a new world brought about by God but does not content itself with the *eschaton* beyond the end of the world, but as it were duplicates eschatology. What is awaited is that in this world too God's goal with man and history must be achieved, that there must therefore be a final age within history in which everything will be as it really should. This means that the categories of that which is within history and that which transcends history are combined. That which is within history is awaited in forms that in themselves do not belong to historical thinking; that which transcends history becomes miraculous by being expected as a form of history. This confusion of conflicting expectations has its roots in the multiplicity of meanings and forms assumed by the Jewish hope for salvation in the Old Testament. In the coronation prophecy of Psalm 2 as in the entire strand of the Davidic tradition first clearly formulated in the prophecy of Nathan it appears as a looking forward to a second David and Solomon,[7] as a theopolitical statement, to use a phrase of Martin Buber's. It will be a political entity, a kingdom of David and Israel, but with powers, safeguards, successes, that presuppose God himself as immediately involved politically. This theopolitical construction has on the one hand blurred in apocalyptic literature and shifted into the sphere of the transcendent; on the other hand apocalyptic literature has developed a philosophy of history that turned the end into something datable and made it follow from a logic of historical development.[8] Thus there emerged precisely from apocalyptic an intensification of its theopolitical principle, namely apocalyptic, chiliast politics. There are typical examples for both of these. Jeremiah sees himself faced with theopolitical behaviour that he wishes to replace with national politics for reasons of theological responsibility. The theopolitics of his opponents consists of their being convinced of an absolute guarantee on the part of God for the temple, for Jerusalem, for the continued existence of the house of David, and they treat this guarantee as a political and military factor even though from the point of view of rational politics there is nothing to indicate this kind of security. Jeremiah in contrast demands rational politics which in conduct with regard to Babylon would be guided by the actual conditions of power and the possibilities that follow from these; it is precisely this that he sees as an expression of faith in God and of the responsibility to be shown before God. Obviously here there

---

[7] On Psalm 2 see H. J. Kraus, *Psalmen,* vol. I, Neukirchen 1960, pp. 11–22; on the prophecy of Nathan see H. W. Hertzberg, *Die Samuelbücher,* Göttingen 1965, pp. 231–236; on the Messianic hope in general see W. Eichrodt, *Theologie des Alten Testaments,* vol. I, Leipzig ²1939, pp. 255–278; F. Dingermann, "Israels Hoffnung auf Gott und sein Reich. Zur Entstehung und Entwicklung der alttestamentlichen Eschatologie", in J. Schreiner, *Wort und Botschaft,* Würzburg 1967, pp. 308–318; Martin Buber, "Königtum Gottes, in *Werke,* vol. II, Munich/Heidelberg 1964, pp. 485–723.

[8] A good summary of the state of recent research into the history and significance of apocalyptic literature is offered by U. Duchrow, *Christenheit und Weltverantwortung,* Stuttgart 1970, pp. 17–55, where further reading is listed.

are two kinds of understanding of the relationship between faith and reason, between faith and reality, ultimately two kinds of concept of God, and in this situation one side must reproach the other with lack of faith or the wrong faith. The action of the prophet's opponents which by confusing two kinds of reality and thereby breaking with rationality led to the catastrophe of Jerusalem and the premature end of Jewish political independence is clearly theopolitical, but not yet chiliastic; it starts from the security of the prophecies concerned with David and the temple but is not linked to any particular construction of history.[9]

In contrast in the war scroll of Qumran we find explicitly chiliastic politics. On the one hand the forty-year war between the sons of light and the sons of darkness is presented with a love for military detail that gives the impression "that the author used a hand book of Hellenistic military technology";[10] on the other hand all this is fitted into the apocalyptic construction of history in which the war-lord God with his troops led by Michael establishes the final definitive kingdom. The figure of Jesus needs to be seen against this background. His position is that of Jeremiah, which predicts for such a fusion of faith and politics the final destruction of Jerusalem; seen historically, his failure corresponds in this way exactly to the failure of the prophets. To this extent the synthesis of eschatology and politics that is set out in chiliasm is rejected as a possibility in the fundamental decision of Christianity; but in detail it remained difficult to draw the line in history. If today chiliasm in an altered form emerges as the basic pattern of Christian behaviour, this is not the first time such an event

[9] Cf. for Jeremiah especially A. Weiser, *Das Buch Jeremia,* Göttingen 1966; J. Scharbert, *Die Propheten Israels um 600 v. Chr.,* Cologne 1967, pp. 61–295, 459–478; C. Kuhl, *Israels Propheten,* Munich 1956, pp. 87–100. Instructive for the relationship between Jeremiah's attitude and the position of Isaiah and his followers is for example the exposition of O. Kaiser, *Der Prophet Jesaja Kapiter 13–39,* Göttingen 1973, pp. 111–120 (on Is 22:1–4). It is only in this line that Jesus's Jerusalem prophecies (Lk 19:41–44, Mt 23:37–39 and parallel passages, Mk 13:14–19) become understandable.
[10] M. Hengel, *Gewalt und Gewaltlosigkeit. Zur "politischen theologie" in neutestamentlicher Zeit,* Stuttgart 1971, p. 18: this short work along with Hengel's related book *War Jesus revolutionär?,* Stuttgart ³1971, is fundamental for the questions touched on here.

has occurred but rather the most consistent attempt to take up the old idea and on its basis to make Christianity a practical power in the struggle for the present and the future.

Summing up the objective characteristics of the chiliastic project, we can say that its decisive element is the expectation of a state of salvation within history that in itself transcends the possibilities of political action but is to be established with political means. The guarantee for its possibility is the logic of history, which as it were adds to the political means what they themselves are not able to provide and thus enables it to seem right to apply political means beyond their own logic and to hope for a result from this that they are not able to substantiate from their own resources. If one is looking for historical typologies one will have to say that Marxism is to be fitted in here and not in the sphere of "utopia". Daniel Bell's presentation of the two principles to be found in Marx provides an amazing reminder in structural terms of the mixture of methods to be found in the Essene war scroll. On the one hand there is the most precise economic analysis with which on the other hand is linked a prediction which finds no kind of justification at all in the analysis itself; the difference is actually merely in the fact that now the logic of history has clearly entered on the scene in the place of God and Michael.[11]

2. The model of the great Church: a synthesis of eschatology and "utopia"

The attempt to turn eschatology into a practical and to some extent also a rational statement by following the path of chiliasm is something that suggests itself both by the historical development of the motives involved and by the flow of attitudes. To this extent the suggestive force which the chiliastic model has attained today, above all in the form of theologies of liberation, is completely understandable. However one cannot talk here of a synthesis between the hope of faith and the rationality of political action but only of an addition that in truth corrupts both sides. The blend

[11] D. Bell, *Die nachindustrielle Gesellschaft,* Frankfurt/New York 1975, pp. 63–71.

between an almost abstruse military exactitude and fanatical theological expectations that we encountered in the war scroll of Qumran can be found again in an astonishing way in the literature of liberation theology. On sober reflection one must admit that the sole contribution of theology here consists of linking irrational aims and reasons with political argumentation in such a way that what emerges is political action that is exactly planned in detail but as a whole is profoundly irrational. There is no real connection between the promise and its means; individual sensible projects can thus arise but one will have to label the whole as a leading astray.[12]

The political circumstances of its origination ensured that militant chiliasm could not become an ecclesiastically orthodox solution. Jesus placed himself in the same line as Jeremiah and suffered his fate. The execution of James, the brother of the Lord, the first bishop of Jerusalem, is possibly likewise to be fitted into this context; there could be no conflict with regard to the exactness of fulfilling the law, but it existed with regard to the question of the political guarantees of faith. Corresponding to this was the fact that the Christian community did not take part in the Jewish war; it traced the advice to flee back to Jesus himself (Mk 13:14). The book of Revelation and among the Church's orthodox teachers Irenaeus above all may know the idea of an earthly reign of Christ as a preliminary stage before the final and definitive reign or kingdom of the Father. In both cases any political element is lacking; with Irenaeus the idea is indeed merely a postulate of his Christology and of this concept of God.[13] In the disputes of the early Church it became more

---

[12] The most important survey of "liberation theology" is R. Vekemans, *Teologia de la liberación y cristianos por el socialismo,* Bogotá 1976. I have tried to say something about the presuppositions in the history of the Church and in intellectual history in my contribution "Der Weltdienst der Kirche" to Bauch, Glässer and Seybold, *Zehn Jahre Vaticanum II,* Regensburg 1976, pp. 36 – 53.

[13] On Irenaeus cf. R. Tremblay, *La manifestation et la vision de Dieu selon St Irénée de Lyon* (Münsterer Beiträge zur Theologie); Hans-Urs von Balthasar, *The Glory of the Lord: A Theological Aesthetics. II: Studies in Theological Style: Clerical Styles,* Edinburgh 1984, p. 92: "He [Irenaeus] develops the idea of the thousand-year kingdom of the just on earth after the resurrection because he takes seriously the Old Testament promise of a final, completely secure occupation of the land . . . Irenaeus is the advocate of the new earth." On the death as a martyr of the brother of the Lord reported by Josephus, *Antiquities* XX § 200, reliable historical interpretations are naturally not possible: James's type of Christianity on the one hand and on the other hand the contemporary political background made a diagnosis in the direction attempted above seem sensible.

and more clear that this kind of chiliasm may indeed do no damage to the fundamental Christian structure as such and to that extent is not heterodox but that on the other hand it no longer has anything important to say and to that extent is worthless as a temporal idea. With this chiliasm was finished as an organized attempt at synthesis in the sphere of Church doctrine.

The orthodoxy of the great Church found its decisive partner in dialogue not in apocalyptic and its philosophy of history but in Plato and his ontology. This means that in the place of the militant realization of eschatology by means of chiliastic politics there emerges the relationship to each other of eschatology and "utopia". How does this appear? How is it justified? If one looks more closely, one can establish to begin with that Plato's political philosophy is not so completely disparate with regard to the ways of thought of eschatology as appears at first. In Plato's ideas in their stereotyped form that one discovers to a considerable extent in theological and also in philosophical treatises one encounters two completely different figures of Plato between which a link in general is not obvious. On the one hand there is Plato the dualist, the teacher of flight from the world and of other worldliness; on the other Plato the politician with his attempts at a theoretical and practical reconstruction of the Greek polis overtaken by crisis. Now the delineation of Plato's thought is in fact only possible within limits because we can only provide conjectures about his "secret teaching" and because the work he has left has come down to us only in a variety of allegorical versions which ultimately do not allow any systematization.[14] All the same there are two things that can be said with some certainty: first, that Socrates' philosophical martyrdom is the crucial point of Plato's philosophizing, and secondly that this philosophizing, which has as its background the death of the just man in conflict

[14] The limits of any interpretation of Plato have most recently been emphasized by H. Dörrie, *Von Platon zum Platonismus,* Opladen 1976: cf. especially the dialogue with J. Pieper, pp. 60ff. On the "secret teaching" cf. among others K. Gaiser, *Platons ungeschriebene Lehre,* Stuttgart 1963; H. J. Krämer, *Arete bei Platon und Aristoteles,* Heidelberg 1959.

with the laws of the state, remains continually in search of the just and lawful state.[15] But in this is already to be found the linking of "eschatology" and "utopia" as it occurs in Plato: the individual and the community can only exist if there is a just order of being which transcends them, from which they can derive standards, and towards which they are responsible. "Reality" can only be given a meaningful shape if the ideal is the real; for the ideal to be real is a postulate of experienced reality, which in this shows itself to be reality of a second order. Plato's doctrine of the other world and his theory of ideas are not admittedly discoveries of political aims but they are very well parts of a political philosophy, namely the presentation of criteria which are the precondition for the consistence of the political community. In this context Helmut Kuhn has spoken of the Socratic distinction between goods and the good; in this distinction the core is exposed both of the Platonic doctrine of ideas and of his philosophy of the state, and thereby also of their mutual relationship.[16] On the basis of this distinction the Platonic "utopia" developed as a means of regulating the political reason. While in chiliastic politics faith and reason are blended in a manner injurious to both sides, here a real synthesis is achieved: politics remains a matter of the practical reason, the polis remains polis. But the area of reason is expanded by anticipating true law, by anticipating justice; the good has not less but more reality than goods.

Now Wilhelm Kamlah has established that "utopia" is not some mediaeval nor indeed an early Christian but a "modern . . . undertaking of human thought, speech and writing".[17] This applies in the sense that the explicit genre of utopia was first created by the humanism of the Renaissance. This certainly meant a new stage in political self-criticism and in the search to give political action a rational shape. But this does not mean one should dispute the fact that the mediaeval treaties on politics, as for example the relevant passages in

---

[15] For the interpretation of Plato attempted here cf. U. Duchrow, op. cit., (note 8 above), pp. 61 – 80: something is also to be found in my *Eschatologie*, Regensburg 1977.

[16] H. Kuhn, *Der Staat*, Munich 1967, p. 25.

[17] W. Kamlah, op. cit., p. 16.

Thomas Aquinas's *Summa theologica* and in his commentaries on Aristotle, do in fact stay loyal to the subject of the Platonic utopia, whose fundamental idea is now filled out and reconstructed with material from Aristotle's political philosophy and from Christian traditions.[18] There cannot be any question here of analysing the historical course of this Graeco-Christian synthesis. Instead I would like to try briefly to describe its objective basis and reasons and its content as things appear to me. Three points of view seem to me to be decisive:

a) Eschatological expectation does not comprise any idea of history containing its own perfection and completion in itself; on the contrary, it expresses the impossibility of the world's fulfilment coming from within itself. The different ideas of the end of the world have as their common content a rejection of looking forward to salvation from within history. To dispute history being capable of fulfilment from within itself in this way seems to me to be rationally comprehensible to the extent that such an expectation is not consistent with human beings' persistent openness and their freedom that remains continually open to failure. But behind this we can discern a more profound reversal of our understanding of man: in chiliastic constructions the salvation of history is expected not from man's moral worth, not in the depths of his or her moral personality, but is hoped for from programmable mechanisms; and this means standing on their head the values by which the world is sustained. The orchestration of non-rational expectations with a rational strategy which we encountered before is probably in origin the product of this profound inversion of relative weight and importance.

b) The negative content of eschatology — the rejection of the idea that history is capable of fulfilment from within — is extremely evident to us today. But if this remains on its own complete resignation and naked pragmatism are the only possible consequences. To balance this we need to refer to the

---

[18] On Thomas's political philosophy see U. Matz, "Thomas von Aquin", in H. Maier, H. Rausch, and H. Denzer, *Klassiker des politischen Denkens*, vol. I, Munich ³1963, pp. 114–146; on the sources see M.-D. Chenu, *Das Werk des hl. Thomas von Aquin*, Heidelberg/Graz 1960, pp. 378ff.

positive content of eschatology: while asserting that history is incapable of fulfilment from within eschatology asserts that it is nevertheless capable of fulfilment, but from outside itself. Even though it comes from outside this fulfilment is nevertheless precisely in this way the fulfilment of history. What is outside it is yet fulfilment, completion and perfection. On the basis of the logic of this idea one will have to say that the rejection of the chiliastic attempt and the acceptance of eschatology as eschatology is the only possibility of maintaining history as meaningful at all. History demands meaning but cannot ultimately contain its meaning within itself. So either it is meaningless or it is brought to fulfilment as itself outside itself and has meaning by transcending itself. This has the consequence that eschatology functions as the guarantee of meaning in history precisely because it does not become a political goal itself, and makes possible the "utopia" that in this ideal model constructs the maximum of justice and elevates it as a task for the political reason.

c) Hence eschatology is not necessarily linked with any particular philosophy of history but is with ontology. Because it is not history's own logic that it is executing it can be linked with philosophies both of progress and of decadence.[19] Its crucial point is not a pattern for the course of history but the concept of God that receives its actuality in Christology. The acceptance of eschatology into Christianity which is fundamentally provided by the Christian decision of faith means at the same time its being taken into the concept of God and thereby the retreat of the pattern of the theology of history found in the apocalyptic writings. Establishing in this way how eschatology fits into the system was probably the central point in making possible for its principle to be linked with the tradition of Platonic thought.

---

[19] The profound difference between Augustine's pessimism and the early and late mediaeval idea of progress is shown very well by A. Dempf, *Sacrum Imperium*, Darmstadt [2]1954, pp. 116–398.

3. *The utopian* civitas *of the monks*

Kamlah's thesis of the modern character of utopia needs yet another qualification in addition to that just made. Christian monasticism is nothing other than an attempt to find utopia in faith and to transfer it to this world. The expression βίος ἀγγελικός which monasticism used to describe itself expresses this intention very precisely: to live the life of paradise now and thus to discover nowhere as somewhere.[20] Corresponding to this is the origin of this development in one of Jesus's utopian sayings: "Go, sell what you possess and give to the poor . . .; and come, follow me" (Mt 19:21).[21] In this there is a conscious awareness that Jesus's own life, to following which one devotes oneself, was quite literally a utopian life: "Foxes have holes, and birds of the air have nests; but the Son of man has nowhere to lay his head" (Mt 8:20). The effect of this was that the monks departed from the inhabited world into the non-world, into the wilderness. Cyril of Scythopolis put this reversal of existing values that is intended by the *fuga saeculi* very well when he said that through the monks the wilderness was turned into *civitas,* the non-world into the world.[22] What is involved is a revolution of the spirit which is shown in the convert's expropriation of himself or herself, inasmuch as this creates for him or her a new criterion for living and opens up a new *civitas* in contrast to the old world and its *civitates.* This is shown in the strongest way with regard to the sensibilities of the ancient world by the fact that the social divisions that could not be

[20] On the question of living like the angels, see especailly S. Frank, ΑΓΓΕΛΙΚΟΣΒΙΟΣ, Münster 1964; on early monasticism in general see K. Baus's contribution in Hubert Jedin (ed.), *History of the Church,* vol. II: *The Imperial Church from Constantine the Great to the Early Middle Ages,* London 1980, pp. 337–373; L. Bouyer, *La spiritualité du Nouveau Testament et des Pères,* Paris 1960; U. Ranke-Heinemann, Das frühe Mönchtum, Essen 1964.

[21] Cf. Athanasius, *Vita sancti Antonii,* cc. 2–4, PG 26 cols 842–846; cf. the parallel occurrence in the life of St Francis, I Celano 2, *Legenda S. Francisci a BB. Leone, Rufino, Angelo . . . scripta (Legenda trium sociorum)* 25, Bonaventure, *Vita S. Francisci* III:1; on this see O. Englebert, *Das Leben des hl. Franziskus,* Speyer 1951, pp. 52ff.

[22] Cyril of Scythopolis, *Vita Sabae* c. 15, ed. Schwartz (TU 49:2), pp. 98, 2–3. Cf. C. von Schönborn, *Sophrone de Jérusalem. Vie monastique et confession dogmatique,* Paris 1972, pp. 25ff.

abolished or transcended in the existing world ended automatically on the threshold of the monastic world: the distinction between slave and free that continued to exist in the "world" is done away with here in keeping with Galatians 3:28.[23]

The form of utopia that appears here is distinguished from the Platonic on the one hand by the fact that it regards utopia as partly realizable in the power of faith, and on the other hand by the fact that it does not relate this realization to the world as such and its political corporations but to the charismatic non-world which arises from the *voluntary* flight from the world. On the other hand a connection with the world existed unavoidably. It emerges quite clearly in western monasticism, which modelled itself principally on the figure and on the rule of St Benedict: the monastic community provides a pattern of common life and offers a fixed point of survival in an uncertain age. In this way the monks' existence gradually became very rooted, a firm component of the world as organized and no longer a counter-image to it. Anton Rotzetter has insistently pointed out how in contrast St Francis's idea of a religious community is once again completely characterized by a passion for the utopian ideal and is held together in its variety of expressions precisely by the idea of a realized utopia.[24] Astonishingly it is here that the question of relating to the existing world and to existing human communities takes on clearer outlines. First of all this was shown by the fact that now it is precisely the cities and towns that are the wilderness into which the monks go in order to turn them from wilderness into genuine *civitas*. Even more important for the questions we are dealing with seems to me to be the idea of the third order which contains the attempt to transfer the monks' utopian pattern of life to the "rooted" life in normal occupations. The third order means

[23] *The Rule of St Benedict,* edited and translated by Abbot Justin McCann OSB, London 1952, pp. 18 – 19 (chapter 2): "Let him [the abbot] not make any distinction of persons in the monastery . . . Let not a free-born monk be put before one that was a slave, unless there be some other reasonable ground for it."

[24] A Rotzetter, "Der utopische Entwurf der franziskanischen Gemeinschaft" in *Wissenschaft und Weisheit* 37 (1974), pp. 159 – 169. On the actual difficulties of the Franciscan project see in the same volume K. S. Frank, "Utopie — Pragmatismus. Bonaventura und das Erbe des hl. Franziskus von Assisi", pp. 139 – 159.

the attempt to bring as it were the entire polis one step closer
to utopia and thus to bring about a comprehensive reform of
the real world on the basis of the utopian ideal. One must
admittedly add that essentially this attempt was made with
individual ethical models and if need be cooperative ones, but
not with a genuinely political ethics.

In this context we must remember the figure of Joachim of
Fiore, who made the fateful link between monastic utopia
and chiliasm. Originally the two had nothing in common with
each other. Reversing the principle to be found in Irenaeus of
Lyons, Joachim created a construction of history in which the
trinitarian God himself appeared as the principle of progress
in history. The old idea that monasticism was an anticipation
of the world of the Spirit was now given a chronological
content: monasticism was an anticipation of the next stage of
history. In this way utopia was historicized and turned into a
historical goal that was to be actively striven for.[25] However
mediaeval and monastic Joachim's statements may be in
detail, structurally they opened up the path to Hegel and to
Marx: history is a process that pushes forward in which man
is actively at work building his or her salvation which in its
turn is not to be recognized from the mere logic of the present
but is guaranteed by the logic of history.

4. Teilhard de Chardin's evolutionary outline

What is new about Teilhard de Chardin is that he tries to
link Christian eschatology with the scientific theory of
evolution by defining Christ as the omega point of evolution.
For him the history of nature and of man are stages of one
and the same process which is characterized by progress from
the simplest building elements of matter to ever more
complex entities right up to ultracomplexity, in other words
the fusion of man and the cosmos in an all-embracing unity.

[25] On Joachim see especially A. Dempf, op. cit., (note 19 above), pp. 269 – 284;
cf. also my *Geschichtstheologie des hl. Bonaventura,* Munich/Zürich 1959, pp.
97 – 120.

The image of the body of Christ and of Christ as the head of the cosmos as outlined in the letters to the Ephesians and to the Colossians enabled Teilhard to identify this vision with the acknowledgment of Christ and his eschatological hope. Although there are certain parallels between this outline and Marxist patterns of thought, in the case of Teilhard one must acknowledge the lack of a history of philosophy of his own as well as the absence of an actual political programme. To this extent it can hardly be fitted in to chiliasm. His idea is rather that the progress of technology, despite the unavoidable statistical quota of catastrophes which it shares with the whole of evolution, nevertheless forwards the single-mindedness of evolution, in which it falls to such progress to build up the noosphere beyond the biosphere as the penultimate state of complexity. If the progress of technology shows the line along which evolution is moving, what would correspond most closely to this would be politics run by technocrats; science builds utopia thanks to its immanent progress, if not without reverses. Belief in science here takes on mythical traits; lapsing into resignation, which withdraws into what is feasible, is always tangibly close with views of this kind.

With this we have reached the problems of the present day, which finds itself in a dilemma between chiliastic irrationality and the rationality of positivism, a rationality that is empty of hope. In contrast to this it could be the function of "utopia" in the Platonic, Christian and humanist sense to press for an expansion of the concept of reason and to regard as a task of reason not only the question of what is empirically verifiable but also the question of the values that structure the empirical world; and for this, reason has to go to school with the great religious traditions of mankind. With this the function of eschatology in this context ought to be clarified. Obviously it should not be seen as a kind of theological supplement to penal law, as was often the case in authoritarian states of the modern age, in which the pastor became the policeman for the other worldly sanctions for human action administered by the Church in league with the state. That would be a negative utopia of fear and egoism. It is rather a question of perceiving more reality; reality that is empirically comprehensible and the rationality that is limited to this can ultimately demand only the withdrawal of man, who as a matter of principle and not just as a matter of fact in our present state of knowledge transcends the merely empirical world. It is a question of recognizing not just usefulness but also values as realities and on this basis to make possible humane behaviour with a rational basis.

In this it is indisputable that the traditional humanist-Christian utopia is inadequate in many ways. It was admittedly aware that reality touches justice only asymptotically, but it was not sufficiently aware that knowledge also rests asymptotically on the path. This had the consequence that it regarded its models as too final and definitive, as too static, as can be seen from the Catholic doctrine of the natural law as a classic form of "utopian" thought. If one becomes aware of this then it follows that knowledge can only occur in a continual interplay between practice and theory; the application of a "utopia" discloses at the same time the deficiencies of its knowledge and thus compels new designs that make new practical applications possible and so on. The static approach of Plato is thus automatically changed in favour of a realistic historical approach in which the correct insights of efforts at the philosophy of history are incorporated without deducing from this a logic of history that recognizes no authority but its own.

A second problem seems to me to lie in the correct relationship of *instituta* and *mores*. Criticism of institutions and the creative search for better ones has, in contrast to Plato's search for the best form of state, been little developed in the tradition of Christian teaching on the state. At present in contrast what threatens is completely forgetting the second fundamental element of the existence of the state, *mores*. This means not morality but custom, a structure of fundamental convictions that finds expression in forms of life which give shape to the consensus in the undisputed fundamental values of human life. Alexis de Tocqueville worked out in an impressive way that democracy depends far more on *mores* than on *instituta*. Where no common conviction exists institutions have nothing to lay hold of and compulsion becomes a necessity: freedom presupposes conviction, conviction education and moral awareness. When "utopia" becomes a mere doctrine of institutions it forgets the decisive element: that the management of spiritual forces is more important for the fate of a community than the management of economic resources. For a comprehensively designed "utopia" the question of the best institutions must go hand in hand with the question how the management of spiritual forces, the capability of joint realization of fundamental values can be secured. The stronger the support of *mores* the less will *instituta* be necessary. The question of education, that is the opening up of the reason to the whole of reality beyond what is merely empirical, is no less important for "utopia" than the question of the right division and control of power. When *mores* are left out of consideration we have not an increase of freedom but a preparation for tyranny; this prognosis of de Tocqueville's has been confirmed only too clearly by the developments of the last hundred years. It is not in the sanction but rather in the acceptance of values as realities that the eschatological dimension of "utopias" could lie. In its *mores* the politics that a "utopia" is meant to serve points beyond itself; but without *mores* a "utopia" that knows only *instituta* becomes the project of a prison instead of the search for true freedom.

14

Freedom and Liberation

THE ANTHROPOLOGICAL VISION OF THE
1986 INSTRUCTION *LIBERTATIS CONSCIENTIA*

Public discussion of the new Instruction on Christian freedom and liberation has so far confined itself almost exclusively to the fifth chapter of this document, which on the basis of the principles of Catholic social teaching draws up fundamental guidelines for a Christian practice of liberation in the political and social sphere. Nothing else was to be expected once the alternative had so far failed to become very clear to the Marxist-inspired forms of the practice of liberation rejected by the Church's teaching authority. It is also quite normal for it to be easier in press commentaries to discuss forms of political practice than to present fundamental philosophical and theological questions. But there are pretty certainly more profound reasons for this omission of the document's foundation in its understanding of man. These reasons appear for example in a journalist's critical remark that the Congregation had decided to tackle the problem of freedom not in a historical but in an ethical perspective. In this remark "ethical" is clearly tacitly equated with individualistic and also with idealistic. What is seen in an "ethical" treatment is a reduction to appeals to the individual's good will and to theological speculations. These latter are regarded as "idealistic", in other words as unrealistic; they can be passed over because they do not have any actual consequences. Ethical appeals are similarly also seen as powerless; they seem to be without social or political significance. Hiding behind this kind of view is the conviction that what people do is determined ultimately not by their ethical freedom but by economic and social natural laws which are also briefly labelled the laws of "history". Anyone who thinks along these lines does not for the most part in any way for that reason want to do away completely with the ethical element. But it remains confined to the sphere of the "subjective", the place of which in reality cannot be established precisely; it may be useful and desirable for private life, but for public life it has nothing to say.

I: THE QUESTION OF THE FUNDAMENTAL CONCEPTION OF FREEDOM

1. Ethics and history

In contrast to the understanding of the "ethical" element that has just been described the "historical" element appears as a kind of magic formula: only someone who thinks "historically" gets to the bottom of human affairs because all reality is of its nature "history". Frequently it remains pretty obscure what is really meant by "history" in this context. Evolutionary ideas, Hegelian influences, the Marxist heritage and sociological observations have been blended together into a framework of ideas that is not easy to define. The whole of history appears as a process of progressive liberations, the mechanism of which we are slowly able to explain and thus to direct ourselves. Here a fascinating promise opens up: man can himself or herself become the engineer of his or her own history. He or she need no longer rely on the ever uncertain and fragile nature of his or her good will and his or her moral decisions. He or she now sees directly into the internal workings of the processes of freedom and can create the conditions in which the will is automatically good, just as hitherto we have been living in conditions in which it is automatically bad. Ethical endeavours can be made superfluous inasmuch as one is directing history itself. The objection that the Instruction chose an "ethical" perspective instead of a "historical" one thus means that it has retreated from the sphere of action that transforms history to the field of theological reveries and more or less ineffective appeals to ethical behaviour.

What is correct, however, is precisely the opposite. The

two Instructions together have demythologized the myth of
the process of freedom and posed the question afresh in a
national context; it was only for this reason that they were
also able to reach better practical proposals which presuppose
this new discussion of the fundamental questions. So despite
everything it is a good sign that this practical chapter has been
read with so much interest. Only a brief time ago Catholic
social teaching was spoken of only with contempt as a
middle-class ideology and as mere "reformism". It was
maintained that there was only the alternative of capitalism
or revolution, and only revolution promised a new man and a
new society because only revolution corresponded to the laws
of the progress of history. How the new man was to come
into existence, how the new society functioned did not need
to be thought out any more because the laws of history would
themselves do what was theirs. Today, after so many failed
attempts, faith is gradually dying out in the miracle of the
new society automatically emerging from the dialectical leap
of the revolution. It is slowly becoming clear that we need
alternatives: rational steps in which what is possible is done
and the impossible is not conjured up with a nebulous
philosophy. It is becoming clear that the "natural laws" of
freedom are a contradiction in themselves. A freedom that is
brought about by historical necessities and in this way is
imposed on man from outside is no freedom. Conversely
within human history there can never be a definitively stable
and irreversible social order because man remains free and
hence also retains the freedom to turn good into bad. If this
freedom were finally and conclusively to be taken from him
or her by any kind of society then this society would be
absolute tyranny and precisely for that reason no kind of
well-ordered society.[1]

Now, the myth of a necessary and at the same time
steerable development of all history towards freedom is
gradually beginning to dissolve. It is becoming clear that this
kind of perspective is not really a historical perspective at all,
because it is continuously contradicted by actual history. It

[1] Cf. for an analysis of the tendencies mentioned here G. Rohrmoser, *Zeitseichen.
Bilanz einer Ara,* Stuttgart 1977.

can only go on being handed down by ignoring actual history completely. In this way it is precisely the "ethical" perspective that is the genuinely historical and realistic perspective which takes our actual experience into account. But the question remains: how does the Christian alternative appear when looked at more closely? The fact that there are practical alternatives has convincingly been indicated in broad outline by the fifth chapter of the instruction. But the practical alternatives would be mere petty-minded pragmatism if they did not rest on a vision of man and his or her history which is more than theological speculation and an appeal to the individual's good will. The practical alternatives have hitherto been formulated so unsatisfactorily and have often remained without political resonance because Christians have no confidence in their own vision of reality. In their private piety they firmly maintain the faith, but they dare not accept that it was something to say to man as a whole, a vision of his or her future and of his or her history. From original sin to redemption the whole traditional construction seems to them far too irrational and unreal for them to dare to introduce it into public discussion. So today it is not only non-Christians who leave the first four chapters of the Instruction on one side as irrelevant; it is the Christians above all who do so. They think theology is only an internal matter: an authority responsible for the faith could well do none other than to put forward this kind of theological foundation, but it could hardly be of public and historical interest. Because Christians are of such little faith the search for new myths will continue. A vision without practical application is unsatisfactory, but conversely a practical programme that did not depend on a comprehensive vision of man and his or her history would be without foundation and incredible: an external system of rules that could not suffice for the magnitude of the question. For this reason the five chapters of this Instruction and the two Instructions together form an indissoluble unity which is only understood if they are read and considered as a connected whole. It is a question of understanding, and learning to live, Christianity as a whole as an alternative to the present day's mythologies of liberation.

2. *Anarchy and constraint*

If one reads the document in this sense one will quickly recognize that it is far more than an appeal to the individual's good will garnished with theological speculations. Behind the wrongly formulated and wrongly conceived opposition of ethical and historical perspectives there lie hidden two contrasting conceptions of history and freedom between which we have to choose. The two documents clarify this alternative that faces mankind today and provide the rational justification for an option without understanding which one misses the text's individual contribution. I shall try to make this alternative clear on the basis of some of its fundamental elements. What does the average man or woman of today expect when he or she calls for freedom and liberation? Roughly what Marx provided as a vision of complete freedom: "In the morning to hunt, in the afternoon to fish ... after I have eaten to criticize just as I feel."[2] By freedom is generally understood today the possibility of doing everything one wants to do and of doing only what one would like to do oneself. Freedom understood in this way is a matter of doing what one likes, of arbitrary whim. We could also say that the goal against which ideologies of liberation measure themselves in general today is anarchy. According to this vision freedom would only be complete if there were no government at all, no obligation to other people or other things, but only the unrestricted ability of every individual to do what he or she wanted, with everything he or she wanted always being at his or her disposal, and with him or her always being able to do everything he or she wanted. From this point of view liberation consists in throwing off constraints and obligations. Every obligation appears as a shackle that restricts freedom; every obligation that is thrown off becomes a step forward on the road to freedom. It is clear that from this kind of point of view the family, the Church, morality, and God must appear antitheses to freedom. God obliges men and women; morality is a basic form in which this obligation to

---

[2] Mark and Engels, *Werke,* East Berlin 1967–1974, vol. III p. 33: cf. K. Löw, *Warum fasziniert der Kommunismus?,* Cologne 1980, pp. 64–65.

him is expressed. The Church and the family are structures in which this obligation takes on an actual social form. Even the state, declared to be the rule of man over man, becomes an opponent of freedom. All this brings about a necessary change in one's attitude to force and violence. Hitherto force exerted by the state in the service of law and directed against arbitrary law-breaking for the sake of the law shared by the community seemed something positive because it was the protection of the law against arbitrary action and the protection of the individual against the destruction of community. Now things suddenly seem the other way round: the law seems to be a means of maintaining obligations and constraints and thus upholding a lack of freedom; law and order becomes a negative concept. Force in the service of law is thus the power of oppression, while force against the legal order of the state is fighting for liberation and freedom and thus something positive. The same applies with regard to morality: it is breaking free from morality that is now seen as really moral. In the new counter-morality only one rule applies: everything that serves the destruction of obligations and constraints and thus the struggle for freedom is good; everything that conserves obligations and constraints is bad. Behind all this there stands a programme which must ultimately be labelled theological: God is no longer recognized as a reality standing over against man, but instead man may himself or herself become what he or she imagines a divinity would be if it existed, unrestrainedly free, confined by no boundaries. He or she would like to "be like God" (Gen 3:5). In this context Jesus can keep his place as a symbolic revolutionary figure, which means that, as once happened, Jesus is replaced by Barabbas, who also bore the name Jesus.[3]

Now not everything is wrong that is wanted in detail in this vision; a complete error without any admixture of truth could never be effective in the long term among human beings. There are unjust laws; there is evil state rule against which resistance is due. The law as officially laid down and

[3] Matthew 27:16 according to the reading of the Koridethi gospels as well as of the Armenian version and of some Syriac and Georgian versions, while Origen has the same tradition; cf. for the questions touched on by this M. Hengel, *War Jesus Revolutionär?*, Stuttgart 1970, and O. Cullmann, *Jesus und die Revolutionäre seiner Zeit*, Tübingen 1970.

administered can be injustice and hence force intended to serve the law can become unjust violence. To go even further, "to be like God" is, correctly understood, essential for man made in the image of God. Although therefore truths are hidden both in the fundamental principle and in its details the vision as a whole is a distortion of truth and hence also a distortion of freedom. A practice of liberation when its secret criterion is anarchy is in reality a practice of enslavement, because anarchy is opposed to the truth of being human and hence also opposed to human freedom. The closer one gets to it the less freedom there is. To this kind of concept of freedom, the fundamental criterion of which is anarchy and the method of which is the systematic elimination of obligations and constraints, the Vatican document opposes a vision according to which properly ordered obligations and constraints are the real protection of freedom and ways of liberation. One can, as goes on happening with the liberalistic and Marxist models, decry the family as slavery and so obtain some easy successes. But the kind of freedom that comes into being in that case first of all for the children, then for the wife and for the husband, can be adequately studied in contemporary society to make the proof to the contrary obvious. In reality the family is the primal cell of freedom; as long as it remains supported at least a minimum area of freedom is secured. Hence dictatorships will always aim at smashing the family so as to eliminate this area of freedom that is withdrawn from their grasp. The community of worship and the larger community of the Church that stands behind it is also an area of freedom. When the state is forced by the inner power of these areas to respect them in some way in their individuality they form zones for the protection of freedom which serve the individual as well as the whole. Other communities that are prior to the state can form areas of freedom of this kind too, but even the state itself when it recognizes its limits and builds up genuine law on the basis of the moral forces that precede it becomes a protection against the arbitrary action of the individual and thus a source of freedom for all. The right combination of obligations and constraints makes freedom possible. Freedom rests on the right order of obligations and constraints that are appropriate to human beings. Anarchy, the rule of arbitrary whim, is not appropriate for human beings because they are ordered not towards isolation but towards relating to others. People cannot call on others at whim when they seem useful to them as a means; they cannot dismiss them again at whim when they do not please them precisely because these others are also selves and not means for someone else. But that is what they must be when the philosophy of anarchistic freedom is in operation; it is constructed only on the basis of the individual ego and presupposes that everyone else is reduced to the status of a slave. A correct vision of mankind, however, must start from a relationship in which everyone remains a person and free and is bound to the other precisely as such. It must be a doctrine of relationship and search for a type of relationship which is not an attitude of using people as means towards ends but a self-giving of persons.

3. *Practical consequences*

The practical and political implications of this kind of vision of mankind are not difficult to recognize. If things are so, then the disruption of relationships, the destruction of the ability to form obligations is in no way a practice of liberation but on the contrary a means of building up tyranny. In practice the dissolution of traditional links and obligations, dependence on large anonymous systems and the process linked with this of the individual becoming anonymous in megalopolitan mass societies that lack relationships have turned out more and more to be the pre-condition for total dictatorship and the totalitarian enforcement of conformity. Hence the genuine practice of liberation must do the precise opposite and consist of educating people to be capable of making relationships and building up the fundamental relationships that are suitable for human beings. Equally valid is the fact that it is not the fight against institutions but the struggle for the right kind of institutions that makes freedom possible. Hence finally the battle against law and laws is not a means of making people free but once again precisely the reverse. The battle for law, for a moral law, is the battle against lawlessness and injustice. Only a justice that can be relied on and that can gain acceptance guarantees freedom. Freedom takes shape everywhere, but only where, there is success in making justice, the same law for all, prevail against the arbitrary whims of individuals or groups.

It is only against this background that one can understand correctly the actual options which are expressed in the fifth chapter of the Instruction. It emphasizes the family as the primal and originary area of freedom, because it is in the family that the basic forms of relationship grow that are the relationships of freedom—the relationships on which the human person is founded. The text emphasizes education as the core of any and every practice of liberation. The less a person is able to do, the less he or she knows, the less he or she is capable of forming a judgement, the more dependent he or she is. For dependence to be replaced by meaningful mutual relationships a man or woman must learn. He or she needs education and training, in other words ability; but not just the ability to do things but also the ability to form judgements about what human life is really all about. Mere ability coupled with atrophy of the conscience makes people easy to lead astray and can reduce them to ideal tools of a dictatorship. It is only the formation of conscience that gives the individual his or her human core; then ability creates a sphere of independence and rights from which co-operation in freedom can arise. These two aspects of education as education in being able to be human, being able to live, and training in vocational ability have beyond the individual a social form which is addressed in the Instruction under the headings of culture and work. Freedom does not consist of doing nothing, and still less does doing nothing lead to liberation; the form of work and co-operation that is suitable and adequate for human beings leads to freedom. For work to be satisfying to people and be an instrument of freedom it must be incorporated in culture, in which it becomes possible for people to gain answers to their profoundest question and to exchange and share what is genuinely characteristic of being human.[4] The logic of this vision also gives rise to the

---

[4] Important for the philosophical background of chapter 5 as well as for reconsideration of the anthropological basis of Catholic social teaching is R. Buttiglione, *L'uomo e il lavoro: riflessioni sull'encicica 'Laborem exercens'*, Bologna 1982.

right and duty to resist the distortion of institutions, the abuse of law. But this kind of resistance is fitted into a rational context. Hence it is bound by rules and must justify itself by actual rational goals. For this reason it is something quite other than that ideology of violence which expects a new stage of history from the revolution as such and does not think it owes anyone any explanation over whether this is capable of realization. Anyone who thinks that what is really involved here are tiny casuistical distinctions which should not weigh in the balance in the great fight against tyranny fails to recognize the abyss that gapes between the two fundamental visions of freedom and human dignity that guide the different forms of practice. It is for this reason that it is so important not just to put forward a few practical rules but to have one's eye on the inner connection between practice and the theory that goes with it.

At this point I would like to break this train of reflection off prematurely even though we have by no means reached the end. The anarchic conception of freedom based on the ideology of history which we have just presented has, as has been shown, its theological depth, and indeed ultimately lives from this. To use Feuerbach's language, it is question of man drawing back to himself or herself the projection of God which he or she originated and to make the divinity in man a reality, to let man become as free as one has imagined God to be. The Christian position that we then started to present resists this claim. It says that man is a being marked by relationships; human beings deceive themselves with an anarchistic idea of freedom. They must recognize their need of relationships and build up the right kind of relationships, they must transform dependence into joint freedom; this was how we described the logic of this idea. That is in practice the proven truth of mankind. But where has God been in all this? Has he of all things become superfluous in the Christian vision of mankind? There is of course the temptation to leave God out and thus to water Christianity down into something merely Western. But this way one cannot do justice to the greatness of man. The question of God cannot be left out when man is concerned. We shall come closer to the answer if for the moment we interrupt the train of thought so far and first of all address ourselves to the question how the Instruction expounds the biblical testimony about freedom, its history and its realization.

II: THE CONTRIBUTION OF THE BIBLE

1. Exodus and Sinai

The kind of liberation theology that is related to the "anarchist model" and rejected by the Church's teaching authority knew how to revive political and general human interest in the bible by bringing about an "inversion of symbols" or to put it in more general terms a reversal of the relationship of the Old and New Testaments.[5] Christians used to interpret Israel's exodus from Egypt as a symbol (τύπος) of baptism and to see in baptism a radical and universal form of the exodus. The historical line went from Moses to Christ. But to the theologians of today the path from the exodus to baptism seemed a loss of reality, a retreat from what was political and real into what was mystical and unreal and purely individual. To confer meaning on baptism or indeed on being a Christian in general once again the historical line must now be seen the other way round. Baptism is to be understood on the basis of the exodus, not the exodus on the basis of baptism. Baptism points the way to the exodus, that is, it is the symbol of a political process of liberation to which the chosen "people", in other words the oppressed of all nations, are called. Baptism becomes the symbol of the exodus, while the exodus becomes a symbol of political revolutionary action in general. Jesus is interpreted by reference back to Moses, while Moses is interpreted in anticipation by reference to Marx; and this pattern of interpretation now becomes decisive for reading and understanding the bible, whether it is a matter of the eucharist, of the kingdom of God, of the resurrection or indeed of the figure of Jesus. The acting out and

---

[5] On this see the 1984 Instruction *Libertatis nuntius* X:14.

fulfilment of these symbols, in other words the celebration of the sacraments, is logically drawn into this political dynamism. Thus the bible and the sacraments certainly become topical once again, even if their original meaning is hardly still of interest; with the power of a symbolic happening they illustrate and re-inforce a historical vision and a political option. The objection that this means quite simply falsifying the bible often remains without effect, probably not least because reading it in a manner that is loyal to the text seems to lead us into a no-man's-land of pious edification whose relationship to the reality we experience in our lives remains obscure. So in the end people are ready to prefer a blatantly false relationship between the bible and reality to an understanding of the bible that seems to lack all sense of reality.[6]

How then does the Instruction see the biblical testimony? It is clear that it cannot adopt this inversion of symbols in which the basic pattern of the biblical testimony is stood on its head. It takes the opposite path and tries to understand the internal logic of this pattern and the picture of God, the world and man that is to be found in it. In doing so the document must of course confine itself to indications that demand further development through theological work. Here I would simply like to try to clarify its version of the exodus. What does the exodus lead to? What is its goal? Is it simply an autonomous state for Israel so that at last it may be a nation like all other nations, with its own government and its own boundaries? And if so what kind of freedom is it that this state provides? If an autonomous state were automatically a free state even in its inner workings, then the problem of liberation for Latin America would already have been settled after the dissolution of Spanish and Portuguese colonial rule. But clearly things are not as simple as that. What kind of freedom therefore is the liberation of the exodus aiming at? To answer this question it is important to observe that in telling Pharaoh what the purpose is of their leaving Egypt Moses does not say at all that it is to obtain a country of their own but to search

---

[6] Instructive from this point of view is K. Füssel, "Materialistische Lektüre der Bibel", in J. Pfammater and F. Furger (ed.), *Theologische Berichte XIII: Methoden der Evangelienexegese,* Einsiedeln 1985, pp. 123 – 163.

out a place of sacrifice in order to worship God in the way God himself wanted.[7] Above and beyond everything else the goal of the exodus is Sinai, in other words the conclusion of the convenant with God from which Israel's law derives. The goal is to discover a law that provides justice and thus builds up the right relationships of men and women between each other and with the whole of creation. These relationships that are justice and thereby freedom for human beings depend however on the convenant, indeed they are the covenant; they cannot be devised and shaped by men and women alone, they depend on the fundamental relationship which regulates all other relationships, the relationship with God. One can therefore perfectly well say that the goal of the exodus was freedom, but one must add that the shape and pattern of freedom is the covenant and that the way in which freedom is realized is the right relationship of men and women between themselves that is described in the covenant law on the basis of their right relationship with God. One could also say that the goal of the exodus was to make Israel into a nation, a people, from a collection of tribes and to give it as a people its freedom and its own dignity along with its own mission in history. But once again one must also recall that a collection of people becomes a people or nation through its common law and that man does not live lawfully if he or she remains in a relationship with God that is not right and just.

From this one can understand that the "country", the land, certainly counted among the goals of the exodus; part of the freedom of a people is without a doubt its own country. But at the same time it becomes clear that from a certain point of view the country remains subordinate to Sinai. When in its own country Israel loses Sinai, that is when it destroys the law and the covenant and dissolves the order of freedom by the disorder of arbitrariness, then it was reverted to its state before the exodus; then it is living both in its own country and yet at the same time in Egypt, because it is destroying its freedom from within. The exile is merely an external and political illustration of this inner loss of freedom

[7] Thus Exodus 5:3, and cf. 5:17, 8:21–24, 9:13 and elsewhere. The close connection between the land and the Torah becomes clear in Joshua 1:6–9, 22:5, 23:6, and elsewhere.

that had already occurred and that was brought about by the loss of justice. In this way one has to say that the really liberating element in the exodus is represented by the inauguration of the covenant between God and man, the covenant which is made actual in the Torah, that is in regulations of justice that are the shape of freedom. Corresponding to this is the fact that the exodus did not become possible because of particular acts of boldness or particular competences on the part of Moses but through a religious event, the sacrifice of the pasch, which is an anticipated core-element of the Torah. In this is expressed a primal awareness of mankind that we meet again and again in the history of religion, that freedom and the building of community are ultimately to be attained neither by force nor by mere competence but through a love that becomes a victim and that links men and women together at the profoundest level by allowing them to come into contact with the dimension of the divine. Thus in principle there exists at the core of the Old Testament occurrence of liberation what subsequently comes out into the open in the figure of Jesus Christ and from him becomes the core of a new history of freedom.

2. *The universalization of the exodus by Christ and its consequences*

I am afraid I must decline to develop this in detail, however necessary it would be to open these connections up afresh to the modern consciousness. Let us content ourselves here with concentrating on the consequence the life, death and resurrection of Jesus Christ brought about for mankind's history of freedom. Historically the most obvious consequence consisted of the fact that now the covenant that had hitherto been restricted to Israel was in a renewed form extended to cover the whole of mankind. Sinai, transformed through the figure of Jesus Christ, was made over to all nations, which now entered into Israel's history of liberation and became the heirs of this history. If Sinai, the Torah, the covenant and the exodus are in their core the same, then we could also say that the exodus which had hitherto been confined to Israel and had remained incomplete now became a component part of all history, which thereby as a whole crossed the threshold of a fundamental liberation and became the history of freedom.

This process of the liberating forces of the exodus and Sinai becoming universal includes, however, the fact that the fundamental order of right relationships on which freedom is founded comes out of Israel's national law and as something offered to all peoples and nations is no longer identical with the law of any state. The religious order of the covenant can enter into the most diverse variety of state orders, but does not coincide with any of them. A new people is being formed that finds room in all peoples, does not destroy them, but in all of them forms a force for unification and liberation. Let us put it in terms that we are more used to: the universalization of the covenant has as a consequence the fact that in the future religious and civil society, Church and state, are no longer identical but are clearly distinguished from each other. Many people criticize this distinction between the two levels of human society that represents the most obvious form of the turning-point marked by Christianity. They say it need not have happened in this way because it means the spiritualization of religion. It withdraws back into the internal realm from the political realm and no longer reaches the political sphere. Christian liberation, they say, must once again be given back the complete Old Testament dimension of the exodus; only a directly political liberation is genuine liberation. In this they are taking up once again an objection that had already been formulated in the third century by that great opponent of Christians, Celsus. He derided Christians' claims of redemption and said: What has your Christ achieved then? Nothing at all. Everything in the world is just the same as it always was. If he had wanted to bring about a real liberation then he would have had to found a state, he would have had to bring freedom about polically. This objection was extremely serious at a time when the Roman empire, ruled by increasingly despotic emperors, was noticeably experienced as a power of oppression. It was Origen above all who articulated the Christian answer to this reproach. What would actually have happened, he asked, if

Christ had founded a state? Either this state would have to accept its boundaries, and in that case it would benefit only a few. Or it must try to expand, and in that case it would be compelled to rely on force and would quickly come to resemble all other states. Or on the other hand its boundaries could be threatened by jealous neighbours, and in that case again it would find itself on the path of force. A state would be a solution for only a few and an extremely questionable solution at that. No, a redeemer had to do something completely different. He had to found a society that could live anywhere and everywhere. He had to create a way of living together, an area of truth and freedom, that was linked to no particular state order but was possible everywhere. In a word, he had to found a Church, and it is precisely this that he did . . .[8]

It is precisely the existence of a new society that does not coincide with the state that is a fundamental factor in the liberation of men and women. When this distinction is revoked an essential area of freedom becomes lost, because the state must now once again revert to regulating the entirety of human life. Once again it embraces the realm of the divine because once again it has become the bearer of religion, and by doing so it destroys that freedom of conscience that is founded on the distinction from the state of this new society of faith. But the distinction between the universal religious community and the universally necessary expression of the secular community in the form of a particular state, a distinction that in keeping with this is a consequence of Christianity, does not in any way mean a division of the two spheres so that religion now withdraws into the sphere of the purely spiritual and the state on the other hand is shunted into a purely political pragmatism without ethical orientation. What is correct is that the Church does not prescribe directly the political pattern and rules. The task of finding the best answer in changing times is now left to the freedom of reason. The fact that it is given its full rights in the political field and that political solutions are to be sought

---

[8] Cf. E. von Ivánka, *Rhomäerreich und Gottesvolk,* Freiburg/Munich 1968, pp. 161 – 165.

in no other way than the common effort of the practical reason is one of the aspects of Christian liberation, the separation of religious and secular society. But this reason is not simply left without guidance. Even if the law of Sinai which outlined for Israel the pattern and rules of the community, the liberating framework of relationships, is no longer any law of the state, nevertheless it remains a guiding moral force that is purified and made more profound in the light of Jesus's message. From it results the practice of the faith which at the same time outlines the fundamental moral imperatives for the building up of human society. Because the practice of the faith remains open to reason on the basis of the word of God, it is capable of development with the progress of human history, which in turn always presupposes this practice on the basis of the core of the liberating innovation, the Christian exodus. Catholic social teaching is the scientific and scholarly development of these guidelines which result from the unshakeable foundations of the faith and its continuing experiences with the practice of history. Hence it is far more than an appeal to the individual's good will; it is a historical programme that comes from a fundamental understanding of human history but is not ideologically determined but is rather open to continuous rational development.

3. *Political rationality-utopia-promise*

The realism of Christian social teaching is shown most obviously by the fact that it does not promise any earthly paradise, any irreversibly and finally perfect society within this history. This again comes in for criticism from many people; the great momentum of utopia seems to be lacking and everything is cut back to a rather resigned-looking realism. But what is the use of utopian momentum when it misuses people for the sake of a promise which must finally turn out to be false because its presuppositions are not true? We have already established that an irreversibly perfect and definitive society would presuppose a stand-still on human freedom. It would start from the assumption that it is not people who determine structures but structures people and that people must necessarily behave well if the structures are right. Their freedom then consists of a necessity of not being able to do otherwise. Good fortune is imposed on them from outside. This kind of finally liberated society would therefore be the final and definitive form of slavery. But if people remain free then a final and definitive state of society within history does not exist. Then they must continually be taught their freedom to find the right way. Corresponding to this, Catholic social teaching is not aware of any utopia but rather develops models of the best possible way of shaping human affairs in a given historical situation. For this reason it rejects the myth of revolution and seeks the way of reform, which does not itself completely exclude violent resistance in extreme situations but which protests against accepting the revolution as a *deus ex machina* from which one day in some inexplicable way the new man and the new society will emerge.[9]

At this point we are inevitably led back to the problem that previously we had laid aside for a moment. The question arose whether Catholic social teaching portrayed in this way was not far too pragmatic and too realistic; the question of what place God actually had in it. We have already meanwhile encountered a first element in an answer to this; it was shown that Catholic social teaching lives from the guidance provided by the practice of the faith and that this practice is not simply something thought up by itself but in its core results from the encounter with the old and the new Sinai, the Sinai of Israel and the mountain of Jesus Christ. But this perspective that admittedly points backwards into the past history of the faith is not the whole. A look directed forwards is also part of it. Christian faith may not know any utopia within history but it does know a promise: the resurrection of the dead, the last judgement and the kingdom of God. For people today this probably sounds without a doubt very mythological. But it is much more reasonable and rational than the blending together of politics and

---

[9] Cf. for the questions touched on here H. Kuhn, *Der Staat*, Munich 1967, especially pp. 63 – 135 and 315 – 341. For the concept of the revolution see the same author's *Die Kirche im Zeitalter der Kultur-revolution*, Graz 1985, pp. 30 – 73.

eschatology in a utopia within history.[10] More logical and more appropriate is the division of the two into a historical task on the one hand, which in the light of faith receives new dimensions and possiblities, and on the other into a new world to be created by God himself. No revolution can create a new man; that would always be nothing but compulsion. But God can create a new man from within. The fact that we are able to look forward to this gives even what goes on inside history a new hope. But above all no answer to the questions of justice and freedom is sufficient that leaves out of account the problem of death. If it is only a not immediately foreseeable future that will at some time bring about justice, then all the dead of previous history are victims of deception. It is absolutely no use to them if they are told they have co-operated in preparing for liberation and to that extent have entered into it. They have in fact not entered into it but have departed from history without having received justice. The extent of injustice then remains for ever infinitely greater than the extent of justice. For this reason even so consistent a Marxist thinker as Theodor Adorno has said that, if justice should exist, there must also be justice for the dead.[11] A liberation that finds its final limit and boundary in death is no real liberation. Without solving the question of death everything else becomes unreal and contradictory. For his reason faith in the resurrection of the dead is the point on the basis of which it is at all possible to conceive of justice for history and to fight meaningfully for it. It is only if the resurrection of the dead exists that it is meaningful to die for justice. Only then is justice more than power; only then is it reality, for otherwise it remains a mere idea. For this reason too the certainty of a final judgement of the world is of the greatest practical significance. Knowledge of the last judgement was for centuries the power that kept the mighty in their place. The fact that every single one of us is judged by this standard is the equality of man that no one can escape from. The last judgement does not absolve us from the effort

---

[10] Cf. the previous chapter, pp. 237–254 above.
[11] T. W. Adorno, *Negative Dialektik,* Frankfurt 1966, p. 205 (English translation *Negative Dialectics,* New York 1973); cf. J. Ratzinger, *Eschatologie,* Regensburg 1977, p. 159.

to create justice within history; it provides this effort with a sense and meaning and prevents its obligation taking on any tinge of arbitrariness. So too the kingdom of God is not simply an uncertain future. It is only if in this life of ours we already belong to the kingdom that we shall belong to it then. It is not eschatological faith that banishes the kingdom into the future but utopia, for the latter's future has no present and its hour never comes.

Concluding remark: being similar to God and freedom

There is one final thing we must add. We said that in the anarchist concept of freedom man wanted to become the God which no longer existed outside himself or herself. Does the realism of the Christian ideas of freedom now mean that man withdraws resignedly into his or her finiteness and wants only to be man? In no way. In the light of the Christian experience of God it becomes clear that the unrestricted ability to do anything and everything one wants has as its model an idol and not God. The real God is bound to himself in threefold love and is thus pure freedom. Man's vocation is to be this image of God, to become like him.[12] Man is not untranscendably shut up in his or her finiteness. Certainly, he or she must first learn to accept his or her finiteness. He or she must recognize that he or she is not self-sufficient and not autonomous. He or she must give up the lie of independence of all relationships and doing what you want. He or she must say yes to his or her need, yes to the other person, yes to creation, yes to the limitation and direction of his or her own nature. The person who can merely choose between arbitrary options is not yet free. The free person is only someone who takes the criteria for his or her action from within and needs to obey no external compulsion. For this reason the person who has become at one with his or her essential nature, at one with truth itself, is free. The person who is at one with the

---

[12] On man's being made in the image of God see J. Auer, *Die Welt — Gottes Schöpfung (Kleine katholische Dogmatik* III), Regensburg 1975, pp. 217−227; J. Ratzinger, *Im Anfang schuf Gott,* Munich 1986, pp. 38−41.

truth no longer acts according to external necessities and compulsions; in him or her nature, desire and action have come to coincide. In this way man within the finite can come into contact with the infinite, bind himself or herself to it and thus, precisely by recognizing his or her limits, himself or herself become infinite. Thus at the end it becomes visible once again that the Christian doctrine of freedom is not some petty moralism. It is guided by a comprehensive vision of man: it sees man in a historical perspective that at the same time transcends all history. The Instruction on Christian freedom and liberation was meant to be an aide to rediscovering this perspective in order to make it effective with all its strength in our contemporary world.

Sources

The essays and articles that make up this volume originally appeared as follows:

Chapter 1: "The ecclesiology of the Second Vatican Council", in *Internationale katholische Zeitschrift* 15 (1986), pp. 41 – 52; reprinted in *Pastoralblatt* 38 (1986), pp. 130 – 139; also in J. Ratzinger, Hans Urs von Balthasar and others, *La Chiesa del Concilio*, Milan, 1985, pp. 9 – 24, and J. Ratzinger, *Iglesia comunicadora de Vida*, Lima, 1986, pp. 23 – 39.

Chapter 2: "The papal primacy and the unity of the people of God", in J. Ratzinger (ed.), *Dienst an der Einheit. Zum Wesen und Auftrag des Petrusamtes*, Düsseldorf 1978, pp. 165 – 179.

Chapter 3: Questions about "the structure and tasks of the synod of bishops", a revised version of the paper "Scopi e metodo del Sinodo dei vescovi" in J. Tomko (ed.), *Il sinodo dei vescovi. Natura — metodo — prospettiva*, Vatican City 1985, pp. 45 – 58.

Chapter 4: "Anglican-Catholic Dialogue: Its problems and hopes", in *Insight*, vol. I no. 3, March 1983, pp. 2 – 11, and *Internationale katholische Zeitschrift* 12 (1983), pp. 244 – 259.

Chapter 5: "Luther and the unity of the Churches": an interview, in *Internationale katholische Zeitschrift* 12 (1983), pp. 568 – 582. An English version appeared in *Communio* 11 (1984), pp. 210 – 226, and a French version in *La documentation catholique*, 1984, pp. 121 – 128.

Chapter 6: "The progress of ecumenism": a letter to the *Tübinger Theologische Quartalschrift*, 1986.

Chapter 7: "Biblical aspects of the question of faith and politics", previously unpublished.

Chapter 8: "Theology and the Church's political stance", in *Internationale katholische Zeitschrift* 9 (1980), pp. 425 – 434, reprinted in L.S. Schulz (ed.), *Wem nützt die Wissenschaft?*, 1981, pp. 106 – 117; an Italian version appeared in *Communio* 53 (1980), pp. 60 – 71.

Chapter 9: "Conscience in its age", in *Internationale katholische Zeitschrift* 1 (1972), pp. 432 – 442, reprinted in *Reinhold-Schneider-Gesellschaft e.V.*, Heft 4, July 1972, pp. 13 – 29.

Chapter 10: "Freedom and constraint in the Church", in *Verein der Freunde der Universität Regensburg*, Heft 7 (1981), pp. 5 – 21, and also in E. Corecco, N. Herzog and A. Scola, *Les droits fondamentaux du Chrétien dans l'Église et la société*, Fribourg, 1981, pp. 37 – 52, (in Flemish) in *International katholiek Tijdschrift Communio* 7 (1982), pp. 386 – 400, and (in French) in *Studia Moralia* XXXII (1984), pp. 171 – 188.

Chapter 11: "A Christian orientation in a pluralist democracy?", in H. Schambeck (ed.), *Pro fide et iustitia. Festschrift Kardinal Casaroli zum 70. Geburtstag*, Berlin 1984, pp. 747 – 761; reprinted in N. Lobkowicz. *Das europäische Erbe und seine christliche Zukunft*, Cologne 1985, pp. 20 – 35. In Spanish it has appeared in Universidad del Norte (Chile), *Teología*, 1985; *Scripta theologica* 16, Pamplona 1984, pp. 815 – 829; and *Communio America Latina* 3 (1985), pp. 52 – 63.

Chapter 12: "Europe: a heritage with obligations for Christians", in *Katholische Akademie Bayern* 1979, reprinted in *Zur Debatte* 9 (1979), pp. 1 – 4, in F. König and K. Rahner, *Europa. Horizonte der Hoffnung*, Graz 1983, pp. 61 – 74, and in French in *Revue des sciences religieuses 54 (1980), pp. 41 – 54*.

Chapter 13: "Eschatology and Utopia", in *Internationale katholische Zeitschrift* 6 (1977), pp. 97 – 110, reprinted in O. Schatz, *Abschied von Utopia? Anspruch und Auftrag der Intellektuellen*, Graz 1977, pp. 193 – 210. English, French and Italian versions have appeared in the respective editions of *Communio*.

Chapter 14: "Freedom and liberation: The anthropological vision of the 1986 Instruction *Libertatis conscientia*", in *Internationale katholische Zeitschrift* 5 (1986), pp. 409 – 424, and in Spanish in J. Ratzinger, *Iglesia comunicadora de Vida*, Lima 1986, pp. 23 – 39.